THE
TRIUMPH
OF THE
MARTYRS

Jiu Wicks 2012

THE
TRIUMPH
OF THE
MARTYRS

*A Reporter's Journey
into Occupied Iraq*

Nir Rosen

Potomac Books, Inc.
Washington, D.C.

Originally published as *In the Belly of the Green Bird: The
Triumph of the Martyrs in Iraq* by Free Press, a Division of
Simon & Schuster, Inc. Copyright © 2006 by Nir Rosen.

Library of Congress Cataloging-in-Publication Data
Rosen, Nir, 1977–
  The triumph of the martyrs : a reporter's journey into occu-
pied Iraq / Nir Rosen.— Potomac Books ed.
    p. cm.
  Updated ed. of: In the belly of the green bird, 2006.
  Includes bibliographical references and index.
  ISBN-13: 978-1-59797-184-3 (alk. paper)
 1. Iraq War, 2003– 2. Insurgency—Iraq. 3. Iraq—Politics and
government—2003– I. Rosen, Nir, 1977– In the belly of the
green bird. II. Title: In the belly of the green bird. III. Title.
  DS79.76.R67 2008
  956.7044'3—dc22
                                          2007052960

Printed in the United States of America on acid-free paper
that meets the American National Standards Institute Z39-
48 Standard.

Potomac Books, Inc.
22841 Quicksilver Drive
Dulles, Virginia 20166

First Edition

10 9 8 7 6 5 4 3 2 1

With love for Tiffany and Meitham

CONTENTS

CAST OF CHARACTERS

Abizaid, General John Commander of U.S. Central Command.

al-Adhami, Sheikh Muayad Imam of the Abu Hanifa mosque in Baghdad's Adhamiya neighborhood. Arrested in November 2004 by American troops for supporting the resistance and opposing the elections, he later joined the Islamic Party and supported the elections held in October and December 2005, leading to threats on his life. He went into hiding.

Berg, Nicholas A young American entrepreneur whose beheading by al-Zarqawi's Tawhid and Jihad in May 2004 set off a series of prominent kidnappings and beheadings.

Bremer, L. Paul The American diplomat appointed to head the Coalition Provisional Authority and serve as proconsul in Iraq.

al-Dhari, Harith Suleiman Secretary General of the Association of Muslim Scholars in Iraq, a Sunni neo-Baathist organization that was the most popular Sunni movement in the country, with its own resistance units.

al-Dhari, Muthana Son of Harith al-Dhari and a leader of the 1920 Revolution Brigades, the Association of Muslim Scholars' armed resistance unit.

Fartusi, Sheikh Muhammad Moqtada al-Sadr's most important representative in the summer of 2003, he was later removed from involvement in the movement, either because he was stealing the limelight or because he was alleged to have been a Baathist.

al-Haeri, Ayatollah Kadhim Important student of Ayatollah Muhammad Sadiq al-Sadr living in Iran, and onetime sponsor of Moqtada al-Sadr, with whom the younger cleric aligned for legitimacy.

al-Hakim, Abdel Aziz Head of the Supreme Council for the Islamic Revolution in Iraq (SCIRI) since his brother's assassination in August 2003. He had previously been head of the Badr Corps, the armed wing of SCIRI.

al-Hakim, Muhamad Bakr The founder of the Supreme Council for the Islamic Revolution in Iraq, the exile Shia movement based in Iran. He was killed in a car bombing in Najaf in August 2003. The Badr Corps, its armed wing, was trained by Iran and had fought the Iraqi regime and its supporters.

Hussein, Qusay Older son of Saddam Hussein, who died fighting the Americans in Mosul in July 2003.

Hussein, Saddam Iraqi Baathist dictator deposed by the Americans and finally arrested in December 2003.

Hussein, Uday Son of Saddam Hussein, who died fighting the Americans in Mosul in July 2003.

al-Jafaari, Ibrahim Dawa Party leader and Iraqi prime minister under the interim government.

Janabi, Abdallah Falluja's onetime leading cleric and head of its Mujahideen Council. He fled to Syria after more radical elements took over the city.

al-Khoei, Abdul-Majid The London-based son of former Grand Ayatollah Abolqassim Khoei, he was stabbed to death in Najaf by supporters of Moqtada al-Sadr in April 2003 while on an American-sponsored mission to win over Najaf's clergy.

Khomeini, Ayatollah Ruhollah Iranian cleric who overthrew the Shah of Iran and established the Islamic Republic of Iran in 1979, setting an example for Islamists around the world. He was at one time exiled in Iraq and is still an important symbol for Iraqi Shia Islamists.

Kubeisi, Dr. Ahmad Iraq's most famous Sunni theologian, a former associate of the Baathist regime who moved to the UAE before the war but returned immediately after it in an attempt to lead Iraq's Sunnis. He founded the Iraqi National Movement and called upon Sunnis to show restraint, but his anti-American rhetoric and support for Moqtada al-Sadr earned him the enmity of the Americans. He was prevented from returning to Iraq, and his movement collapsed, pushing his followers into the arms of more extreme elements.

bin Laden, Osama Saudi-born head of al Qaeda.

al-Maqdasi, Abu Muhamad Real name Isam Taher Al Oteibi al-Burqawi, the founder of Tawhid and Jihad and former mentor to Zarqawi.

Mowhoush, Major General Abed Hamed An air force commander under Saddam, he was arrested in October 2003 by the Third Armored Cavalry Regiment for suspicion of involvement in the insurgency, and was killed during interrogation.

al-Musawi, Seyid Hasan al-Naji Imam of the important Muhsin mosque in Baghdad's Sadr City, a leading representative of Moqtada al-Sadr, and onetime head of the Mahdi Army militia in Baghdad.

Rostam, General Hamid Rahim Known as Mam, or "Uncle," Rostam, he was the top field commander for the Patriotic Union of Kurdistan *peshmerga* and their strongman in Kirkuk.

Rozbayani, Hasib Deputy governor of Kirkuk who hoped to expel all Arabs from the city.

al-Sadr, Moqtada Son of Ayatollah Muhammad Sadiq al-Sadr, he emerged from obscurity immediately following the American invasion, capitalizing on his father's network and followers to establish control of much of Shia Iraq and become the main Shia opponent of the American occupation.

al-Sadr, Ayatollah Muhammad Bakr Founder of the Dawa Party, and the most important Shia political Islamist theologian, his movement was an attempt to combat secularism and provide Islamic answers to all social problems. When he began openly opposing the Baathist regime Saddam killed him and his sister in 1980, earning him the title "the First Martyr." Sadr was a descendant of the Prophet Muhammad, earning him the honorific "seyid."

al-Sadr, Ayatollah Muhammad Sadiq An important Iraqi-born leader of the politically active *hawza,* Sadr was at first supported by the Baathist regime as an Iraqi nationalist alternative to a foreign Shia leadership, but when he began condemning the regime in his sermons he was assassinated with two of his sons in 1999, earning him the title "the Second Martyr," and leaving his son Moqtada to inherit his mantle. Sadr was a descendant of the Prophet Muhammad, earning him the honorific "seyid."

al-Samarai, Sheikh Ahmed Abdul Ghafur Former deputy head of the Association of Muslim Scholars whose fiery sermons supported jihad. After the January 2005 elections he decided it was time for Sunnis to negotiate with the Americans and join the government. He became head of the Iraqi Sunni Waqf, or Endowment, a government-appointed position.

al-Shami, Abu Anas Real name Omar Yusef Jumaa. A Jordanian of Palestinian origin who was the main cleric in Zarqawi's Tawhid and Jihad movement.

al-Sistani, Ayatollah Ali The Iranian-born, highest-ranking cleric in Najaf, and a so-called moderate with the largest following in Iraq.

al-Ubeidi, Sheikh Dhafer Acting head of the Mujahideen Council of Falluja when it was autonomous in the summer of 2004. He fled to Syria when more radical elements took over the city.

al-Yaqubi, Sheikh Muhammad Former student of Ayatollah Muhammad Sadiq al-Sadr who formed a movement rivaling Moqtada's and a party called Fudala, which later became Fadila. He sought to establish clerical control over the government and dominated much of the Shia south as well as university campuses in Baghdad.

al-Zarqawi, Abu Musab Real name Abu Hilalah Ahmad Fadil Nazal al-Khalaylah. The Jordanian leader of the Tawhid and Jihad movement in Iraq, responsible for most of the suicide attacks and beheadings in Iraq as well as the November 2005 Amman hotel bombings.

INTRODUCTION

ON APRIL 9, 2003, as the world watched, Iraqis dragged a bronze statue of the body of deposed dictator Saddam Hussein through the streets of Baghdad. *Sahel* means, literally, to pull a body through the street. Iraqis have done this many times before, to other deposed leaders, usually in the flesh. Once again change had come with violence. This time, the violence did not end with the change.

It was that April that my experience of the new Iraq began.

The overthrow of Saddam unleashed a wild mix of reactions: a spontaneous burst of repressed fury from one segment of Iraqi society, which caused more damage to property than did the American bombs; solidarity and a volunteer spirit eager to restore security and normalcy from another segment. Common civilians stood all day, directing traffic in a country with no traffic lights or rules, and the absolute liberty to drive anywhere, in any direction, at any speed. These volunteers protected neighborhoods and established order. Shia groups self-organized and managed hospitals, city governments, and police. But many criminals, gangs, and mafias took over, and the fear of Saddam's totalitarian state was replaced with complete indifference to the idea of a state.

This is the story of the occupation, reconstruction, and descent into civil war of the new Iraq. It makes no attempt to cover the invasion or debate the decision to invade. Instead, this is an attempt to capture the story of the new Iraq from the point of view of the Iraqis themselves.

From the start of the liberation, Iraqis have been divided not only in their views of America, but also among themselves. Many Iraqis might have preferred an occupation, imperialist or not, to the anarchy that prevailed. When I would ask Iraqis what they wanted, they would always say, *"Amn"* (safety, security). Some called for an immediate evacuation of U.S. and British troops, others asked to be the fifty-first state, and some asked for both in the same breath. Most longed only for a place in the shade and a better future than their past, though they were proud of their history.

New political parties and organizations appeared every day, announcing their birth and their intentions on walls. Their banners covered the abandoned buildings they had confiscated. The Iraqi Communist Party headquarters bore the hammer and sickle associated with dogmatic atheism, right next to a huge banner proclaiming their participation in an important Shia holiday. Seventy newspapers appeared in Baghdad after the war, their viewpoints as divergent as possible. *Azzaman,* the most popular, professional, and mainstream paper, was owned by a former senior intelligence official who worked directly for Saddam's son Qusay. In May, *Azzaman* used a Reuters picture of an old Iraqi man being held by two American soldiers on each side. Its caption read "American soldiers help Iraqi man cross street." *Tariq al-Sha'ab,* the Communist Party paper, had the same picture over the caption "American soldiers beat Iraqi man."

Everywhere I looked, I saw division, conflict, struggle. (Only one group of Iraqis remained virtually invisible amid the throngs. Iraq's greatest majority, its women, outnumbering men by as much as 1.5 million, were imprisoned in silence. In my many months in Iraq, I met hundreds of men, but very few women. I became afraid to look at them or walk too close to them and thus arouse the ire of their male guardians. Among the Shias in particular, Arab tribal mores had combined with religious conservatism. The Shia women reminded me more of the prisoners behind the Taliban's burkas in Afghanistan than their comparatively liberated Iranian coreligionists, who granted women far more participation and liberty.)

CIVIL WAR REQUIRES that fratricidal violence be organized. At first, after Saddam fell, the violence was mainly chaotic. But there was an endless supply of it, and it was soon organized, as the chapters that follow attempt to show.

According to many Iraqis, the Americans "came as liberators and now they are occupiers." For Americans occupation conjures images of postwar Germany or Japan, and the repair of damaged societies. In Arabic, *tahrir,* or liberation, and *ihtilal,* or occupation, have much greater moral and emotional significance. *Ihtilal* means the Crusaders who slaughtered Muslims, Jews, and Orthodox Christians; it means the Mongols who sacked Baghdad in the thirteenth century; it means the British imperialists who divided the spoils of the Ottoman Empire with the French; and it means the Israelis in southern Lebanon and Palestine. It is hard for Americans to understand just how deeply they are hated by ordinary Iraqis. "We warned them," one member of the Free Iraqi Forces says of the Americans, "but they didn't listen. They are turning a thousand friends into enemies every day."

Was it an occupation or liberation? On June 2 the Coalition Provisional Authority hosted an Iraqi Senator Council for nearly three hundred tribal leaders of all religions and ethnic groups. Ambassador Hume Horan, a political adviser to Ambassador L. Paul Bremer, addressed the audience in fluent Arabic. After Horan finished speaking, a Shia tribal leader from Amarra thanked President Bush for removing the Baath regime of Saddam and stated that he had seen the mass graves of Shias in the south and was firmly opposed to Saddam. He asked Horan if the coalition forces in Iraq were liberators or occupiers. Horan responded that they were "somewhere in between occupier and liberator." This was not well received.

The tribal leader said that if America was a liberator, then the coalition forces were welcome indefinitely as guests, but that if they were occupiers, then he and his descendants would "die resisting" them. This met with energetic applause from the audience. Several other sheikhs echoed the same sentiment. The meeting deteriorated, and one-third of the audience stood up and walked out, despite the efforts of Horan and other organizers to encourage them to stay.

I FIRST CROSSED INTO IRAQ in April 2003, a few days after Baghdad fell. I split the $2,000 taxi ride with three other journalists and we drove the twelve hours into Baghdad. The city's walls were covered with leaflets and banners announcing the deaths of "martyrs." At first the names of those martyred by the liberating American military festooned the walls, but soon there were new martyrs, victims of the nihilistic anarchy spreading in the country, the *faudha* (chaos) as Iraqis called it. These new names up on the walls were those martyred first by violent men let loose in the power vacuum, and then by the Iraqi insurgency's terror—men seeking martyrdom. Without the Baath Party or any other political force, without police or an army, all that remained was the mosque. Old authorities were destroyed and angry young clerics replaced them, arrogating to themselves the power to represent, to mobilize, and to govern. Sunni clerics exhorted their followers to seek martyrdom. Shia clerics wearing turbans hailed the memory of two particular martyrs; their bearded visages soon dominated much of the country's walls.

Known as the First and Second Martyrs, these were, in order, Muhammad Bakr al-Sadr, martyred in 1980 after Saddam's men tortured and killed his sister and hammered nails into his skull, and then his kinsman Muhammad Sadiq al-Sadr, slain with all but one of his sons in 1999 when their car was riddled with bullets by Baathist assassins. Supporters of the First and Second Sadr Martyrs now swept throughout Iraq's Shia areas, imposing a new order. The downtrodden Shia masses were now ascendant for the first time since the seventh century.

The story of the new Iraq is the triumph of its martyrs. When I arrived, Saddam's statue had just fallen, marking the beginning of what Iraqis would call "the fall." For some it was the fall of the regime, for some it was the fall of Iraq and for others it was the fall of Baghdad. But all those in Iraq would forever view time as "before" and "after." I would, too, for Iraq changed my life. I celebrated my twenty-sixth birthday a month after I arrived. My dark complexion and grasp of Iraqi Arabic allowed me greater access to the country and its people than some of my colleagues. I tried to live with Iraqis as much as possible, in small unfortified hotels that did not imprison me and remove me from the rest of the country. I traveled by taxi and ate in local restaurants. I befriended Iraqis who became my interlocutors and taught me how to survive, how to act, what to look for. I witnessed with excitement and wonder Iraqis struggling to grasp the new reality and to redefine themselves. With concern and sorrow I was with them when the postwar world of possibilities became chaotic and violent.

I did not belong to an organization and had no backing or supervision, so I wandered wherever I wanted. I focused on the Sunni and Shia Arab parts. (Kurdistan was a different country, not occupied by foreign troops, independent of Baghdad in its political development, and apart from the occasional terror attack in Erbil or Suleimaniya, free from the flames engulfing Iraq.) I consciously chose to avoid reporting about events in the Green Zone and focused instead on developments in the "red zone" that was the rest of Iraq. These events seemed more real to me than the world of make-believe acted out on a political stage removed from Iraqis and surrounded by American soldiers.

As Iraqis were searching for new authority, I was too. Like them, I found it in the mosque and the tribal meeting hall, the new centers of power in Iraq. Perhaps I neglected those who were silent, but they would not be the ones to determine the shape of the new Iraq. Perhaps I neglected those who shied away from violence, but they would not seize power in the new Iraq. My book begins with Iraq's Shias awakening and expressing their identity with an unprecedented vigor, vowing never to be shackled again. They, and perhaps the Kurds who are on their way to independence, were the only victors in America's war. I continue with the Sunnis, the losers, struggling to adjust to a painful new reality. I visit the occupation, seeking to understand how American actions were alienating the Iraqi population they had come to allegedly liberate. Their presence and the realignment of power unleashed sectarian forces of internecine hatred that the people of Iraq had never experienced. Into the vacuum stepped foreign radicals in need of a home base where they could operate without obstruction and arrive in paradise via martyrdom.

As Iraq's violence made a journalist's work more and more dangerous and finally prohibitive for most, I continued to venture out, relying on my Middle Eastern features and Arabic, as well as a young freelancer's recklessness borne of desperation. But as friends were killed and others fled, and the violence came closer and closer to me, I too found it increasingly difficult to work with integrity in Iraq, where foreigners were a target and a commodity, and the ranks of the martyrs in Iraq only increased.

1

THE TRIUMPH OF THE MARTYRS:
April 2003

✦ Approximate number of Americans killed before President Bush's
   May 1, 2003, declaration that the mission was accomplished: 300
✦ Approximate number of Iraqi civilians killed by May 1, 2003: 2,000

ONE WEEK AFTER I arrived, hundreds of thousands of Shia
pilgrims were marching south, to the holy city of Karbala for
the first time in decades. Young barefoot men carried nothing
but flags. Weathered old women hunched under their black
ebayas. In small clusters, or dozens, or hundreds, they treaded
through the red earth, formerly cracked and parched, turned
to mud by recent rain. Their excitement, and sense of liberation, was electrifying. To an irreverent American, it might have
seemed like Woodstock for the Shia. In fact, it was far, far
more significant.

   Shias believe that after the death of the prophet Muhammad
in 632 A.D., leadership of the Muslim community should have
been inherited by the family of Muhammad and his descendants, of the Hashemite clan. Instead, his best friend and father-
in-law Abu Bakr became the first caliph. A quick succession of
caliphs each met with assassination. By the year 680, the fifth
caliph's son, Yazid, was challenged as leader of the Muslims by

Hussain, a grandson of Muhammad and a son of a previous caliph, Ali. Hussain expected the people of Kufah in southern Iraq to support his claim, because his father's caliphate had been based there.

Hussain and seventy-two male supporters and their families set out for Kufah. While they were en route, Yazid persuaded the Kufan leadership to join with him and betray Hussain. Hussain was intercepted and forced to camp in the desert of Karbala with his entourage. Yazid's army surrounded Hussain's camp, denying Hussain and his supporters access to the waters of the nearby Euphrates River. After a ten-day siege, on the tenth day of the Muslim month of Muharram (October 10, 680), Yazid's army slaughtered Hussain and his followers. The women and children were sold into captivity. Yazid became the sixth caliph, ruling from Damascus. Hussain's followers became known as Shiat Ali (Partisans of Ali).

Karbala became a pilgrimage destination for the world's Shias and a center of theological study. Ali, his sons Hassan and Hussain, and their nine descendants, who became leaders of the Shia community, were called imams. Most Shias believe that the first eleven imams were assassinated and the twelfth imam went into occultation in a supernatural realm in 874 A.D., to reappear on Judgment Day as the Mahdi, or promised messiah. Shias devote many days of the year to commemorating the martyred imams, as well as more contemporary leaders, such as the First and Second Martyrs of the revered Sadr dynasty.

Singers wail lamentations for Hussain. Actors describe in detail the thirst of Hussain and his besieged followers in the heat of the desert, and Yazid's cruelty in choosing the time of Muslim communal prayer on Friday to slaughter his rivals. Adult men and women weep bitterly during the last scenes of the reenactment, where they are reminded of the treachery and guilt of the Kufan community who abandoned Hussain to the evil Yazid. The virtues of Shia leaders are contrasted to the alleged immorality of early Sunni leaders, who supposedly stole the rightful leadership from Hussain and showed no mercy to his family, even the children. Early Sunni leaders are condemned and therefore so are their followers, today's Sunni Muslims. In Iraq most Shia homes have posters of Hussain, a handsome, exotic figure, with long lashes and thick lips, riding his horse or carrying his sword. Many also have macabre posters of his severed and bloody head, the neck stuck on a pole.

The self-flagellation and mutilation during Muharram are done publicly, reinforcing the Shia sense of community. Muharram and its rituals, as well as the mourning processions during the month of Ramadan (marking Ali's martyrdom), last for about two months of the year. Hussain's martyrdom is interpreted as the truest example of heroism and sacrifice for all believers to emulate in their struggle against contemporary oppressors and as the standard by which all acts of martyrdom are analogized. The martyrdom in Karbala has intrinsic political content and symbolism that have found expression throughout the history of Shia oppression.

The most important politicization of the Muharram ceremonies occurred in late 1978. The Islamist faction of the opposition to the Shah of Iran dominated anti-Shah protests, casting their struggle as a reenactment of the historic battle between Hussain and Yazid. Ayatollah Khomeini appropriated the Muharram rituals to establish an Islamist government in Iran and used them as an expression of the ultimate act of resistance to injustice and tyranny.

Khomeini interpreted the Karbala events politically, accusing Mohammad Reza Pahlavi of acting as a modern Yazid and enemy of the Shias, thus sanctioning the uprising against the shah's regime. Ashura fell on December 11, 1978, and was transformed into a political weapon. Millions of people took part in nationwide demonstrations that eventually led to the shah's abdication and Khomeini's return.

On April 9, 2003, in Iraq, the Shias awoke from the trauma of centuries of Sunni rule. Their history began in Iraq, where they had risen up against Baghdad's founder and feuded with Sunnis. Now, there was a massive and unprecedented assertion of Shia identity to commemorate the end of the forty-day mourning period for Hussain's martyrdom.

Not surprisingly, the annual celebration marking Hussain's martyrdom was banned in Iraq for most of the thirty-five years of Baathist rule. In 1974 mourning processions became angry political protests. In 1977 police officers were met with fury when they tried to interfere with processions between Najaf and Karbala. Angry crowds took over a police station and chanted, "Saddam, remove your hand! The people of Iraq do not want you!" Now, in 2003, the Shia were free to make the pilgrimage without anyone trying to stop them.

I made my way among the pilgrims, through villages, alongside canals, and beneath palm trees. The villages were crisscrossed with thousands of wires and cables, connected to private generators. All along the way entreaties were made for us to share the pilgrims' food and drinks by the banks of the Husseiniya canal. Girls washed clothes in the water as cows watched them indolently. Along the road children all gave us the thumbs-up. They had learned that from the Americans. They ran after cars and shouted, "Good! Good!"

At a checkpoint by a bridge I was pulled over by a group of men, some barefoot, all carrying Kalashnikovs. I got out of my car. It was then I learned the most valuable skill for surviving the new Iraq: how to smile at angry men pointing their guns at me and wish them peace.

On the dusty highway to Karbala, women held flags and balanced packs on their heads, marching behind their menfolk. When we finally reached the city, the streets had been closed to cars. Pedestrians streamed in by the tens of thousands. The elderly were carried on donkey carts. Everyone else walked toward the city center and its two shrines, their golden domes shimmering with an orange glow as the setting sun cast its dying rays on them. They are the shrines of Hussain and his brother Abbas, the two grandsons of the Prophet Muhammad who had died in this town in 680 A.D.

With its natural resources, proud and well-educated population, and history, Iraq is a natural leader in the Arab world, but it is *the* natural leader of the Shia world. Shia Islam started in Iraq and its major events and battles occurred here. For most of Islamic history the religious academies in Iraq were the most important centers of Shia learning. Najaf, where the fourth caliph Ali is buried, was the most important Shia learning center for a thousand years, until 1920, when Qom (in Iran) began to overshadow it. The Najaf academy is known as the Hawza Ilmiya, which means "circles of learning," and was established in the eleventh century. It is the only institution in Iraq that can claim to lead the Shias and the only one to whom nearly all Shias claim allegiance.

Senior scholars in the *hawza* are called *marjas*. Each *marja* has a school named after him, and an office where his rulings on religious questions are distributed and to where his followers can turn for questions. *Hawza* students hope to become jurisprudents, allowing them to interpret and apply Islamic law. Every Shia must follow a jurisprudent, but he is free to choose which one he prefers and is then obligated to give his jurisprudent 20 percent of his yearly assets. A jurisprudent can rise up the ranks to become a grand ayatollah, the Jedi knight of the Shia world.

The *hawza* is currently led by four grand ayatollahs, the most senior and widely followed of which is Ali al-Sistani. All Shia clerics want a state ruled according to Islamic law, and their followers—a majority of Iraqis—do, too. So Sistani's political desires are of great consequence. Yet he is hardly the sole voice of the Shia.

Under Saddam, an underground movement called Dawa had sought to establish a Shia state. Its leader, Muhammad Bakr al-Sadr, had been executed in 1980. Muhammad Bakr al-Sadr was the greatest Shia theologian of the twentieth century, writing about economics, politics, and philosophy. Bakr al-Sadr's main contributions were to jurisprudence and economics, particularly Islamic economics. With his 1961 book *Our Economics,* he sought to combat socialism and show that Islam could be applied to all social problems. It was the first codified theory of Islamic economics. Sadr, like the Shia establishment of the time, was concerned that Iraq's Shias were increasingly attracted to the communist and Baathist secular and socialist ideologies. In *Our Economics,* he critiqued Marxism and capitalism, and then articulated a theoretical and practical approach based on private and public ownership, economic freedom, and social justice. In 1980 when Bakr al-Sadr declared Baath Party membership forbidden, he was executed along with his sister. He became known as the First Martyr.

Bakr al-Sadr's nephew Ayatollah Muhammad Sadiq al-Sadr envisioned himself as the *wali ai-amm,* or general leader, of the clergy, a position above all others, including the top clerics in Iran. "I know more than all the living and all the dead," he famously said. He aspired to lead world Shiism and head an Islamic government in Iraq. Beginning in 1997 he publicly criticized Saddam, increasing his support among the masses of Shias and thus appropriating followers from other clerics. Since Shia believers must give a yearly tithe worth 20 percent of their assets to the cleric they follow, more followers mean more money and more power. Despite his Santa Claus–like visage, Sadiq al-Sadr was vehement in his damnation of dissenters. He was said to publish statements naming dozens of new people infidels every day. Many included homosexuals, others were clerics who disagreed with him. In 1998 when Saddam relaxed restrictions on the Friday *khutba,* or sermon, Sadiq al-Sadr began preaching at the Kufah mosque, outside Najaf. His forty-seven sermons reached all Iraqi Shias and were very influential. In his sermons he wisely mixed colloquial Iraqi dialect with classical Arabic, thus reaching the average Iraqi. He mobilized the masses of disenfranchised Shias in Iraq. Unlike his sermons, Sadiq al-Sadr's writings were eloquent. Sadiq al-Sadr also wrote about jurisprudence, Islamic economics, and such issues as the dangers of individualism and the Islamic utopia. Much of his writings showed an obsession with the coming of the Mahdi, or Shia messiah. Killed in an ambush by alleged agents of Saddam in 1999, he was known as the Second Martyr. The Sadr family was known for being revolutionary, their political activism a contrast to the quietism of the *hawza*'s more traditional leadership.

Many pilgrims chanted and beat their chests, professing their love for Hussain. "I love you, you are my eyes!" one wailed. Colorful posters of Hussain and Ali decorated the gray walls. With thick lips and dreamy eyes, they looked like handsome Christ figures. One man had a long sword on his belt. "I cut my chest for the sake of Hussain," the men chanted. "Oh, Hussain, where is Sadr? We don't know on whom to seek vengeance!" "We swear we will never forget you, Hussain!" "Yes, yes for Islam, yes, yes for the *hawza*."

A black cloud of shrouded women were amassed at the shrine of Hussain's sister. A crowd of men beat their chests in penitence and sang for her. Some men checked their shoes, others left them on the sidewalk before entering a glistening room of refracted light. It had marble geometric patterns on the floor, inlaid wooden doors, and a mosaic of tiny mirror fragments covering the ceiling and top half of walls, columns, and arches. It was a small room, with people praying on the floor and kissing or touching the place where she once stood.

All night long, throngs closed their eyes and clapped their chests with one or both hands, then lifted both arms up to the sky and brought them down again in a rhythm to chant. The chant repeated as the crowd swelled, until it abruptly ended and somebody called, "Our God prays for Muhammad and the family of Muhammad," and then it was over. The crowd dispersed.

An interminable stream of mourners marched into the city, chanting, wailing, and carrying banners. One procession of people chanted, "Sadr is in our hearts, Sistani is in our eyes." "Oh, Hussain!" was written on the black bandanas the mourners tied around their heads. A huge crowd marched by, chanting and whipping their backs with chains. It was a flagellation procession. The men grunted and whipped the chains over their shoulders, onto their torn and bloody shirts, chanting "Hussain, Hussain, Hussain."

Men carrying exterminator packs filled with rosewater walked through the sea of people, spraying the scented water into the air. It descended upon the crowds in a fine and very annoying mist. Men who had made a vow to Hussain or Abbas in hopes that their prayers would be answered had crawled on hands and knees to Karbala. Now they crawled all the way to the shrines, their backs wet with sweat, their clothes a mess of rags. In the park between the two tombs of Hussain and Abbas people slept on blankets or on the hard street.

At 5:30 A.M. a procession with trumpets, swords, and drums woke me up. At 6:00 A.M. a huge procession of men went by, singing, carrying many flags, hands beating their chests. "Let people say what they want," they chanted, "we will mourn for you in your tomb, Hussain." Inside the mosque, in the courtyard, there was no room to move except toward the tomb itself. Above the sea of heads, only flags and outstretched arms rose. Outside the tomb, trumpets blared and drums beat, as men wearing white robes stained crimson hit their heads with swords. It was the controversial sword-flagellation ceremony. Blood sprayed on all those who were close, especially photographers, whose faces and shirts were speckled with red. Women cried and hit their heads, watching from the side or from the roofs of houses.

The celebration was getting rowdier and more crowded, yet it was peaceful. Sheep were slaughtered on the street for free meat, their blood running in canals. Runners started at one of the gates of the city and sprinted to the tombs of Hussain and Abbas. They ran and beat themselves to show that Hussain and his followers did not die in vain and that their deaths would be avenged. More people arrived all day, marching to the tomb and breaking down when they saw it, as if they had just learned of a relative's death. Old men cried, bent over, covering their faces. Others went about their business. One man carried a long block of ice on his back. In the *suq,* the open market, were mounds of incense, piles of spices, a tea stand, and slaughtered sheep. Sandal repair boys were making a killing.

I walked past many impromptu sermons given in colloquial Iraqi, past the stands for free sweet tea, past an ambulance covered in leaflets in English, with messages for the media. "We want a government that represents all Iraqi people, a government which has an independent will," one said. "We refuse wardship and occupation."

The following day there was a *hawza* demonstration. "Yes, yes for the *hawza*," people chanted. "Yes, yes for freedom! Islam is victorious! Yes, yes for unity! Death to America! Death to Israel! No to imperialism!" In the street I saw a banner that proclaimed "No, no for America, no for Israel, no for the devil, in the name of Hussain's revolution."

AT THREE IN THE AFTERNOON on April 23, the celebration took an abrupt turn to politics. Abdel Aziz al-Hakim, one of the two or three most important politicians in the new Iraq, called a press conference in the second floor of a building by the shrines. Heavy security guarded the building, and all guests were checked for identification and weapons. Hakim wore a green robe with embroidery, a black turban, and thin-framed glasses. His gray beard was shaved close. "In a few hours these ceremonies will come to an end," he began. He explained that the ceremonies symbolized resistance to oppression by the enemies of Islam. "These ceremonies today come while we pass through a very delicate and serious stage," he said, consisting of "the absence of security, stability, and a political system, which will lead to more confusion and losses . . . [and to] terrorist groups and extremists and remnants of the old regime. The Iraqi people can organize their own affairs. . . . There are no more excuses for the U.S. presence, and it is not accepted by the Iraqi people." When he took questions, I asked him if there was a *faqih,* or jurisprudent, who could lead Iraq. "There is a *faqih* who can lead the people," he said, referring to his brother, Ayatollah Hakim, whom he hoped would be the supreme cleric leading the new Shia state of Iraq. Abdel Aziz al-Hakim was the leader of the SCIRI (the Supreme Council for the Islamic Revolution in Iraq).

Then it was over. The city returned to normal, the pilgrims left, the journalists returned to the better food that could be found in Baghdad. As we drove out we saw children wearing swimming trunks, their scrawny bodies glistening as they jumped into the waters of the canal beneath a bridge.

THE FUTURE OF IRAQ'S SHIA is the future of Iraq. For the first time in the modern history of the Shia homeland, they started to share power, if not control the new state outright. The jubilation in Karbala would not last long, however. Back in Baghdad, the new Iraq was full of looting and chaos. The Shia were partly kept under control by Sistani, who called upon them to stop looting and return stolen goods (which many of them did). But Sistani was challenged by strongmen. His deputy in southern Baghdad, Sheikh al-Qaisi, controlled a militia whose leader Ahmad al-Mullah would be killed at the end of 2004 after assassinating up to forty Wahhabis and Baathists. Yet when al-Qaisi sent a delegation led by al-Mullah to one rebellious sheikh to collect looted goods, the sheikh refused. He did not recognize Sistani as his leader. Al-Mullah and his gang were infuriated and asked for permission to kill the man, but they were refused. The sheikh, named al-Muayad, quickly became known as "sheikh of the looted goods."

Sistani was challenged in a more serious way by the scion of the Sadr family, Moqtada al-Sadr. After the war he had emerged from a life in hiding to seize control of the vast network of mosques and clerics his martyred father had established. On April 9, 2003, his spiritual leader, Ayatollah al-Haeri, issued a fatwa urging Shia clerics in Iraq to take power as soon as they could. Haeri urged Iraqis to kill all Baathists to prevent them from taking over again. Moqtada sent cash to clerics through-out Iraq, proclaiming them his deputies and ordering them to seize former public buildings. His announcements were hung on walls throughout the country, alongside pictures of Haeri and Moqtada's father and great uncle.

The United States initially hoped to influence the Shia through yet another leader, Abdul Majid al-Khoei. He had been in exile in London. He was more moderate than many clerics, and he owed a great deal to the support of the American government. But on April 10, just after he returned to Iraq, carrying millions of dollars given to him by the U.S. government, Khoei was stabbed to death by a mob. Khoei had embodied the Bush administration's Shia strategy for Iraq. With his death there was none to replace it. Most observers and residents of Najaf believed that Moqtada was involved in the murder, something he dismisses. Moqtada's followers proceeded to surround the houses of conservative Shiite clerics, including that of Sistani, and give them twenty-four hours to leave Najaf. This provoked 1,500 tribesmen loyal to Sistani to descend on Najaf in his defense. A brutal pattern was established: a minority of extremists would follow whichever leader exhibited the most brute force, in this case Moqtada, and would manage to outflank the more numerous and moderate followers of people like Sistani. The Western press would paint Sistani as a good man, and Moqtada as evil.

The large Shia section of Baghdad, known as Sadr City, was a tough, hostile neighborhood, with no love lost on America. My Shia driver was terrified of taking me there. A doctor making a living working for journalists, he had learned his English from medical textbooks. Sadr City was "critical," he said, meaning dangerous. In mid-April, one hundred Shia clerics met in high security in Sadr City, protected by armed men who blocked off the road and shot in the air. The clerics stated their preferences for a theocracy by calling for a ban on dominoes, television, makeup, music, dancing, and Western films.

Many sheikhs controlled their own militias. One sheikh's young clerics controlled hospitals throughout Baghdad, guarding them with armed volunteers who did their bidding. Teenagers with thin fuzz for beards and immense turbans claimed to be managing these hospitals. Doctors were both grateful to them for the security they provided and terrified of the young thugs, who had little education and no experience. Similarly, Moqtada announced that his clerics were in charge of Najaf. They were organizing the city's services independently of American intervention.

I soon realized that Saddam had been smart to monitor Shia trends by recording so many sermons in their mosques. I began to do the same, attending prayers and asking friends to record the sermons in other mosques. I heard similar messages from many rival Shia leaders, already in late April, within weeks of the fall of Saddam's regime: demands for an Islamic government. Denunciations of secularism. Sometimes the word *democracy* was used positively, but the larger message was not about tolerance and liberalism.

ON APRIL 18 Abdel Aziz al-Hakim had spoken in Kut, proclaiming that Shias were the majority in Iraq and hinting that they hoped for an Islamic government. In Sadr City's Hikma mosque, now controlled by Moqtada, tens of thousands filled the street for Friday prayer, protected by guards carrying Kalashnikovs. It was the first time the mosque was open since the 1999 riots that followed the Second Martyr's death. Sheikh Muhammad Fartusi, Moqtada's deputy for Baghdad, warned that Shias would not accept democracy without full sovereignty. If Shias did not have a say in the government, it would be worse than under Saddam, he said. Fartusi exhorted his audience to obey the *hawza* (i.e., Moqtada) and issued a ban on music and other Western infidel habits. He imposed the veil on women and argued for the supremacy of Islamic law over tribal law.

In Karbala, Sheikh al-Abadi spoke at the shrine of Hussain, which had been closed to Friday prayers since 2002. "We reject this foreign occupation," he declared, calling it an unwanted imperialism. "We do not need the Americans," he said, warning that they were infidels who had come for Iraq's oil. Abadi

also condemned the Iraqi exile politicians who were now returning to Iraq. They were under American control, he said.
Abadi also called for Shias to obey the *hawza* (again, meaning
Moqtada). Abadi called for unity and the crowd chanted with
him, "Yes, yes to the *hawza!*"

On Sunday, April 20, Ayatollah Kadhim al-Haeri, in Iran,
demanded that the new government in Iraq be consistent with
the Iraqi people's religion and morals. That same day Sheikh
Fartusi and five others were arrested by American soldiers. They
were traveling on the road from Karbala and they had refused
to hand over weapons. Thousands of Shias had demonstrated
in front of the Palestine Hotel in Baghdad, demanding Fartusi's
release. Fartusi called his arrest "worse than the arrests that
Saddam ordered against our students." He claimed that he
had been beaten and had spent the night in jail with his hands
tied behind his back. He added that "none of our youth pointed
a weapon against the Americans" and warned that "next time
God alone knows what the people's anger could lead to."

Supporters of Moqtada were getting stronger by the week.
The Bayaa mosque had belonged to followers of Muhammad
Sadiq al-Sadr. Its sheikh, Muayad, had been responsible for
distributing the *hawza's* fatwas in Baghdad, and he had been
popular with antiregime Shias. He had been jailed by Saddam
in 1999 and released following the war. On Friday, April 25,
Sheikh Muayad warned his flock that if he learned of any
Iraqi woman sleeping with American soldiers, he would announce her tribe and call for her death. Muayad now owed his
allegiance to the second Sadr's son, the young Moqtada.

Sadiq al-Sadr had built an impressive network of mosques
and social services around the country, controlled by his former
students. Moqtada capitalized on this network, dispatching
young clerics around the country to seize mosques, hospitals,
clinics, and looted goods, and to provide security and social
services. His men soon controlled Baghdad slums, housing up to
three million Shias, now known as Sadr City. Built in the 1950s
to house Shia migrants fleeing from their feudal lords in the south,

it had originally been called Revolution City, a bastion of the Communist Party. Then it had become Saddam City, though it remained a very traditional area. Now it was a tinderbox.

That same Friday the twenty-fifth, supporters of Moqtada rallied to hear him speak in Kufah. They were watched by Moqtada's burgeoning gang, wearing badges stating they were from the "Office of the Martyr Muhammad Sadiq al-Sadr." Elsewhere, in Nasiriya, Moqtada's supporters gave many fiery sermons. People were told to prepare for an Islamic state. In Baghdad's al-Rahman mosque, the sheikh called on the foreign occupiers to leave Iraq. He wielded a Kalashnikov and spoke of his time in Saddam's jails where he was tortured along with his son. He cried, and his audience cried with him. The sheikh declared the Rahman mosque the Baghdad office of the *hawza* and called for a demonstration on Monday, April 28, to rival a conference the United States was holding to discuss a new Iraqi government. The *hawza* should participate in determining the new government, he said.

In Sadr City's Mohsen mosque the devout were told that they would no longer be ruled by secular laws. They would demand an Islamic government. Sheikh al-Khafaji warned all alcohol and music shops to close.

Muhammad Sadiq al-Sadr had famously said that the *hawza* was divided in two. There was the *hawza natiqa,* or the outspoken *hawza,* meaning him, and there was the *hawza samita,* or silent hawza, referring to Ayatollah al-Sistani, who had sedulously avoided confrontation with political authorities. Now, the outspoken *hawza* was getting louder still. In Baghdad's Kadhimiya district, Sheikh Muhammad al-Yaqubi competed with Moqtada for leadership of the house of Sadr. He addressed tens of thousands of devout in the Shrine of Musa al-Kadhim, each Friday. Most of the listeners had to kneel outside on rugs because the mosque was so crowded. Yaqubi's voice echoed on loudspeakers outside the beige and blue walls of the shrine, the largest Shia mosque in Baghdad, its gold dome and minaret towers shimmering.

At one sermon that I attended, Yaqubi demanded that Iraq's future ruler be a Muslim and rule according to Sharia, or Islamic law. Though "others" were attempting to establish a government, Yaqubi called for a conference to establish it. The *hawza* would send a delegation of experts in public administration to the conference and the new government would restore normal life, write a constitution consistent with Islam, and hold elections. A committee of Sunni and Shia *ulema,* or theologians, would supervise the drafting of the constitution. The jubilant crowd chanted, "Death to Saddam the infidel! Death to the Baath Party!" and "We want! We want! We want [the *hawza* to represent Shias]!" He called on Shias to demonstrate the following Monday at 9:00 A.M. starting at the National Theatre and ending at the Palestine Hotel, where most of the press were staying.

At the end of Yaqubi's sermon, the listeners began to shout, "Yes, for the *hawza natiqa!*" When Sheikh Yaqubi left the mosque, only one gate was open. Outside, the mosque was surrounded by at least two dozen bodyguards armed with Kalashnikovs. As Yaqubi made his way out, his bodyguards shoved people out of the way. People began falling over and getting trampled. They pleaded with the bodyguards to cease pushing them. Several angry prayer goers complained furiously, "He is like Saddam, there is no difference!"

The Kadhim mosque had also issued a decision that women could only enter wearing the *ebaya,* or *chador,* as it was known in Iran. Sadr's followers were imposing their control. Not far from the Kadhim mosque stood the Sunni Sheikh al-Ansari mosque. It was hated by Shias, and they closed it down after the war. When asked why, a *hawza* representative said, "We did it for the security of Yaqubi," but it was clear he did not mean it. "It's the beginning of the separation," he added with a smile.

The demonstration Yaqubi and others had called for was held on Monday, April 28. Thousands of angry demonstrators called for freedom, independence, and justice, whatever those slogans meant. They condemned America and Israel, voicing their support for the *hawza*. They also voiced their opposition to the leadership meeting conducted under American supervision. Moqtada and his followers boycotted the demonstration. A Sadr representative warned that though they did not object to the removal of Saddam and his weapons of mass destruction, an American occupation would be met with resistance.

At a summit meeting called by Jay Garner, the former American general and then-head of the reconstruction effort, Iraq's Shias were underrepresented because the two largest movements, the Sadrists and the Dawa Party, boycotted the event. Dawa explained that it refused to cooperate with a military administration. The Shias were already beginning to feel alienated from the U.S.-led process in Iraq. Even the Supreme Council for the Islamic Revolution in Iraq sent only a minor delegation. The previous week another leadership meeting had been held in Nasiriya, and it too had been boycotted by all major Shia groups. Both meetings were failures, since most of the population was not represented. Ayatollah Ali al-Sistani, Iraq's most powerful cleric, steadfastly refused to meet with any American representative.

On April 28 I drove down to Najaf to meet the *hawza* leadership face to face. When I checked into a hotel near the city's market, the hotel manager had three machine guns behind his front desk. I started my visit with a tour of the City of Peace, as Najaf's cemetery is known. It is a city of tombs, for all those Shias who have sought burial close to the tomb of Ali. When I got to the cemetery, a grave digger was washing a body in preparation for burial. His whole tribe had been grave diggers for centuries, he explained. "I was born and found my father a grave digger, and my father found his father a grave digger." He claimed Najaf's cemetery was the second biggest in the world. "Najaf is designed for burying," he said, "not living, but because people like Ali, they do live here too." In 1991, following the Shia uprising, Saddam destroyed many tombs and built a road over them.

I had come to Najaf to meet with representatives of the

four leading Shia ayatollahs, to find out what sort of government they wanted, and to compare it to the unvarnished messages preached in the mosques. I expected to hear careful statements tailored for the Western press. Yet some of the clerics were honest. The four *marjas* led by Ayatollah Ali al-Sistani were represented by their sons. I met with Ali al-Najafi, the son of Sistani ally Ayatollah Bashir al-Najafi. Their contempt for the young Moqtada Sadr was barely contained. "Some people just buy a turban from the market and dress like an imam," Ali explained, alluding to Moqtada. "In the *hawza* a man can be recognized by his learning. Some irresponsible people who wear the imam's turban have divided the *hawza,* but there are only four *marja:* Najafi, Sistani, Hakim, and Fayad." But even the so-called moderate ayatollahs were not sanguine about the American presence. Ali reminded me that it was Najaf's religious leaders who had led the battle against the British in the "revolution" of 1920 and it was a religious leader who had led the resistance to the Mongols. "This may very possibly happen against the Americans and the British," he said, "if the occupation is against the religious people of Iraq, then they will have to say something. The *marja* has no relationship with the political, it does not need the chair of the country, and it does not aspire to politics, but if the political system is against Islam, then we will fight it. No Muslim can be ruled by a non-Muslim."

What kind of government did he hope to see in Iraq? I asked. "We desire a government of God's justice," he said, but "this is just a wish, we will not get it because the foreign occupation controls everything in Iraq. America will not leave Iraq until the twelfth imam returns." He warned, however, that "we will not wait for the *Mahdi,* we will work to give advice to people. The four *marja* reject the U.S. occupation and could at any time urge their followers to fight, but those who say fight today will never fight," he said. "They just want to increase their popularity. In the 1920s, the leaders of the revolution were all *marja.*"

Volunteers on the street wore plastic *"hawza"* identification cards, but they exchanged them with friends, and nobody knew who was in charge of these volunteers. A loudspeaker announced that there was only one *marja* and no other. Back in the hotel, two middle-aged men sat in the lobby, playing with their children and sharing raisins from American-supplied snacks. They told me they hoped to become the fifty-first state of America. Sitting in my stale room that night, hoping to watch television, I found only one channel. In the middle of a Western television show, the transmission was cut by an amateur announcer. "The new Najaf channel is starting from this day," he said, and the screen showed a Quran as a narrator read it. Later on, a famous singer of Shia lamentations began wailing tributes to Imam Hussain's death. I resigned myself to boredom.

Across from a Baathist building destroyed by American missiles, and from where the stench of dead bodies crushed under the concrete still wafted out, was the headquarters for the Fudala group of the *hawza,* led by Sheikh Yaqubi, who had spoken in Baghdad's Kadhim mosque the previous Friday. "Fudala" meant "the generous ones." Inside, Sheikh Husain al-Tai, a tall man with dark red skin, explained to me that Fudala sought to run the city's administration, to prove that the *hawza* could govern everything in Iraq, the political and the social. "We are researching and comparing Islam to other political systems such as capitalism, socialism, and Marxism," he said. "We know that religion and politics are the same. Now that Saddam is gone, we can return to politics." He invited me to the Fudala Party's founding conference the following day.

To prepare for Fudala's founding conference I looked at Yaqubi's book *We and the West,* which he had written before the war. "America lifts the flag of enemies to Islam and makes itself the first enemy of Muslims, so we must also consider America our enemy," he said. "All the signs have occured for the *awar al dajal,*" Yaqubi warned. The *awar al dajal* was the one-eyed liar, sort of like the Muslim Antichrist. He was very powerful and could put people in his paradise or his hell. He had godlike powers and could make rain fall and the flowers grow. He was like a pharaoh (not a good thing to be in Islam). The *Mahdi* and Christ would return eventually to kill the *awar al dajal*. According to Yaqubi's book, America was the *awar al dajal*. He was blind in one eye, because he looked at life only in one way, and that was money. He did not see life with feelings. His hell was the suffering caused by America. His paradise was the money that America gave to people. Anybody who was sent to his hell would be sent to paradise by God, anyone who followed him to his paradise would go to God's hell.

Yaqubi attributed his theories to Muhammad Sadiq al-Sadr. "People must not take culture from America, but should take their science," he said. He mocked those who wore jeans and adopted American culture but demonstrated against America. "We are at war with the West," he said. "It is a cultural war . . . after the fall of the Soviet Union, a new system in the world called the unipolar system took over. It is represented by American imperialism. Behind it are the global Masons. They have been planning in the shadows for two hundred years to satisfy distant goals. These goals are putting all the world under the control of a strong hand. This hand must interfere in every affair of other systems under the guise of internationalism and legality to create a balanced organization. This whole new system is called globalization."

There were about three hundred people present at the conference. Since they were followers of Yaqubi, they were by extension followers of Muhammad Sadiq al-Sadr. Like all such events, the conference began with a verse from the Quran specifically selected for its appropriateness for the occasion. For the Fudala Party's establishment they read a verse from the Quran that stated "God opened our path to go to the future and nobody can stop us because we are victorious." Members of Fudala wore badges that said they were protectors of Najaf.

The conference was attended by tribal leaders, religious leaders, and academics. "This group will represent the *hawza* and all of Islam," Yaqubi announced. Yaqubi, who was in charge of Sadr University, was a small, older man with a child's body and a stern face. Under his white turban he wore thick glasses with a gray frame. He sat behind a desk flanked by two laymen in Western clothes. He explained that they would defend Shias and Sharia from Western culture. This was much like the Dawa Party's original goal. Tribal heads were not suitable to run Iraq, Yaqubi said, and the leader of Iraq should not come from outside Iraq because his behavior would be Western and not Iraqi.

Yaqubi announced that he would open many offices in all of Iraq to organize the *hawza*. He would organize a consultative council to be elected by the people, like in Iran. They would establish a newspaper to spread their thinking. A constitutional Islamic council would be responsible for politics and for watching what other parties did, evaluating and controlling their behavior. He urged people to go to their mosques. "The mosque is a school, a cultural center, a center for conferences," he said. "Everything that is done must be done inside the mosque."

MEANWHILE, ONE OF Yaqubi's main opponents among Shia leaders, Moqtada al-Sadr, was trying to put a velvet glove on his iron fist. Around the time of the Fudala convention, he spoke in the mosque in nearby Kufah, trying to bolster his religious credentials. Moqtada warned those who did not attend Friday prayers that their absence was tantamount to supporting the atheist West. All alcohol shops must be closed down, Moqtada decreed, even those owned by Christians. The *manbar,* or chair upon which the imam sat, would be the seat of the government in Iraq, he said. Tens of thousands were in attendance. Moqtada's following was growing. He already controlled Sadr City, home to nearly 10 percent of Iraq's population. Even if not all of Sadr City's residents supported him, the presence of Moqtada's armed thugs meant that nobody could compete with him there. Moqtada had taken to wearing a white funeral shroud, like his father, demonstrating his willingness to be martyred.

He was doing his best to sound like a more erudite cleric, yet when I visited him, he was gruff.

Moqtada punctuated his points with a dismissive puff, "eh," and sneered. He was very aggressive, which was unusual in the labyrinth of rumors, hints, and innuendoes that typically constituted a conversation with a Shia leader. Moqtada's followers called him by his first name—he was one of them. No other leader in Iraq had such a personal relationship with his followers. The young upstart of the Shia world, he was taking on the establishment, showing no respect for his elders, or his betters, at first glance just an arrogant street punk benefiting from his father's reputation and universal admiration. But to believe that he was merely that was a grave mistake.

Moqtada refused to tell me what kind of government he hoped to see in Iraq. "When America attacked Iraq, it ignored world opinion," he said. "The whole world stood against America and the U.S. ignored it. Likewise, the U.S. will ignore the opinion of the Iraqi people and it will compose the new government according to its own desires." He did not thank the United States for freeing Iraq, he said, he thanked only God. "I don't want the chair of the government because it will be controlled by the U.S., and I don't want to be controlled by the U.S.," Moqtada said.

I asked if he wanted to attack America. Moqtada snorted and replied in a very colloquial expression, *"Ya muawad,"* or "Hey, man, you want us to get in trouble?" "I am not afraid," he said when I asked him if he feared for his safety. "I wish to be a martyr and I don't fear death." When asked if he wanted relations with Shias in other countries, Moqtada said, "The Shias outside Iraq didn't help the Shias inside Iraq; they urged us to fight and didn't help, letting us be first in line to get killed." Would there be a time to fight the Americans? "I will fight America when the *Mahdi* will appear, because this is the land of the *Mahdi* and they occupy his land."

✦ ✦ ✦

MOQTADA'S POWER GRAB only became more difficult. The number of contenders for Shia leadership continued to expand. On May 10 Ayatollah Muhamad Bakr al-Hakim, the SCIRI leader whose brother had called a rally in Karbala, returned to Iraq after twenty-three years in exile. He was greeted by an adoring crowd of thousands. Hakim called for a Muslim government.

On Friday, May 16, the rough concrete halls of Baghdad's al-Rahman mosque were packed with hundreds of men who spilled onto its gravel courtyard. Men with Kalashnikovs patrolled through the kneeling crowd, as did a man spraying water from an insect exterminating pack to cool the crowd. Sheikh Fartusi, Moqtada's boss for Baghdad, quickly got to the point: "Iraq is an occupied country." Fartusi called for a demonstration the following Monday at the Kadhim shrine to show Iraqi unity and support a *hawza*-led government. Fartusi asked the crowd to shout, "No, no to imperialism, no, no to occupation, no, no to falsehood, no, no to the devil!"

The al-Muhsin mosque, at the entrance to Sadr City, was its most important. It was controlled by Seyid Hasan Naji al-Musawi. Though only in his midthirties, the jovial and ribald Hasan had a white beard. Fond of wordplays and vulgar jokes, Hasan always promised to find me a good Iraqi wife, and he once explained to me the different ways to satisfy Iranian, Lebanese, and Iraqi women. I met him in May 2003, visiting him often in his home around the corner from the mosque. In the beginning he often charged me a "tax," asking me to use my satellite phone to call friends and relatives in southern Lebanon, where he had once lived, and I teased him by suggesting he was calling Lebanese Hizballah. Seyid Hasan's brothers worked as drivers, taking passengers from Baghdad to Syria or Jordan in sedans nicknamed "dolphins." I drove in and out of the country with one brother, a devout young man who ate only kabobs. His other brother, Seyid Abdul Jabar, drank alcohol and worked as little as possible. Eating dinner once with the brothers, they asked me which ayatollah my father followed. Jabar whispered in my ear, "I only follow girls!"

Seyid Hasan insisted that the Iranian system of government was the best system for Iraq, and that Ayatollah al-Haeri would be the Supreme Leader. Seyid Hasan denied forming a political party, but he insisted the Sadr movement represented the people of Iraq. "People want us to try and establish a government," Seyid Hasan said. He warned that should Sadr City rise up against the occupation, it "will be one hundred times worse for the Americans than Mogadishu. Until now we are just waiting for the Americans to fulfill their promises." On television that day I saw Defense Secretary Donald Rumsfeld warning that "efforts to make Iraq in Iran's image will be aggressively put down."

The next Friday, May 30, at the al-Muhsin mosque, Seyid Hasan led tens of thousands in prayer. Sheikh al-Abadi provided the sermon. "We demand that the American forces get out of Iraq," he said. "The Iraqi people have the right to govern their own country. America wouldn't agree to be occupied by any other country, so they must know that Islamic countries do not accept occupation." Addressing the "people of humanity in America," he said, "we are not your enemy. Your enemy is gone, as you can see." He warned that the crime of occupation overshadowed the gift of liberty.

Sheikh al-Abadi warned about the Jewish threat. "There is a negative phenomenon that will destroy this society in the same manner used before by Israel to occupy Palestine," he said. He warned that the Jews were "coming and buying land here just like they did in Palestine" and that "they make Jewish footprints in Iraq. Israel is the number-one enemy of Islam and Iraq. Selling land to these people is forbidden."

In Baghdad the power vacuum was rapidly filled by Sadr's army of followers. "The *hawza* orders and people obey," said Sheikh Fartusi. "It was the same in the time of Saddam. People were suffering and complaining and the *hawza* tried to decrease these sufferings. The first thing we did was to reassure people that the area is secure and stable; then restore social services, traffic, power; then restore law and prevent people from looting and stealing. Moqtada was in charge of the martyrs' office and the office gave orders." Fartusi was born in the Meisan province in 1969 and studied pharmacology at the University of Baghdad. He studied in the *hawza* for ten years, never leaving Iraq. He worked for Moqtada's father as a religious school supervisor. "They tried to close the office after 1999," he said, "and we tried to move to continue spreading our ideas and in the end with patience we succeeded. We were always trying to serve people, not thinking of leading or the future, only of today. Sadr City was suffering from a water shortage under Saddam and we helped that. If they install an honorable government we will continue studying. It should be peace-loving, fair, honest, not aggressive against neighbors, no discrimination between sects. We want the leader to be from those people who suffered. If the government is good, it will have direct relations with people. If the government fails, we will reelect a new government."

Fartusi ran the Hikma mosque. When I visited one morning, I found the baby-faced Sheikh Halim al-Fatlawi presiding over social services in Sadr City. In an annex of the mosque, Fatlawi sat on a thin mattress on the marble floor. When the war ended, Fatlawi was at the Shia religious academy in the holy city of Najaf. Now, he and his fellow clerics were dispatched to Sadr City to stave off the crisis following the collapse of Saddam's food distribution program. He explained that "when the government fell, there were many cars going back and forth between Najaf, where the Shia leadership resides, and Baghdad, where many clerical students were staying." United in their adherence to the rulings of Muhammad Sadiq al-Sadr, these students were able to organize and obey Moqtada. "I was in Najaf when the government fell and we sent instructions to all the students in Baghdad in these cars," Fatlawi said. "We issued a fatwa that looted food and medicine be returned to us, and we reopened the warehouses and began distributing food to the people."

With the help of an army of volunteers from Sadr City, Fatlawi also supervised the provision of security to medical clinics and for the Islamic court, held once a week in his mosque to settle civil disputes. Young men with badges from the *hawza,* wielding AK-47s, protected hospitals, food warehouses, and neighborhoods. But security was not the only need. Fatlawi listened patiently and handed out instructions as people beseeched him for food, to provide them with milk, sugar, rice, and other essentials. A line extended out of the door into the main hall of the mosque. He leaned forward intently, his legs crossed and his round face serene, almost Buddha-like. Those who requested financial assistance received five to ten thousand dinars a week per person. Fatlawi explained that "sometimes they get more if they need to pay for a medical treatment."

Sheikh Halim warned me that "the Iraqi people don't like American freedom; they want Islamic freedom, not a secular freedom." When I visited the children's program in the mosque courtyard, I found rows of young boys chanting that America was the devil. As I left with my female photographer, who was wrapped in her own black *abaya,* the boys chased after us, smiling, and slitting their throats with their fingers in pantomine.

Walking to Moqtada's office, in an alley just before the Tomb of Ali, I entered a store selling religious books, CDs, and watches with pictures of Moqtada, his brothers, and father on their faces. Crowds stood before his office, earnestly making their case for entry to an indifferent young cleric who peered down at them from behind the barely opened door. A young cleric in black robes and white turban dragged an older shopkeeper to the door, ordering him to wait there, as the cleric entered to inquire whether it was permitted to sell shirts bearing the image of Moqtada's father, Muhammad Sadiq al-Sadr.

In mid-July, Moqtada called for the establishment of a Mahdi Army of loyal followers to protect Iraq and the *marja* leadership of the *hawza*. He also accused the Americans of besieging his house, but added that they could not prevent him from going out to see his people because of the Mahdi Army. "Americans dispersed," he said, after knowing that they would face a "test called the Shiites." He reiterated that the American-appointed Iraqi Governing Council was an "agent for Americans" and that services such as electricity were much better under the old regime. He claimed that the "Zionist" IGC (Iraqi Governing Council) was composed of insignificant men and members of illegal political parties who had handed control of Iraq to foreigners. Moqtada warned that his Mahdi Army would be mobilized when it was necessary to support the *hawza,* meaning himself. He demanded that Iraqis shut down radio and television stations that the Americans had established. Moqtada denied any desire to participate in the new government, which he called illegal.

Later that month Moqtada claimed that American soldiers had surrounded his home and were planning to arrest him. Thousands of protestors descended upon Najaf, heeding their leader's call. Many were bused or trucked in from Baghdad or Basra. Some even came in ambulances. They confronted American soldiers and marines. Demonstrators chanted "no Americans after today," echoing the motto of Saddam's storm troopers in the 1991 intifada who ransacked southern Iraq warning that there would be "no Shias after today." The leaders of the protest handed a list of demands to the colonel at the American base in Najaf, including a demand that the troops leave immediately.

In mid-August, as temperatures rose, tempers flared. On the thirteenth of that month an American helicopter flying over Sadr City stopped above a radio tower where a black flag inscribed with the name of the Mahdi waved from the top. Soldiers tried to knock the flag down. Thousands of protestors were met by U.S. troops. At least one Iraqi was killed and several others wounded. Sadr City was in an uproar. Signs condemning America and Israel and calling for violence appeared throughout the neighborhood. For Iraq's insecure Shias, accustomed to victimization and reared on myths of martyrdom, it was the spark they had been waiting for.

The Friday prayers in Sadr City two days later were predictably inflammatory. Thousands chanted for Islam and against America. "Yesterday Saddam the infidel attacked our holy sites and the people of this holy city," one sheikh cried, "and now the Americans do the same thing. So what is the difference between Saddam and America?" The American civilian administration, the CPA, was at a loss. They were under strict orders not to deal with Moqtada's movement throughout the country. Even humanitarian NGOs working on U.S. aid contracts were forbidden by the local CPA officials from interacting with Sadr's men. Sadr was dismissed as a nuisance and nothing more. A U.S. inquiry into the murder of Khoei found Moqtada guilty, but he was never arrested for the crime.

Iraq's *faudha,* or chaos, was one step closer to *fitna,* or civil strife (a condition greatly feared in Islam) when SCIRI's leader Ayatollah Muhamad Bakr al-Hakim was killed in a car bombing outside Najaf's Tomb of Ali following the Friday prayers on August 29. It was only ten days after the UN headquarters suffered a devastating attack. Up to one hundred others were also slain in the massive bombing that killed Hakim. Iraqi authorities seized nineteen men, some of them foreign Arabs, suspected of involvement. The bombings were followed by calls for an Iraqi paramilitary force to be recruited from the various militias in the country. One more martyr graced the walls of Iraq's streets.

2

THE NEW MONGOLS:
Summer–Fall 2003

✦ Number of Americans killed from April 9–June 8, 2003: 39

✦ Number of Americans killed in July 2003: 48

THE ABU HANIFA MOSQUE, in Baghdad's Adhamiya neighborhood, is one of the most important locations in the country for Iraq's Sunnis. The neighborhood's name comes from Al Imam al-Adham, "the greatest saint." The mosque contains his 1,300-year-old tomb and is named for him: Abu Hanifa al-Nu'man. Abu Hanifa was a ninth-century theologian whose legal judgments are followed by about half of the world's Muslims. His tomb is visited by hundreds of thousands of pilgrims a year. If Karbala is the center of Shia Islam, the Abu Hanifa mosque is Iraq's most important Sunni shrine. During Saddam's reign, the mosque's imam held up a Kalashnikov during his sermons, exhorting his listeners to protect Saddam and his regime. He was now in hiding. The neighborhood was the last to fall to the invasion. Saddam's last public appearance was outside the mosque.

So it was fitting that the first man to give a sermon at the Abu Hanifa mosque after the regime collapsed was Dr. Ahmad

Kubeisi, Iraq's most important Sunni scholar. A great deal of hope for peace rested on his shoulders. It was Friday, April 18. Looting was in progress, and the Ministry of Information was in flames. Loudspeakers atop the U.S. Army's Humvees warned in Arabic that if the looters did not immediately leave "there will be consequences." Thousands gathered to hear Dr. Kubeisi. He was born in the western Anbar province in 1935. He grew up in Falluja, and was an Islamic studies professor at the University of Baghdad until leaving Iraq for the United Arab Emirates in 1997. Kubeisi had served as an advisor to the UAE government, forging close ties with the country's elite as well as the well-known hard-line preacher Sheikh Yusuf al-Qaradawi. There were few other Sunni personalities as well known. His past five years in exile created the impression that he had been opposed to Saddam, and he would attempt to use this to forge ties with the former opposition figures who had returned.

For Dr. Kubeisi's triumphal return the mosque was covered in banners. On the walls of the mosque stood young men holding banners proclaiming "One Iraq One People," "No to America," "All the Believers Are Brothers," and "Leave Our Country, We Want Peace," among other proclamations of national and Islamic unity. Demonstrators chanted, "No to America, no to Saddam, our revolution is Islamic!" The angular and white-bearded Kubeisi had been a strident opponent of the American war, which he had warned would fail, but shortly after he was proven wrong, he made haste from his comfortable life in Dubai.

As the devout knelt and then stood in a typical "fortified wall," Kubeisi explained that he preferred not to discuss Saddam until the former leader's fate was known. In truth, he dared not criticize him. Symbolic of the Sunnis as a whole, Kubeisi was torn. As a professor at the university, he had had a good relationship with the previous government, at least for a time. Kubeisi had not been a member of the Iraqi opposition, and even as the war in Iraq was being waged, he had given a speech in support of the Iraqi people's and government's defiance of the coalition, condemning the Iraqi opposition and comparing the Iraqi government's defiance to the Prophet Muhammad's grandson Hussain. He had also spoken of the U.S. plan for Iraq as part of the "Jewish Torah's goal." He called anyone allied with the Americans a traitor and warned the Iraqi opposition that they were considered traitors and spies by the Iraqi people.

Now he was attempting to galvanize the Sunni elite and lead the community that had become disenfranchised with the end of the regime. His sermon was an ode to resistance. Baghdad had been occupied by the Mongols, Dr. Kubeisi said, referring to the sacking of what was then the capital of the Muslim world in 1258. Now, new Mongols were occupying Baghdad, they were destroying its civilization, and they were creating divisions between Sunnis and Shias. The Shias and Sunnis were one, however, and they should remain united and reject foreign control. They had all suffered together as one people under Saddam's rule, and they were suffering again now. Kubeisi went out of his way to thank the Shia people of Basra for "defending their country against the foreign invaders." He demanded an administration governed only by Iraqis and a council of Shia and Sunni scholars to oppose any government the Americans tried to establish. "We will reconstruct our country," he said, rejecting American interference and rejecting "a government that will oppress us," calling instead for elections. He mocked the "continuous lies" that the Americans had come to get rid of Saddam's weapons of mass destruction. "Where are these weapons?" he demanded. The Americans were the enemies of mankind and had come for Iraq's oil. "Get out before we expel you," he said, warning of the humiliation they would suffer. The sermon ended with shouts of "Allahu Akbar!"

The parallel with the fall of Baghdad to infidels in 1258 was ominous. It had shocked Muslims in the thirteenth century. Theologians such as Tariq al-Din ibn Taimiya had reacted by blaming Muslims for failing to be sufficiently devout. A wave of conservative Islam spread throughout the Muslim world, as many tried to return Islam to its original purity. Often quoted by Osama bin Laden, Ibn Taimiya is the spiritual father of radical Sunnism, in particular the Wahhabi form of Islam dominant in Saudi Arabia and the general Salafi trend dominant in international terror movements like al Qaeda. Ibn Taimiya viewed offensive jihad as a duty of every Muslim and expressed extreme disdain for Shias. Ayman al-Zawahiri, the Egyptian fundamentalist who acts as al Qaeda's ideologue, has relied on Ibn Taimiya's thirteenth-century fatwas, written as the Mongols devastated Baghdad. The Saudi government has been distributing the works of Ibn Taimiya for free throughout the world since the 1950s. The January 2004 memorandum attributed to Abu Musab al-Zarqawi also quoted Ibn Taimiya extensively as it praised the Sunni resistance. Across from the Abu Hanifa mosque, I found a shop selling magazines that promoted Ibn Taimiya's thoughts. Also present that day was Sheikh Muayad al-Adhami, whom Kubeisi had appointed to lead the mosque. Muayad was angered by the entry of American marines into his new mosque the previous week. The marines had not removed their shoes and had carried weapons. The Americans had violated Iraqi dignity, he said.

Just as Kubeisi was finishing up, the new Mongols showed up in person. A marine patrol ("the one five") rounded a corner and walked right into hundreds of people praying on the street and listening to the sermon. The marines naively approached near the separate section for women. Dozens of men rose and put their shoes on, forming a virtual wall to block them. The marines seemed unaware of the danger. They did not understand Arabic. "Go back!" the demonstrators screamed, and some waved their fists, shouting, "America is the enemy of God!" as they were restrained by a few cooler-headed men from within their ranks. I ran to advise some of the marines that Friday prayers was not a good time to show up fully armed. The men sensed this and asked me to tell their lieutenant, who appeared oblivious to the public relations catastrophe he might be provoking. He told me: "That's why we've got the guns."

A nervous soldier asked me to go explain the situation to the bespectacled staff sergeant, who had been attempting to calm the situation by telling the demonstrators, who did not speak English, that the U.S. patrol meant no harm. He finally lost his temper when an Iraqi told him gently, "You must go."

"I have the weapons," the sergeant said. "You back off."

"Let's get the fuck out!" one marine shouted to another, as the tension increased. I was certain that a shove, a tossed stone, or a shot fired could have provoked a massacre and turned the city violently against the American occupation. Finally, the marines retreated cautiously around a corner, as the worshipers were held back by their own men. Women peered at the marines from behind cracked open doors and children waved to them and gave them a thumbs-up.

Following the marines' departure, tens of thousands demonstrated in the street, carrying their Qurans, prayer mats, and banners, some condemning America and Israel, some calling for jihad, and some calling for unity among Sunnis and Shias. A few banners were held for the Muslim Brotherhood, a movement started in early twentieth-century Egypt that had grown to be the largest pan-Islamic movement and had spawned the terrorist movements of the Middle East. It had long since been crushed and gone underground in Iraq. Where once Iraqis had cheered "with our souls, with our blood, we will sacrifice ourselves for you, oh Saddam," they now vowed to sacrifice themselves for Iraq and Islam.

Kubeisi was head of the recently formed Hayat al-Ulema al Muslimin, or the Sunni Association of Muslim Scholars. He went on to form the United Iraqi National Movement, leaving the word *Islamic* out of its name to stress its national rather than religious quality. It organized demonstrations in Mosul as well. Kubeisi mocked the heads of the UN and the Arab League, but in the summer of 2003 he condemned attacks against American soldiers as premature. He wanted to wait and see whether or not the Americans acted on their promise to leave as soon as possible. Kubeisi started out as a moderate among the extremists, stressing that his movement was not demanding an Islamic regime in Iraq. His trajectory would say a lot about the Sunnis in the new Iraq: he moved steadily toward militancy, until his own life became endangered because he was not militant enough.

In April he was still saying things such as, "Let's build our society, build the city, and show the world that we can do it." In one sermon he said that the best weapons the Iraqis had were science, knowledge, and culture. Kubeisi also called for a government to reconstruct the city, pay salaries, and stock hospitals. He commended the volunteers who were guiding traffic and attempting to establish order, and he condemned the looters. Somewhat confusingly, he called for a future Iraqi state that was neither secular nor Islamic. Yet that sermon was followed by a demonstration calling for the United States to end its occupation, and Kubeisi was flanked by bodyguards as he left. A rival demonstration then proceeded to protest Kubeisi's alleged pro–former regime statements and reject his calls for the immediate departure of coalition forces, which they viewed as implying that Saddam's regime should be restored.

That week, in an interview given to the Arab *Al Hayat* newspaper, Kubeisi again called for the Americans to leave, but not until they established security and a government. "There is no alternative to them at present," he said. He repeated his view that the Iraqi people did not respect the former opposition members who had returned and demanded that a delegation be selected from the country's notable leaders to negotiate with the Americans. By "notable" he meant, for the most part, Sunni.

Kubeisi feared Iraq would end up like Afghanistan, he said, because the American government was not interested in fixing what it had destroyed. "Words cannot describe my rage for what they did to Iraq," he told the paper. He called for a cabinet with an even number of Sunnis and Shias, warning against domination by any sect. He threw in a typical appeal to anti-Semitism, suggesting that those nations that back Israel were also seeking Iraq's destruction and the fulfillment of what he claimed was an Old Testament edict that Babel—modern-day Iraq—had to be destroyed.

Back then, in April, most Sunni sheikhs were counseling patience, but not all. In Baghdad, the sheikh at a mosque in the Dora neighborhood was already warning that his job was to motivate his congregation to declare jihad. In Mosul, Iraq's third-largest city, situated in the Sunni north, life was returning to normal with shops and restaurants open, buses running, and fighting subsiding. The sheikh at the important Al-Ziab al-Iraqi mosque called for the Americans to leave and condemned them for killing civilians. He rejected American and British "colonialism" and said they had defeated Saddam "for the sake of Israel." Allah had warned his believers not to trust Christians or Jews, he said, and he called on the Iraqi people to unite and expel the foreign occupiers, whom Allah would destroy. This was a sheikh who had been imprisoned and tortured by Saddam and who condemned his regime for committing atrocities. Yet he was already threatening resistance if the coalition forces did not leave promptly.

The Iraqi Islamic Party had old roots in Mosul, and had reemerged after the war in full force, occupying the former offices of the Iraqi Olympic committee and printing pamphlets calling for the establishment of Islamic law. It had organized militias of bearded young men wielding Kalashnikovs to provide security, distribute aid, and open health clinics. The party was closely aligned with the Muslim Brotherhood, whose Iraqi branch had been founded in 1945. These days, it was led by Dr. Usama al-Tikriti. Interviewed on Al Jazeera, Tikriti claimed credit for Saddam's reintroduction of Islam into Iraqi politics in the 1990s, explaining that it was a change from infidelity to hypocrisy, which he meant as a compliment.

The Brotherhood was especially active in Mosul, which was the only post-Saddam province to have a functioning government, albeit an increasingly Islamist one. Like in Baghdad, theaters showing "sexy movies," as pornography is called, were being threatened or bombed. A Mosul city council member and leading Sunni cleric, Sheikh Saleh Khalik Hamudi, warned that all movie theaters would soon be closed, because they were a threat to society. In the first week of May, Hamudi had closed two theaters for letting in youth and for opening on the birthday of the Prophet Muhammad.

In Baghdad the first week of May, temperatures and tempers were rising. "I told the Americans, 'If this doesn't stop, we might have a revolution,'" said Sheikh Abdul Rahman Abdul Jabar, a thirty-year-old Sunni imam in southern Baghdad. His neighborhood was frustrated with American troops exploding ammunition dumps nearby, shaking their walls, breaking their windows, and terrifying them. Another sheikh warned that young men were getting increasingly angry over the poverty and hopelessness of their lives. He blamed the UN sanctions for much of the poverty and explained that many men were dropping out to fight the illegal occupation. Atop his mosque was a large banner proclaiming "Iraq for the Iraqis." This sheikh was already urging his congregation to resist the Americans.

In Baquba, northeast of Baghdad, a twenty-three-year-old woman threw a grenade at U.S. soldiers. They shot her as she tried to throw a second one. Baquba's clerics, such as Sheikh Raad Anbagi at the al Zaituni mosque, spoke of the young woman with admiration, urging their men to take up her battle.

On June 1, a U.S. patrol was attacked with small-arms fire and RPGs (rocket-propelled grenades) from the rooftops across from the Abu Hanifa mosque. That week the CPA warned that it would ban any incitements to insurrection or violence. Major Christopher Varhola, of Civil Affairs Command in Baghdad, was harshly critical of a policy that would lead to arresting clerics. "It will only make them martyrs," he said, adding that "it treats the symptom and not the cause." One Arab newspaper reported that resistance groups that had been created before the war had started were conducting quick operations to create the impression that the war was not over, and warned, presciently, that in a month or two the resistance would be more organized, with more suicide operations. The following Friday, June 6, Sheikh Muayad spoke to over a thousand people, lamenting the deaths of two civilians in the RPG attack but defending those who raised the flag of jihad. He defended the resistance for attacking those who were oppressing Iraqis. Iraqis had suffered too much in the previous century, and they were now being strangled by America, the forces of tyranny. He warned of a sleeping warrior called Islam that had not yet been awoken. Meanwhile, in Ramadi, a leading sheikh was already warning that "the future is jihad!" and asking his congregation if they would sit and do nothing while the Americans occupied their land. Sunni support for America was quickly fading.

The following day, Web sites in Iraq posted a document allegedly written by the former regime's intelligence services, outlining plans for sabotage and resistance should Iraq lose the war to the "Zionist American British coalition forces." The document, purportedly written on January 23, 2003, was signed by the director of the General Intelligence Service.

Dr. Kubeisi, however, was still advising patience. He condemned attacks against American soldiers, saying that they were premature. Iraqis should wait to see whether or not the Americans acted on their promise to leave as soon as possible. Kubeisi admitted that Sunnis were pushed aside because the United States viewed them as hostile and that the Shias were "temporary" victors in the new Iraq, but he still hoped for a peaceful process. On June 13, at Samara's grand mosque, Kubeisi called for reason over emotion. Though jihad and martyrdom were great, he said, it was better to live for God than to die for him. A longer life would allow one to pray more, fast more, perform the pilgrimage more, and donate more to charity. The resistance was giving the American occupiers an excuse to kill, to extend their occupation, and to prevent the establishment of a government. He went so far as to prohibit attacks against the Americans. "We waited thirty-five years under Saddam, and we should give the Americans a year before we fight them and tell them to leave," he said. By mid-June Kubeisi was complaining that the Iraqi Shias felt they were in a strong position and were taking advantage of it. Their priority was to fight Sunnis, while the Sunnis' priority was to fight the Americans. Yet he also warned that history would record the Shias as having divided the Iraqis and the Sunnis as having fought the Americans. Alternately optimistic and cynical, he predicted that the American occupation might last sixty years.

He knew he had to appeal to listeners who were far more angry and cynical than he was. Kubeisi assured them that the Americans sought to abolish Islam but mentioned that other empires such as the Byzantines, Persians, Mongols, and British had all tried to do the same, and failed. He said that he had visited Najaf, another major Shia city, to call for unity, and that throughout the country Iraqis were ready to control their affairs.

Misunderstandings between American troops and Iraqi citizens were inevitable, yet each one was an irritant. Shortly after Kubeisi's Samara sermon, the Association of Muslim Scholars organized a protest in response to an American raid on a mosque in Baghdad. Protestors claimed the soldiers had stolen money, and one cleric cried out that the mosque had been defiled. I went to meet the mosque's leader, Imam Mahdi al-Jumeili.

"We are sure they came here to steal the country and protect Israel," Jumeili said of the Americans. "They plan to take over the whole world. Everyone wants to control Iraq and take a piece of our wealth: Japan, Europe, Russia." Jumeili was conspiratorial in his view of international affairs. "Judaism and Masonism are at war with Islam, and they share the same goals with America in the world. What is happening tells us the truth about their intentions. The American army consists of mercenaries and bastards. The control of Iraq is an evil thing and those who help control it are evil. The U.S. helped Saddam three hundred times. In the war with Iran, the U.S. helped Saddam because it needed him. Now the U.S. wants to play a role in the area by itself so it got rid of Saddam."

Jumeili explained that "many simple people ask us why don't we wage a jihad, but we refuse to grant a jihad so that there will be no more bloodshed. All the people are mad and want to fight the U.S., and we tell them the U.S. promised to leave Iraq and we have to wait, but we think eventually people will take things into their own hands."

I asked officers I had befriended from the 352nd Civil Affairs Unit to come to the mosque and investigate the charges. Jumeili was barely courteous. Lieutenant Colonel Glenn Schweitzer greeted him with the Arabic "Peace be upon you" and extended his long arm forward. Jumeili refused to shake Schweitzer's hand, placing both his arms behind his back, bowing his head slightly, and answering with a curt "and upon you," omitting the "peace" that comes at the end of the proper response.

He refused to meet Schweitzer and Major Chris Varhola on mosque grounds, so they sat in a lot outside as he recounted the events, surrounded by dozens of his angry congregants. "The mosque is only for Muslims and prayer," he said. "We are very angry at the U.S. soldiers for entering our mosques. Saddam fought all of us, but he never attacked or insulted our mosques." A nervous sergeant remained in the army's Humvee as the two officers made themselves vulnerable targets. Imam Jumeili asked whether any of the Americans before him were Jews. "Are you Americans? Christians? Are any of you Jews?" Satisfied that he was dealing with non-Jews, he told the story of the raid. A Nissan pickup truck and an American military truck had pulled up to the mosque, which was functioning as a medical aid center. They pushed a boy aside and four soldiers went inside. They asked many questions about where the mosque's money and medical supplies had come from. They insulted all the people inside, even the doctor, and threatened him with arrest, Jumeili claimed. "Is this the freedom or democracy you are talking about?" asked the sheikh's secretary.

In response, the officers tried to be respectful. "We are very embarrassed," Varhola said. Schweitzer added that "maybe somebody who did not like you or know your good reputation told the soldiers you were hiding weapons. Some spies that worked with Saddam now work with us, so we are getting bad information and we don't know that." Jumeili responded that "the mosque has to be respected." Schweitzer agreed, explaining that "General Franks gave an order that no Americans are to enter mosques, even just to look. Only Muslim soldiers. Our young soldiers who are only eighteen do not know and make mistakes." Varhola added that "this is new and strange to them." Schweitzer explained that they would reimburse him for the damages.

Jumeili laughed. His pride restored after standing up to Americans, Jumeili turned benevolent. He explained that "if America had not occupied Iraq, I would not let you leave without inviting you to my house and shaking your hands. If America leaves Iraq and allows Iraqis to control Iraq, then you would be my friends." Schweitzer responded that "if you come to America, you are welcome in my house. We are not here as occupiers, we are here to liberate."

"Liberate?!" cried out an old man. "With weapons?"

Jumeili quieted him down. "The Americans came to Iraq for many reasons," he said, "and international Jews pushed them to do that. Now we see all our country in their hands— the oil, the wealth. The large military presence reveals that they want to stay for a long time and they are not letting the government be formed. We are not attacking America. Osama bin Laden is a lie; Saddam's weapons are a lie. These are reasons from the Mossad [Israeli intelligence] for America to occupy Iraq and control the world. They are working intensively to destroy our religion."

The sergeant who had been driving the Humvee came with bottles of water for the clinic. Jumeili refused them, saying,

"We don't accept anything except from Iraqis." Schweitzer explained that "it is important for us to understand how you view the world. I don't know how [CPA head Paul] Bremer will create government, and I don't know why he delayed the creation of government." Jumeili smiled. "But we do know," he said, mysteriously.

"Is there anything we can do for you?" asked Schweitzer.

"Leave Iraq!" shouted someone nearby.

"Iraqi people ask us daily about beginning the jihad against the U.S.," Jumeili said, "but we don't want bloodshed, and we tell them to wait for America to leave—but we might fail to convince all of them. Every imam in a mosque cannot always control all the people."

IN FACT, by the summer, many Sunni clerics had become active leaders of the resistance. On June 14, Sheikh Tahma Aboud Khalif of the Salahedin mosque in Baghdad planted a bomb composed of two artillery shells on a road, with the help of three accomplices. When the bomb failed to explode, Sheikh Tahma and his friends, wielding RPGs and Kalashnikovs, were spotted by soldiers, who managed to arrest the cleric. Inside his mosque the Americans found thousands of ammunition rounds as well as flares, detonators, and timing devices. Locals were angered at the arrest of their cleric, a Wahhabi who had spent over a month in Saddam's prisons before the war.

A letter purportedly written by Saddam warned all foreigners who came with the "cowardly occupiers" to leave Iraq before June 17, though the writer might have confused the dates, actually intending the ultimatum to be July 17, the thirty-fifth anniversary of the coup that brought the Baathists to power. "We are not responsible for the consequences after that," the letter said, threatening to attack coalition countries and their airplanes abroad. The letter also called for Iraqis to liberate Iraq from the occupation and "turn the enemy's life into hell."

Some sheikhs offered strategic advice. Sheikh Kheiri, leader of Tikrit's main mosque, one of the best-lit and best air-conditioned mosques in the country, lectured on how best to go about attacking Americans. "I told you many times not to attack the Americans now," he began. "You are like a bird right now. The bird that broke its wing has to be patient and wait for his wing to be fixed and fly again. If somebody takes off a bird's feathers, it takes a few months to grow back, but you have broken wings. That takes a long time to heal. Wait and prepare yourselves. Your enemy is very strong and whatever you do, you cannot defeat him. When you organize yourself secretly, and plan secretly and collect weapons secretly, then you will succeed in whatever you do. Don't let your enemy know what you are doing. Your government is gone, your supporters are gone—everything is gone right now. If you work now and organize yourselves, you will get the Americans out. If you don't do it, your descendants will. It is very important to expel them. Deceive them like they deceive you. Be smart now."

Sheikh Kheiri admonished his listeners, who numbered about five hundred, for supporting the Baath Party and for straying from Islam. Before the war, such criticism of the secular and corrupt regime was a capital offense. Kheiri reminded his listeners that "Muhammad worked secretly for three years before he began his campaign for Islam." He urged them to organize and recruit people, warning against small random attacks. "Don't shoot here and there. You are between the lion's teeth, and if you do anything he will kill you and your family. Be smart and don't do anything until we tell you."

"Tikrit is like the Mason-Dixon line," said a sergeant in the U.S. Special Forces operating in the town from whence Saddam and many of his regime's members hailed. "The further west you go, the more Arab it is; the further east you go, the more Kurdish it is." Lying on an arid, sandy, dusty, flat plain in northern Iraq, with squat mud houses and a hostile population, Tikrit reminded me more of the Wild West than the antebellum

American South. Tikrit had a Saddam Street, Saddam Hospital, Saddam Mosque. A Kurdish student at the university joked that "we had Saddam air and Saddam water also." American soldiers called the road from Balad to Beiji, running south-north through Tikrit, "RPG Alley."

If per capita waves and smiles to American troops were a standard by which to judge a town's reaction to the war, then I would have needed no further information about Tikrit. In many other parts of the country at that point, children and adults, even old men, were still waving and smiling at soldiers from their perches on street corners and from their cars. In Tikrit they just glared at their occupiers and watched them drive away, their cold, still silence conveying plenty. While anti-American graffiti was commonplace on the walls of every Iraqi city, only in Tikrit and its neighboring villages could you still find so much pro-Saddam graffiti calling for jihad against the Americans. Every morning formerly empty walls were painted with "Long live Saddam!"

Unlike other towns and cities, Tikrit did not suffer from an orgy of looting directed at symbols of authority and former government buildings, perhaps because the population bore no hostility to the former government. Also unlike other cities, Tikrit did not suffer from the same shortages in water and power that plagued Iraqis everywhere. The city did suffer a large American presence. Special Forces helicopters shot through the skies and American convoys rolled down streets with greater visibility than elsewhere, as former regime members and current resistance fighters were hunted down. The Americans were based in a lavish walled-off compound of dozens of palaces that belonged to Saddam, set among several hundred square acres complete with artificial lakes, waterfalls, and islands, as well as ostentatious villas and swimming pools. Even the chandeliers and columns bore Saddam's initials. I tried grits for the first time in a large cafeteria, its walls intricately decorated with Saddam's name in geometrical calligraphy. Most soldiers had minimal personal interaction with the locals, merely rumbling from one base to another in large convoys, perhaps bursting into homes to arrest suspects.

The Mashallah restaurant in Tikrit was an Iraqi version of an American diner, always full and boisterous. It quieted down and emptied when several American soldiers and I entered for lunch. There were none of the warm welcomes that typify Iraqi culture. Major Varhola commented, "I feel like a black guy walking into a country-western bar in the South." The food was hastily brought and removed. Since I looked like a local, I could not escape the hateful stares from locals who presumed that I was an Iraqi "traitor" working with the Americans.

On April 28, Tikritis celebrated Saddam's birthday, decorating their streets with shrines and flowers. The Fourth Infantry Division had banned all celebrations that day, but demonstrators still carried Saddam's pictures until American soldiers arrived and threatened force. People were afraid to talk to the soldiers in public and had to steal a few words in the concealment of alleys off the main street. A local ice factory that served the Americans received so many threats that American troops had to begin protecting it.

In the middle of this powder keg, three children were accidentally run over by American soldiers. An angry old man in a black robe and traditional head scarf swore to me that he was heading to his tribe to collect weapons and allies to come attack the Americans because they shot one of his relatives. Cars slowed down and the passengers extended their necks and eyed strangers. "Tikrit is a small town," one local told me, "and we recognize anybody new." By 9:00 P.M. the normally slow streets were entirely empty and Tikrit was a ghost town in anticipation of a 10:00 P.M. curfew. Major Varhola was in civilian clothes, and we chatted. "We have already proven that we can break down doors and shoot people in the face," he said. "We need an overall understanding of the structure, greater context, the black, the white, and the gray." Other officers in the base complained that they did not have enough translators.

Since Tikrit is nearly all Sunni, when I attended an intelligence briefing I was surprised to hear an American intelligence officer warning about the "Shia fingers" extending from Iran to Tikrit in order to establish an Iranian-style government. Assim Abdullah, a university student originally from Alam, a town to the north, said that "ninety-five percent of Tikritis supported Saddam, but they changed one hundred eighty degrees now that he is gone. They all benefited from him. Only five percent of Tikritis are innocent. The others supported Saddam, they helped him, and they took advantage of their power to increase their wealth, so you can recognize the innocent people. If they are rich, they are not innocent."

The Americans appointed a governor for Tikrit from the unpopular Juburi tribe. This only increased local consternation. The new governor appointed his relatives to all positions, including communications, police, traffic police, and college deans. "Saddam did the same thing," an observer commented. When I visited, Governor Juburi's office was guarded by dozens of his plainclothed relatives sporting a vast array of pistols and machine guns clearly from the tribe's personal collection.

The nearby town of Balad had appointed its own elected council, but Juburi did not recognize it. There, and in Baquba and Samara, all of which fell under his jurisdiction, Juburi was detested. Like all Iraqis, Sunnis in the north hated it when the Americans did things unilaterally, such as appointing Juburi.

To continue my sampling of the Sunni Triangle, I headed from Tikrit to Samara, population 300,000, located between Tikrit and Baghdad. The resistance was in full swing by the early summer, with attacks by machine guns and RPGs and mortars. The resistance would be active for an entire week, then stop for a week, and then resume. American intelligence was seeing evidence of organized activity by the terrorist group Ansar al-Islam.

Not every imam supported the resistance, at least not yet. Mullah Hatim Samarai, leader of the Great Mosque in Samara, was initially a moderate. Mullah Hatim spoke to a congregation of one thousand people in his mosque, where he wielded tremendous influence as one of the leading clerics of northern Iraq. He urged his listeners not to take matters into their own hands. "God punishes you for stealing and looting and being bad Muslims. Some people changed after the war and have many faces, they drink and become pimps, they bring girls into their homes; we weren't like that before. Your relationship with God is zero. . . . Our problem in Iraq is bigger than the occupation—corruption, drinking, immorality."

Yet in the nearby al Jubeiria neighborhood, at the mosque of Ahmad bin Hamad, the sermon was usually angrier. This mosque was reputed to be Wahhabi. It was known for its sermons that demanded of Muslims not to speak with Americans, not to help them, and to begin fighting them. It was a dangerous neighborhood. Graffiti on the mosque walls supported Ansar al-Islam. Until recently, there had also been a weapons market nearby.

At the Alburahman mosque of Samara, Sheikh Ahmad al-Abasi had taken a comparatively moderate approach, advising his listeners to work with the Americans and help them, but that "if after a year they do nothing for the people here, we will tell them to go home."

Late one afternoon I met with the Islamic Charity Organization of Samara, stationed in an abandoned building next to the American civil military operations center. I met with three fit and tall young men, looking far more like fighters than the graduates of theological college they claimed to be. "We want a government to be formed as soon as possible as long as it's not a government of thieves like Saddam's," they said. Though at first hostile, they began to open up a bit. They made it very clear, however, that they wanted the United States out as soon as possible.

IT IS ONE THING TO LISTEN to fiery preaching in militant mosques, it is another to find out exactly who really listens and acts on such words. It would take me quite a long time to work my way into the inner sanctums of the resistance, relying on my looks and my Iraqi-accented yet rusty Arabic. Yet even in the summer of 2003, I saw some clues about the motley collection of fighters who were already attacking the Americans dozens of times a day.

Rawah is a border town in the desert, 400 kilometers northwest of Baghdad, close to the Syrian border. Its population of a few thousand farmers and traders are Sunnis. You reach it by crossing the Euphrates River, wide and flowing, with skinny boys diving in over and over again. When I visited on the morning of June 14, its small cemetery had about sixty new bodies buried in graves so shallow, the rotten stench of corpses was carried by the wind. Most of the graves were unidentified. Four had soda bottles buried headfirst, with the names of the dead on scraps of paper inside. In an RC Cola bottle was the name Usama Mahfudh Salam, from Yemen. Another had the name Abdul Satar Muhamad, from Falluja. In a Pepsi bottle was the name Salah al-Afifi, a common Syrian name. These rows of dead were fighters killed by American troops the night before, around 2:00 A.M. Elsewhere in the country four thousand U.S. troops were conducting raids as part of Operation Peninsula Strike, which they described as part of their "continuous effort to eradicate Baath Party loyalists, paramilitary groups, and other subversive elements." Iraqis were losing patience with the violent American incursions. Rumors of soldiers searching women's quarters and spying on Iraqi women with night-vision goggles did not help. These fighters had used a camp in the desert. A U.S. reconnaissance aircraft had spotted it. The cemetery stood at the edge of a barren yellow moonscape—rocky, dry, and inhospitable. It was ten kilometers outside of town, where an underground stream emerged to create a small oasis of tall green reeds against thirty-foot cliffs. It was a good location for the middle of the desert. This was where the seventy or so fighters sought refuge and a last stronghold. Steps were carved into the ledge of the *wadi,* or riverbed, to cross the water and climb up to the ledge where the camp had been. All that remained now was a mess of bloody and burned mattresses, sneakers, clothing, magazines, books, razors, combs, cups, cooking gas cylinders, sacks of grain, a deflated soccer ball, and medical supplies. Iraqi military poles lay where a tent must have stood. The walls of the cliff were baked white from explosions. A charred flatbed truck stood at the edge of the ledge. Caked blood and ashes were on the earth. Most of the clothing was black, the color worn by the Fedayeen fighters.

Around a bend, through a narrow *wadi* were dozens of rocket-propelled grenades and their launchers as well as Russian-made handheld antiaircraft launchers, M60s, large-caliber bullets, and weapons crates with English writing. One label stated the contents had included 100 cartridges of plastic explosives, imported by the Iraqi Ministry of Defense. Most of the weapons were live and undamaged, some of the RPGs were still wrapped. I tiptoed around the deadly mess.

Rawah had one restaurant and one mosque, called the Mosque of the Martyr Nasir Abdul Fatah. At prayer time Raghbi Abdel Aziz led his congregation, after which they emerged to talk about the fighters and the attack. Sheikh Raghbi was an elderly man, with a short white beard, very thick glasses that enlarged his dark eyes, a white cap, and a starched white robe. He maintained that the townspeople were not aware of the camp or at least of what exactly was going on. "Rawah is a border town," he said. "Many people come and go and we cannot recognize them. The desert here connects with Syria and Kirkuk." He explained that some of the strangers would come to the mosque for food and prayer, but they did not make problems for the townspeople.

The morning after the attack, he and his followers buried the dead. They found fifty-seven men whom they said had apparently been shot in their sleep. Another ten or so were so badly mutilated that their remains were buried at the camp. They claimed that seven of the dead had their hands tied behind their backs and their throats had been choked with a cord of some kind. They had been shot in the head or chest. Some of the dead were blackened like coal. The congregants confirmed that the men they had seen were not from the town. Yet I couldn't help noticing that there were no guns to be found at the base. Seventy men would have meant at least seventy Kalashnikovs. Most likely, the townspeople confiscated the guns along with whatever else seemed useful. I remembered seeing many antiaircraft bullets on the ground but no gun for them. Officially, the United States announced one wounded soldier and one destroyed Apache helicopter, its two-man crew rescued. Up to eighty shoulder-held, surface-to-air missiles, seventy-five RPGs, and twenty Kalashnikovs had been found.

ON JUNE 15 the Americans launched Operation Desert Scorpion to "root out pockets of resistance" such as a network of fighters and former intelligence officers who had formed a group called al-Awda, or "the return." The group was blamed for many recent attacks in the Anbar province. Other nebulous groups were called "the snake party" and "the new return." One group, called the National Front of Fedayeen, appeared on a Lebanese broadcasting channel in the form of four scarved men wielding RPGs who threatened President Bush and his allies. On Al Jazeera a rival group called the Iraqi Resistance Brigades wildly claimed credit for all the attacks against occupying forces in Iraq.

IN LATE JUNE rumors abounded in Baghdad of Jews and Israelis buying land and property. University students handed out leaflets on the streets warning of the Jews swarming their city to "buy homes, control the media, and control trade." The University of Baghdad's walls were pasted with leaflets beseeching Muslim brothers not to sell their land regardless of the price, because it would go to the Jews. The leaflets singled out the Iqal Hotel as the base for Jewish investors, and the Samaritan Hospital as full of Jewish doctors. At the time that hotel was under renovation, empty of guests, with only a few confused staff who insisted that neither Jews nor anybody else was staying there. The Samaritan Hospital, located next to the Red Cross headquarters, had been opened a decade earlier by an Iraqi Arab, and was also devoid of Jews.

On Friday, June 20, Sheikh Mahmud al-Khalaf spoke at the Abdul Qadar al-Gailani mosque in Baghdad, warning his congregation that the American occupiers were opening Iraq to the Jews. He condemned Iraqis who sold land to them and prohibited any association with them. In the Mother of All Battles mosque, Sheikh Thaer Ibrahim al Shomari also warned that the Jews were buying land, as they had done in Palestine prior to 1948, in order to take over the country. He asked his congregation to be careful and not sell their dear country and dear land.

A common belief in Iraq is that when held to a mirror and reversed, the Coca-Cola logo says "No Mecca, No Muhammad." This is attributed to the alleged Jewish ownership of Coca-Cola. Many Iraqis in the summer of 2003 believed that trucks were smuggling Iraqi oil through Jordan into Israel, every night. And the rumors continued ad nauseam. The fact that the Old Testament contains references to Jewish hegemony over the lands between the Nile and the Euphrates did little to ease concerns.

Works purporting to be scholarly were available in every book market, elaborating on themes of the Jewish threat. The ubiquitous *Protocols of the Elders of Zion* detailing a Jewish plot to rule the world, long proven in the West to be a fabrication written at the behest of a Russian czar, was popular in an Arabic edition. Another book, called *The Crimes of the Jews,* was on display on Baghdad streets alongside a book about *Drugs and the Sons of the Devil.* These sons, of course, were the Jews. A book in Kurdish was also available, its cover bearing a Star of David within which a monster dripped blood from its fangs. The book was titled *In the Jaws of the Jews.*

The Supreme Council for the Islamic Revolution in Iraq

itself sold a book called *Jewish Nights,* refuting various Jewish claims about their history, and in Najaf, the office of the cleric Seyid Moqtada al-Sadr sold a book called *Ali and the Jews,* detailing Ali's conversion of Jews to Islam.

After the war, with the flowering of new Iraqi publications, newspaper articles helped to spread the panic that Jews were invading the country. The independent Iraqi daily *Al Yawm al-Aakh'er* reported that "the frantic campaign to resettle the Jews [in Iraq] has aroused the annoyance of Iraqis, particularly the clerics." *Al-Adala,* a newspaper published by the Supreme Council for the Islamic Revolution, warned that "a number of Jews are attempting to purchase factories in Baghdad." An eyewitness was quoted who claimed to have observed Jews making such transactions. Nearly everyone in Baghdad swore he had a friend or relative who had seen Jews buying land. Meanwhile, the newspaper *Al-Sa'ah* warned Iraqis to check Taiwanese- and Chinese-made appliances for concealed Stars of David because the Israelis were said to be surreptitiously selling their products in Iraq.

Another rumor going around was that Michel Aflaq, the now-hated founder of the Baath Party, was a secret Jew who had converted to Christianity. It was even rumored that in Israel, Jewish brothels were built to look like mosques, complete with the minaret. Iraqi Shiites believe that a final battle between Jews and Muslims would occur when the Jews came to the city of Kifil on the Euphrates to visit the tomb of an alleged Jewish prophet. There Muslims and Jews would fight, and the Jews would hide behind rocks, until the rocks spoke to say "there is a Jew behind me," allowing the Muslims to be victorious. Not a day went by that I did not hear another story about the Jews.

KUBEISI HIMSELF, despite his scholarly credentials, was no less prone to these conspiracy theories. Before Saddam's defeat he had condemned the war as a Jewish plot. As the summer began he was still trying to be tolerant of the occupation.

By then he had become dissatisfied with the Association of Muslim Scholars, and had formed his own political party. Kubeisi astonished radical clerics by advocating the necessity of the American occupation. "Like all other Iraqis," he said, "we reject their presence," but without them there would be no security. "We will take from them what we need and give them what they need." He explained that Muslims could not fight if there was no government, because the rules of Islam applied only when there was an existing state, and if the state was not resisting the occupation, neither should its people.

Sheikh Muayad, chosen by Kubeisi to lead the Abu Hanifa mosque, had strategically chosen to cooperate with the Shiite majority, although Shiites grumbled that both he and Kubeisi had denounced them as apostates until the war started and that their newfound brotherhood was merely tactical.

I visited him on July 5, 2003. On the steps of his mosque, on the way in, I bought a thin book supporting bin Laden entitled *Bin Laden: Our Enemy Is America.* Muayad had studied religion as a child while growing up in what he called an "ocean of knowledge." His primary school had been both religious and academic, his high school was mainly academic. Muayad went to Baghdad University's Islamic College. "I never left the scholarly environment," he explained. He studied under many sheikhs and served in the military twelve years, including during the war with Iran. For several years, Muayad was an imam without a salary. In 1994 he became the imam and speaker of a village mosque in the Anbar governorate. In 1999 he became the imam of al-Anbiya (the prophets) mosque in Adhamiya. His family was one of the oldest families in Adhamiya, and he was a Sunni version of a *seyid,* or descendant of the prophet Muhammad.

After "Baghdad fell," as he put it, he became the imam of Abu Hanifa. Sunnis tended to say "Baghdad fell," instead of "the regime fell," as Shias put it. "The previous imam went back to his governorate," he said, "because he was rejected by the people of the city, since he worked for the previous regime." I asked him about his relationship with Kubeisi, which by then might have been souring. "It is like the relationship between a Muslim and a Muslim and between a student and teacher," he explained. "Kubeisi never taught me, but because he is a great man I call him 'my teacher.'" Muayad was not a member of Kubeisi's political party, "but we have the same goals and programs." His tone regarding the occupation was far less conciliatory than that of Kubeisi. "All good people and citizens of the world reject occupation whether they are Muslim or not," he said. "And this is the same thing that America did before against British imperialism, so why do they deny for other people the right to do what they did before? If others have the right to liberation from occupation, then Muslims should have that right also." As we spoke, the electrical power went out in the neighborhood. He smiled. "This is the American liberation," he said.

That week leaflets distributed in Baghdad mosques called for jihad and a battle from hell to terrorize the Americans. The anonymous leaflet warned Iraqis who worked with the Americans that they would be killed. Addressing former Baath Party members and former security and intelligence officers and fighters, the leaflet called on them to prove their manliness and shed their blood so that they would be forgiven for their past crimes.

On Friday, July 11, Sheikh Muayad preached that like the Americans who fought for independence, the feelings of the Iraqis could not be subjugated, and occupation required resistance. On July 15, Al Jazeera reported a meeting between American forces and clerics. The Americans had accused mosque leaders of inciting the people to violence and asked them to call for calm and stop spreading rumors. Though about thirty clerics were invited, only about ten showed up. Abdel Qadir al-Juburi, the imam of the Al Karim mosque, demanded of the Americans to show the freedom they spoke of. His own mosque had been attacked by the Americans during Friday prayer and he had been wounded by shrapnel. Sheikh Munim al-Azzawi of the Nur al-Mustafa mosque explained that they did not incite people to violence but called them to jihad, because every devout Muslim must attack the Americans, and the Americans had to leave Iraq.

KUBEISI, BY NOW, was almost the only moderate Sunni leader left. Harith al-Dhari, head of the Association of Muslim Scholars and a key Sunni leader partly by virtue of birth (he was the grandson of Sheikh Suleiman al-Dhari, who led the 1920 rebellion against British occupation), was much more typical. Originally from Khan Dhari, a village west of Baghdad, Harith al-Dhari was a professor of Islamic law at the University of Baghdad. Dhari was also an imam, with a large following for his Friday sermons. In July, at one typical sermon, he built from a simple, calm beginning to a raging climax. At the outset he allowed for the possibility that Iraqis could befriend Americans. But he then noted that "it is the right of occupied people to resist the occupiers . . . the Iraqis will resist." Dhari recalled the recent American celebrations of their own independence from the British. Did the Arabs not have the same right to resist occupation and expel the occupiers that other nations had? The Americans had to leave at once, and the Iraqi people would establish their own government, unite, and live as brothers. Dhari commended the resistance, calling them "an honest opposition" of which Iraqis could be proud. He called on them to continue defending Iraq.

Dhari condemned the new Iraqi Governing Council: "We have nothing to do with it and we do not support it." Dhari was infuriated by the council's declaration of April 9 as a national holiday, a day he described as "the downfall and surrender of Baghdad," which should be commemorated with sorrow and pain. Dhari's anti-Shiism came across obliquely, when he condemned as the council's worst evil the fact that it allowed one community (the Shias) to dominate the others, despite statistics to the contrary (meaning he rejected claims that Shias were the majority population in Iraq). Up to half of the country's population was former Baathists, he said, defending them as pious and well intentioned.

Dhari reminded his audience that the Iraqis knew how to resist occupation, recalling the "1920 revolution" against the British, when Sunnis and Shias fought together. As prayers ended and the men streamed out of the mosque, they shouted, "No to colonialism!" "No to the occupiers!" Leaflets and books were available, "proving" that Sunnis were the majority. Sheikh Abdul Salam al-Kubeisi roared that they would fight the occupation throughout all of Iraq, as the crowd cheered for the brave Fallujans. A statement was read to the crowd condemning the governing council. The crowd chanted rhyming slogans for the extermination of the infidel army and calling for Baghdad to revolt and for Paul Bremer to follow Nuri al-Said, the British-installed prime minister who had been killed by mobs in 1958. Leaflets distributed during the demonstration called on Muslims around the world to come to Iraq to help confront the atheist occupying forces.

That day in Mosul, clerics were furious over the July 22 deaths of Uday and Qusay, Saddam's two sons who had been besieged in their home by American soldiers. A sheikh in the mosque next to their destroyed home called the Americans barbaric for not arresting the sons. Taunting his congregation, he said they need more women from Falluja to provoke them into action. He rejected calls for patience and urged resistance.

A few days later, on July 25, Liberation Party leaflets distributed at the Abu Hanifa mosque called for jihad and called the governing council members traitors. Graffiti for the "army of Muhammad" was scrawled on the mosque's walls.

On August 18, a committee was established to improve relations and coordination between Sunnis and Shias. Moqtada appointed a representative. It was agreed that Shias would return Sunni mosques that they had seized, as the Association of Muslim Scholars had asked. They agreed to avoid conflict and to organize joint prayers, with Sunnis leading Shias and Shias leading Sunnis. They would also try to coordinate the political themes of their Friday sermons. The initiative received support from clerics throughout the country. The next Friday, August 29, in the western Baghdad neighborhood of Amriya, Sheikh Abdul Wahab of the Hassanein mosque called for jihad against the American tyranny. Those who died fighting for their country and religion would be rewarded in the next life, he said.

Meanwhile, the Americans were losing what few Sunni allies they had. They had installed Sheikh Mishkhen Jumeili, an important tribal leader, onto the Ramadi Governing Council. But in the last week of September and the first week of October the sheikh lost nine relatives, including a son, to American bullets. Though the shootings were purportedly accidental, they convinced him that the American goal was to kill as many Iraqis as they could and inflict suffering on all the tribes. Relations were worsening everywhere.

By October, Kubeisi's calls for patience had been forgotten. I met two young Sunni clerics in Baghdad's Sunni stronghold of Amriya. Sheikh Hussein and Sheikh Walid were old friends. They had graduated together from the Baghdad Islamic Institute. I interviewed them in Sheikh Walid's Fardos mosque, formerly known as the Tikriti mosque, built in 1999 by the head of intelligence. Sheikh Walid dismissed Kubeisi's call for calm. "Kubeisi says wait on fighting," he said. "This is his opinion, but every Muslim rejects occupation, though maybe the presence of American forces now and in these circumstances is beneficial to Iraqis." Their view of the Americans would not have changed had they managed to create security. "We would remain opposed to the American presence because it did not come to provide security, but it came for greed," said Sheikh Hussein, "and it came because there was no Islamic awareness and awakening and now it is becoming active. And we know Islam will be victorious, as our Prophet Muhammad promised us before. He promised that Muslims will fight the Jews east of the River Jordan and Muslims will be victorious. And Jews want to delay this battle or prevent it from happening." I asked them if they wanted America to leave immediately. "No," said

Walid, "at this time we don't want them to leave because as the Iraqi expression says, 'If someone tears the clothes, he should fix them before he leaves.'" He added that, of course, "we reject the occupation. And we hate America."

Sheikh Hussein went further. "America is worse than Saddam," he said. "In spite of all the flaws of Saddam and his oppression of us, when we compare Saddam with the Americans, he is much better than them, and under no condition do we want Saddam, but our suffering and our situation today make us miss the old days."

As I had suspected, they supported the Iraqi resistance. "We are very happy with the resistance of the Iraqi people to the American occupation, but we don't support killing civilians and innocent people and taking impulsive actions." Iraqis were seeking revenge for American abuses, they told me.

In late 2003, just before the capture of Saddam, I revisited the Mashallah restaurant in Tikrit, alone this time. I sat next to four Shia truck drivers heading back to Baghdad. "We thank America for its help," said one man. "We cannot forget what she did for us, but because we are Shia and we follow the *hawza,* our leader is the *hawza* and they determine our opinion about the Americans." The *chaichi,* as the tea maker and server was called, was a local Sunni. He refused to speak about politics. A second Shia truck driver told me that while Saddam had imprisoned and executed the faithful while freeing thieves, the Americans had liberated the faithful and "ended the rule of the tyrant Saddam."

I was surprised by their candor in such a staunchly Sunni town. As I was leaving, a waiter grabbed the manager and lifted his sleeve, revealing a watch with Saddam's picture on its face. "I don't want to say I love or hate Saddam," the manager told me, "but Saddam was Iraqi. There was security and stability under Saddam. Saddam is Iraqi, no matter what else he is, Saddam is Iraqi." The waiter cut him off. "The Americans are the dirtiest of the dirty. Saddam was also a tyrant, but they are worse than Saddam." He explained that the Americans abused

Iraqis, breaking into their homes, tying their hands behind their backs, putting bags on their heads, and stealing money from homes.

The patience requested by Dr. Kubeisi was running out. Kubeisi himself, aware of Sunni weakness, complained that the Shia of Iraq were better organized and that Sunnis needed a similar leadership. His supporters had been attending Moqtada's demonstration and he was assisting the radical Shia cleric's activities, even providing Moqtada with financial assistance.

A Sunni council was soon announced. It included radicals and opposed elections in Iraq so long as it was under occupation. Soon after the council was founded the Ibn Taimiya mosque was raided, leading to thirty-two arrests and the discovery of a large weapons depot including explosives, rocket launchers, and mortars.

On December 14, Saddam's arrest was announced. Shia neighborhoods emptied their guns into the air in celebration. Throughout Alawi's cafés angry Sunni patrons watched Saddam on television and rushed to kiss the screens. In Dora, a majority Sunni district, a rumor spread that it was not really Saddam. The neighborhood awoke that night and celebrated. These rumors spread in Adhamiya as well. Its residents emerged to celebrate carrying pictures of Saddam and wielding Kalashnikovs and even RPGs.

In late 2003, while in Dubai, Kubeisi was allegedly informed by the Americans that he was persona non grata in Iraq. Rumors that Saddam had let him into Iraq in the years before the war might have ruined his reputation as a collaborator. Sheikh Harith al-Dhari of the Association of Muslim Scholars was also blamed for Kubeisi's demise. Dhari's association, consisting of rehabilitated Baathists, expelled Kubeisi from key mosques and then his movement's newspaper was taken over. The leading Sunni voice for moderation was out of the picture. The voices of martyrdom were growing louder.

I often attended Sheikh Hussein's sermons on Fridays. The Amriya district was a Sunni stronghold in the northwestern edges of Baghdad. Home to many former Iraqi military bases as well as former officers in the army and intelligence services, it was made famous in the 1991 Gulf War when its bomb shelter was hit with U.S. missiles, killing up to four hundred civilians. The bomb shelter still stands, a gaping hole torn into its roof, its inside still charred, and outside a gravestone for each immolated victim. Signs in English direct visitors to the shelter, Saddam's pride.

On the corner a bronze statue serves as a final monument, as if the people of the neighborhood, most of whom lost friends and family, need additional reminders. It is an immense head screaming in agony, flames surrounding it. Saddam loved his propaganda and then, just as now, the U.S. military provided all the innocent victims necessary for any propaganda industry. These days, the war still continues in Amriya and the sounds of gunfire and explosions reverberate through the neigh-borhood's walls, ignored by the children playing in the street until a particularly loud explosion sends them scurrying inside. Neighbors talk of the nightly attacks and raids. Just last night, they say, U.S. soldiers raided a house, and when the suspect was not found, they took his younger brother.

Nearby is the house of a former intelligence officer. When U.S. soldiers came for him his family said he was not home, and he escaped, wisely trading his conspicuous SUV for a smaller, older wreck of a car. And just last night, they say, from this very street ("We saw them," they laugh), a car pulled over and shot three artillery rounds at the nearby base where U.S. soldiers train the new Iraqi security forces. One round landed in a small mosque by the walls of the base, damaging its tower; one went over and past the base; and one landed somewhere inside.

The Maluki mosque adjoins the Amriya shelter. The walls of the mosque are covered in pro-Saddam graffiti that has been unsuccessfully crossed out. That Friday Sheikh Hussein compared the Iraqi plight to the young prophet Abraham being thrown into the fire. No nation had a greater right to be proud of its history than the Islamic nation, he said, and all its successes were thanks to God. Though Sheikh Hussein emphasized the need for greater piety in that sermon, he would soon be exhorting his flock to support the resistance.

It was the Americans who provoked Iraq's Sunnis into resisting the occupation. Hudheifa Azzam is the son of Abdallah Azzam, founder of the jihad movement in Afghanistan and mentor to bin Ladin. Abdallah Azzam had established the Office of Services in Pakistan, helping to bring in Arab mujahideen. Hudheifa fought communists in Afghanistan for seven years, and moved on to defend Muslims in Bosnia and Chechnya. When the war in Iraq started, he crossed into Falluja from Jordan. In Falluja he tried to convince clerics and tribal leaders to resist the Americans, but they told him to go fight a jihad in his own country because they wanted to give the Americans a chance. Only after the Americans shot dozens of demonstrators in late April and rumors started spreading of Americans raping an Iraqi woman did the leaders of Falluja agree to learn from Hudheifa's experience. "This was the main cause of starting the resistance in Falluja," Hudheifa told me. "We were more than forty Arabs with no weapons. We went from mosque to mosque, from school to school. People told us, 'The Americans brought us democracy.' They believed the lies of Bush, that he would bring democracy and freedom. After the rape they said, 'Okay, we want to start now, or tomorrow we will find our mothers or daughters or sisters raped.' This story exploded the resistance in Falluja." Hudheifa briefed them on his experiences and helped rich Arabs funnel money to the Association of Muslim Scholars—in his view the only legitimate resistance movement in Iraq. He added that it was only in Al Qaim that the resistance began spontaneously.

3

IF THEY'RE NOT GUILTY NOW, THEY WILL BE NEXT TIME: Fall 2003

✦ Number of attacks on Americans on September 8, 2003 (not counting bombs defused, etc.): 27

✦ Number of cities involved in those attacks: 11

CAPTAIN JOHN BROWN'S executive officer gave the order of march. Vehicles would proceed out of the base following routes with such names as Penthouse, Playboy, and Hustler. Their targets were thirty-eight men in a number of houses in Al Qaim, a small area in Iraq's Sunni Triangle, close to the Syrian border. Brown reminded his men to look for satellite phones, computers, notebooks, photo albums, and any documents or other potential intelligence resources. Mainly, they were to round up every man found in the target houses, in order to identify the target "most wanted." To avoid having the women in the houses call other cell members, Brown's men were told to disable land lines, "rip them out of the walls." Finally, they were urged to sleep before the mission, which would begin at 0200. "I'm fuckin' excited about this," Brown said. "The bottom line is we're gonna get thirty-eight mother-fuckers who shoot at us on a daily basis." He told his men that one day they would tell their grandchildren about the operation.

It was my first taste of a hostile U.S. raid and an offensive military operation. It was called Operation Tiger Strike.

By 0100 the vehicles were being moved into position, guided by flashlights and their own headlights. The mood among the men was like that of athletes before a big game. They joked, psyched themselves up, bashed their chests together, and received final reminders by their team leaders, like coaches, to focus, to keep their eye on the ball. Finally, one after another the vehicles in the convoy rumbled out the gate of the American base.

It was October 2003. Five months after President George W. Bush spoke from the USS *Lincoln* beneath a sign reading "Mission Accomplished."

In the American press, nagging questions went unanswered. Were foreign fighters streaming into Iraq, or not? Was Iraq a new magnet for terrorists, or were the insurgents homegrown? Were the Americans wearing out their welcome? In western Iraq there was little doubt.

The Al Qaim area is arid, dusty, and lawless. It lies northwest of Rawah, about 170 miles from Baghdad, close to Syria; 230,000 Iraqis live there. Foreign fighters used it as a gateway to the country. Former regime officials may have fled through Al Qaim. For several weeks during the war, British, Australian, and American Special Forces had fought some of the longest and fiercest battles against Saddam's Republican Guard and special security services in Al Qaim. Some of the fighting centered on a compound by the Euphrates River containing a phosphate fertilizer plant and a water treatment plant. It was an area that in the 1980s had been used for uranium processing. Scuds had been launched at Israel from there during the first Gulf War. Coalition soldiers believed the Iraqis were defending similar weapons, possibly related to Iraq's alleged nuclear program or possibly defending high-ranking members of the regime or their families.

Al Asad air base, the regional headquarters for the Third Armored Cavalry Regiment, was tasked with policing Al Qaim and the entire Anbar province. It was one of the toughest assignments in the country. Among American soldiers there, the standard response to "How are you?" was "I'm here." Outside the base one morning in June, local Iraqi laborers were sitting in the sun waiting to be acknowledged by American soldiers. Every so often a representative would come to the soldiers to explain in Arabic that they were waiting for their American overseer. The soldier would shout back in English. Finally I translated between them. One impatient soldier barked at one of the Iraqis, "Do I owe you money? So why the fuck are you looking at me?"

The sprawling base, with its swimming pool, basketball courts, and excellent cafeteria, was run by Colonel David Teeples, the seventieth commander of the regiment. There were five squadrons and several battalions under him, totaling around eight thousand men. Teeples explained the typical Iraqi guerrilla as he saw him: The resistance, composed of former regime loyalists backed by financiers, had been given large amounts of money by Saddam for the purpose. Others were criminals formerly imprisoned in Abu Ghraib prison whom Saddam had released in his prewar amnesty. "I think they went primarily to Falluja," he said incorrectly. The strength of the resistance was due to the availability of these freed criminals, he said, and "the fact that there is money available for them to be hired as anti-coalition killers. To a lesser extent there are some foreign fighters who make their way into this country and link with a facilitator who has access to money and weapons. They get training, safe houses, mission, and payment." Teeples maintained that there was no popular support for the resistance. "The vast majority of the population wants nothing to do with these people," he said confidently. "But until Iraqi security is strong enough to be a viable force" the resistance would not be defeated. "When we came in we took away the army and secret police," he said, "all that was left were city police, who were at the bottom rung and had no authority and were corrupt. We're trying to build that police force to identify and apprehend the criminal elements."

He acknowledged that U.S. activities might have contributed to resentment, but only on a very small, limited basis. "Negative acts," he said, "are minuscule compared to the help the U.S. gives—improving the quality of life, fixing hospitals, putting together a democratic government. The people of Iraq are a little confused," he continued, lecturing. "They have been under a harsh dictatorship and told what to do; security conducted by the dictatorship was a very harsh security, with people executed for no apparent reason. Now they are making decisions on their own and some of them are not comfortable with that—where to send their kids to school, how to run their life, what television and newspapers to buy, how to rectify their problems. It's under a system that's different than what they had before, but the good things are not as sensational as RPG attacks." Teeples was not worried that his men were alienating Iraqis. "U.S. soldiers are culturally sensitive," he insisted. "They received training before they came here, and they continue to receive training and experience. Probably to an Iraqi they are not culturally sensitive enough and like anyone who goes to a new country you are not culturally sensitive until you spend a lot of time in the country."

Several hours away, in his makeshift home in Huseiba, a town in Al Qaim, Lieutenant Colonel Gregg Reilly, the SCO (pronounced "sko"), or squadron commander, of the Third Armored Cavalry Regiment's Tiger Base, led his men in policing the border, pursuing anti-coalition paramilitaries, and providing humanitarian assistance to hundreds of thousands of people. Reilly commanded about one thousand soldiers from the First Squadron of the Third Armored Cavalry Regiment, based in Fort Carson of Colorado Springs, Colorado.

The Third ACR had converted an abandoned train station into home, calling it Tiger Forward Operating Base. It had a cafeteria with a pueblo motif painted on its walls, serving three different hot meals a day, from bacon and pancakes to pasta and Asian-flavored chicken with vegetables. There were tactical operation centers and barracks, where soldiers worked out in small gyms, watched satellite TV, and competed in board games like Risk or in football video games on Sony PlayStations. Some played Desert Storm video games, pretending to be soldiers fighting in Iraq. That couldn't have been much of an escape. There was a detainment center for prisoners and even a recreation center with wireless Internet and "morale phones" to call home.

Reilly was a tall forty-one-year-old Californian with a gentle, wispy voice and waving limbs. "He's a little kooky," one sergeant said, reacting to Reilly's intense personality and uncommonly gentle, almost effeminate mannerism. "A little left field." Paradoxically, some local council members were said to resent him as arrogant, strutting around with a cigar in his mouth. It had earned him the nickname Saddam. Reclining at his desk with drawers full of junk food and the two sabers emblematic of his regiment on the wall behind him, Reilly relaxed, throwing his long legs over the desk. Rimless glasses combined the gaze of an intellectual with the strong taut jaw and Ranger badge of a warrior. On the bulletin board listing his schedule of operations were pictures of his wife and two children, both in college.

"We don't have a reference point for problem solving in Iraq," he explained. "You can't say this is the same as Bosnia, Kosovo, or Afghanistan. You need an understanding of the situation on the ground to see what you need to do. Each area has its own distinct terrain, and the terrain in this environment is the people. It's not a one-size-fits-all thing. It takes a tremendous amount of thought. It consumes me."

Reilly is a veteran of the first Gulf War who had also served in Bosnia, Kosovo, and Germany. "The problem is," he believed, "we're here and we brought an idea with us. The idea is, in order for this place to progress it has to move forward in a way that it governs itself so that basic human rights and respect for one another are established. So we have to establish stability and security." Like his boss Teeples, Reilly was convinced that "most of the people here understand why we came and are happy the regime fell. But when the regime fell, so did their system for supporting themselves. The regime controlled everything. There is a vacuum. The challenge we face is that people here expect to see their lives improve. America is here, America is the greatest industrial power, so their lives should improve. They need to have confidence in the future, they need opportunity. But it's very slow and they don't see it happening. Until they see it and identify with it, there will continue to be tension and dissent." By dissent, he meant grenades. "I could crush dissent easily by storming the town and punishing all the residents," he suggested, though it was obvious to both of us that that would just breed more "dissent."

For Reilly, who majored in economics at Sacramento State, the panacea was employment. His priority was getting the regional superphosphate plant at Ubeidi running at full capacity, employing 3,300 workers, in addition to miners in the nearby town of Akashat and the truckers who would transport the phosphate. The plant had once exported phosphate to twenty-seven countries. Reilly's Civil Affairs section had created an unemployment office staffed by Iraqis. So far 2,600 applications had been filled, providing information about the individuals' skills and family size. Reilly had helped set up a sanitation system, police force, and a customs organization. He had built water treatment plants and hospital wings. His next goal was the creation of a 200-man civil defense corps and an 800-man border force staffed by local Iraqis.

The phosphate plant emerged from the desert with immense convoluted metal tubes like a city out of *Mad Max*. In the 1991 Gulf War it had been hit by a bomb. Sanctions imposed after the war made it illegal for the plant to do business with any country, although it had managed to export phosphate illegally to the United Arab Emirates using a false name. Iraqis called the sanctions regime "the siege." The dilapidated condition of the plant was typical of the entire country's infrastructure, thanks to the asphyxiating blockade on many industrial goods. A UN report had described the sanctions as reducing

Iraq "to the preindustrial era." Now things were worse. Gasoline was four times as expensive as before the war, and some of it was imported from Saudi Arabia, an added humiliation for oil-rich Iraq. The phosphate plant depended on power provided by a dam at Haditha, yet looters had destroyed three of the dam's five turbines and stolen much of the power lines going to the plant. It could not get enough energy to run.

Reilly acknowledged the paradox of his responsibilities. "The tactical activities I conduct to bring security—tactical checkpoints, raids, and patrols—often have a destabilizing effect. No culture likes to have an army in their neighborhood. If the Chinese occupied the U.S., we would react the same way, we would hate them too. So the more people you arrest over time can have a destabilizing effect because if you're not arresting the right people, it can cause dissent. I have to be very careful because what I do can have the opposite reaction from the intention. When we go search houses, we're very polite. Most of these people have never seen an American. Now we're in their house! We knock on their door, tell them why we're there. They ask us in. We don't ransack the house, we don't touch the women. When we leave the house, they know why we were there and we thank them for their support. They wouldn't appreciate it if we treated them like criminals." Yet how would it seem otherwise? Leaflets left on the road by Reilly's Psychological Operations depicted tanks and helicopters and stated, "We're watching you."

Reilly got visibly tense for the first time when I asked him why the United States was in Iraq. He removed his long legs from the desk. Placing an elbow on the table, resting his forehead in his palm, he looked up suddenly and spoke deliberately, "We're here for the right reasons: in order to enable this region of the world to progress. And America has always had to be there to stand up for the basic human rights of people. We believe that people should be able to govern themselves and that human rights are important to the long-term support of progress in the region. This idea is embedded in the progress of humanity. The reputation of the United States is on the line," he said. "Now, you can talk about how we got here, that we should have waited for a UN resolution, et cetera, but that's for the history books. We're here." He repeated emphatically, "We're here. And we're here for the right reasons. There is nobody else who had the will or the ability to do this. It will take the full industrial support of the U.S., and that has to be better articulated to the people back home. It will cost hundreds of billions of dollars, but that's just a drop in the bucket of the American economy."

Similar sentiments could be heard from a young enlisted soldier relating his experiences to his wife on the morale phone. "If they would be peaceful and be nice, we would be out of here in no time," he told her. "We're trying to help them. They don't understand and they're trying to prolong our stay by butting heads with us."

Known as the "anti-morale phone" by soldiers, because it was often impossible to find a connection, this phone and the Internet access they had were their lifelines, allowing them to tell family members they loved them, to ask for supplies, to arrange their finances, and from time to time, to argue with girlfriends and wives to the increased interest of all those within listening range. They tried not to discuss politics over the phone.

Of course, not all the men were thrilled to be in Iraq. Enlisted men said that their officers had to be positive, because dissent could ruin a career. When asked how long he had been in Iraq, one enlisted twenty-one-year-old snapped, "Way too long." He explained that "when we first got here it felt like we were doing something good, now it feels like a waste. We were making progress for a while and now things are slower. When we first got here we were getting Baath Party members left and right. We've been away from our families a long time."

Another twenty-one-year-old said, "If we find weapons of mass destruction, it was worth it. But if we don't and we're just here because Bush wanted to finish what his daddy started, then a lot of boys died for nothing, and that's fucked up."

It was common to hear the men state that they were just a conventional force, untrained for "these kinds of operations." Fortunately for the regiment, many of its soldiers had experience from Bosnia and Kosovo setting up tactical checkpoints, dealing with foreign cultures, and navigating complex ethnic, tribal, and religious rivalries. Sergeant Joseph explained, "This isn't from a textbook. It's all battlefield training. Tank commanders aren't trained for kicking down doors. We're adapting as we go."

One of the two captains under Reilly, Captain Alfeiri, had arrested a midget with a phone that had Osama bin Laden's picture on it. He was a guerrilla leader. "Based on six months out here, I'd say the majority [of the insurgents] are local thugs, criminals, and some ex-regime loyalists," Alfeiri said. "I respect their tactical patience and their organization that they have used against us. These people attacking us are evolving just like us. They conduct after-action reviews, just like us. Their biggest flaw is that they underestimate us. They have enough tactical patience that if conditions are not in their advantage they will not attack us. They love to wait in an alley and shoot us from behind when we drive by. Then as soon as they drop their launcher, they're just another Iraqi citizen."

The men on Tiger Base were curious about what the Iraqis thought of them and baffled by the hostility the daily attacks made so obvious. "They hate us," soldiers often said of their new neighbors in Iraq. Sergeant Reginald Abram, twenty-four, from San Diego, exclaimed, "These people are pretty persistent! If they killed three of my buddies for shooting at them, I'd be like, damn, maybe it's time to find a new hobby. But it's not difficult to understand why somebody might pick up an AK-47 against us. Maybe we killed his father in the first Gulf War, maybe in this gulf war, maybe he's just a dick." Captain Alfeiri also expressed sympathy. "I wonder how I would feel if someone was breaking down my door," he said, "or if it was my grandfather who didn't understand instructions at a checkpoint and panicked and was shot by the foreign force."

Every night Alfeiri's men rolled out of the base with a con-voy of tanks and Humvees, heading toward the Syrian border. But on most nights, unlike Operation Tiger Strike, they weren't playing offense. They would run off the "hardball," as they called the road, in order to avoid improvised explosive devices. They would stop first at a test-fire range and make sure their heavy weapons worked before heading into action. On a typical night, on a hill one kilometer from the border, they observed the berm for movement, using night- and thermal-vision ca-pabilities that allowed them to see thousands of meters ahead. A Kiowa helicopter observed from above. "We have nightly contact," Alfeiri said. "There are cross-border attempts both ways." Alfeiri's men fired warning shots at infiltrators, probably smugglers of sheep, gasoline, fertilizer, and produce. "We're not seeing guys with truckloads of AK-47s," he said. "Most weap-ons they carry are for their own protection." The trespassers usually ran back into Syria after the warning shots were fired. Before the mission, one of Alfeiri's officers instructed his men that if they had to "drop somebody," they should get a picture of him so that he could be identified.

The men of the Third ACR policed a porous Syrian border 195 kilometers wide. Captain Justin Brown and his Apache troop ran one checkpoint twenty-four hours a day for two months before they reconstituted the Iraqi customs facilities and let Iraqis take over. From June 7 to early October, that checkpoint alone had absorbed 130 attacks.

Early one morning Alfeiri's Bandit troop took three "up-armored" Humvees and two Bradley armored personnel carri-ers that could hold up to five very cramped "dismounts" and went out to search three houses. They were looking for a sup-porter of attacks against American troops and a man injured recently while conducting an attack. It was not a raid. It had little of the adrenaline of the October operation. Yet it was an exercise in alienating the locals.

"With the intel we've been getting it's probably a house full of nuns," complained acerbic First Sergeant Clinton Reiss. At thirty-seven he still had a thickly muscled body from his days as a high school running back. After a few minutes of banter the ride out into the rising sun was silent. The smell of dust filled the vehicles as they rumbled noisily through the desert. Alfeiri kept the communication receiver by his ear at all times. Metal clacked against metal as weapons were loaded. Sergeant Tim Carr, the linguist for Third ACR Military Intelligence section, accompanied Bandit that morning. The thirty-seven-year-old native of Michigan had studied Arabic at the Defense Language Institute in Monterey, California, prior to departing for Iraq and had received two weeks of supplemental Iraqi dialect classes as well.

The Stack Team, as the soldiers who conducted the house searches were called, knocked on the gate and asked the residents if they could conduct a search. They found an emaciated young man whose entire torso was covered with burns. A bullet wound scarred his calf. Sergeant Carr demanded to know how he was injured. The young man replied, "It was a cooking accident." Carr questioned the family in simple Arabic staccato, searching for contradictions in their statements. One soldier joked, "This ain't the South, they're not deep-frying chicken here!" They took the burned man and the owner of the home in for further questioning.

The troops then knocked on the door of the neighboring house, and a surprised couple protested that they had no illegal weapons. The wife had studied English in college and was eager to practice it with the soldiers. "Welcome, welcome!" She smiled at the soldiers, who gently searched the house for weapons other than the legal AK-47. When none were found, they thanked the family and moved on. The smiling young wife seemed disappointed by their hurried departure.

On the ride back, the jocular Reiss brought up the wife of the arrested home owner. "That woman was hard," he said, "she didn't have an expression on her face. If it was my mother she would have been hysterical." Reiss was still stunned by the improvised explosive device they had found the previous night.

The mechanism was more sophisticated than past ones. Composed of two artillery rounds and a car battery, it was designed to explode when a vehicle drove over two pieces of metal that would come into contact and complete the circuit. Only luck had spared his men from death just two kilometers from their base.

The border crossing into Syria, along the main highway, was now manned by Iraqis. Ayman Aftam, a portly young customs office manager, owed his position and salary to the Americans. He explained that much of his challenge involved smugglers. World Food Program rations were smuggled from Iraq and sold in Syrian markets. Cooking oil, sold at 1,500 dinars (less than a dollar) for five liters in Iraq, costs the equivalent of 6,000 dinars in Syria. Weapons were smuggled out of Iraq as well. "Everything is so cheap here," he said. "Rocket-propelled grenade launchers, grenades which cost about two thousand dinars [one dollar], even the engines from abandoned Iraqi fighter planes. Syrian traders load their trucks full of weapons from the local arms markets to take back." Iraqis smuggled benzene into Syria by building large tanks beneath their cars and raising the chassis.

The twenty-six-year-old Aftam, who studied law at Baghdad University, saw hundreds of foreign mujahideen, or holy fighters, enter Iraq through the Al Qaim crossing before the war. "We welcomed them because they were here to defend our country," he told me. As for the Americans, "We don't welcome them. They are occupying forces. We haven't seen anything good from them, only an occupation. The Iraqi people want to like Americans, but they won't let us. They are an occupying force." He concealed his resentment from the American soldiers he cooperated with, but in Arabic he demanded of me, "Why do they come with their Bradleys in front of our houses and put their boots on our people's heads? Why don't they wave back when our children wave to them? They just keep their guns pointed at us." Aftam also referred to the many innocent people he claimed the Americans had killed, including a man who drove up to their checkpoint and did not under-stand the instructions shouted at him. He was shot. Aftam maintained, like most Iraqis, that "the fighters are not Saddam loyalists, those were killed in the war. There are only very few mujahideen here. We don't want mujahideen here. The people attacking are just normal Iraqis angry at Americans." I asked him if he was not afraid of the resistance and of the Americans whom he openly criticized. He replied, "If you are not a thief, you don't have to fear the government."

Between Aftam's analysis of ordinary Iraqi hatred, and Gregg Reilly's talk of most Iraqis' understanding of why America came, there was a wide gulf. Reilly's troops encountered a world that resembled Aftam's more than Reilly's. "They hate us," soldiers often said about the Iraqis they believed they had lib-erated. In the town of Huseiba, twenty-five kilometers from Tiger Base, America's presence was not viewed as a libera-tion. "Any night we go there we get shot at," said Alfeiri. Huseiba's 150,000 residents lived comfortable lives, benefit-ing from a thriving, centuries-old smuggling route as well as the normal trade of a border town. Large mansions owned by successful smugglers and tribal leaders sat on the fertile riverbanks. The U.S. Army had imposed a curfew on the city from 11:00 P.M. until 4:00 A.M.

Huseiba's market street was crowded with stalls selling veg-etables, cows, radios, and, more discreetly, AK-47s, grenades, and Russian grenade launchers. Seated outside a café by the Great Mosque of Al Qaim, one young man who worked as a trader was willing to admit "the American occupation is better than the old regime." His friend disagreed. "This is an occupa-tion; they don't respect civilians, they laugh at us and insult us." The owner of the café interjected angrily, "We have no dignity now because of American soldiers. We are very angry that American soldiers don't respect civilians. Now we are all mujahideen. Any man who can't fight will give his money to fighters. Even Saddam was better to us and gave us more re-spect." A passerby agreed. "It's not freedom, it's an occupation."

Sheikh Mudhafar Abdel Wahab Alani could be heard preaching to his congregation of 1,200 at the mosque, where he had led prayers for twelve years. He berated his audience for what he said was their sinful behavior since the foreigners occupied their country. They had not returned to Islam, by which he meant that they were not living according to the strict rules of Sharia. Loudspeakers atop the mosque made his furious opprobrium audible throughout the city. As he completed his sermon and the noon prayer ended, he emerged, wearing a white robe and white turban, a thick black beard on his reddish brown face and an aquiline nose defining his angular, distinguished features. He walked swiftly past the departing devout, smiling, greeting passersby warmly, and wishing everyone peace and God's blessings.

I sat down with him. "We reject this occupation, as I said in many of my sermons," Sheikh Mudhafar explained. "No country would accept an occupation. We have lost our dignity." Of the Americans, he said, "Until now we have not seen anything good, only killing, searches, and curfews. There is a reaction for every action. If you are choking me, I will also choke you. We have a resistance just like the Palestinians, Chechens, and Afghans." When asked if the Americans should leave soon, he snapped, "They should leave today." The Americans had done nothing to improve life, he said, so if they left, "how could it get any worse? It has never been so bad."

Sheikh Mudhafar was a member of the Association of Muslim Scholars. As he summarized it, one word explained the attacks against American soldiers: *intiqam*, or revenge. "Revenge is a common tradition in Iraq," he said. "It was the same between Iraqis before the Americans arrived. The attacks are the reaction to the Americans—revenge for their actions." He rejected American claims that there was no popular support for the Iraqi resistance. "I don't think there is al Qaeda in Iraq, and Saddam's supporters are too cowardly to attack the Americans." He was at least a tacit supporter of the insurgency. "I did not tell my people not to attack the Americans."

Throughout the occupation, there were many Iraqis willing to help the Americans, risking reprisals for the chance to make some money and help the transition. Muhamad, a young engineer in the phosphate factory, worked as a translator in his spare time. A Sunni from Baghdad, he was married to a Shia engineer from Karbala who also worked in the factory with him. They had gone to university in Baghdad together and now had two small children. I was surprised to find a personal computer in his home. He was an indispensable asset to the Third ACR because he was so liberal and modern (a Sunni-Shia marriage was itself proof of that) and had the desire and ability to act as an interlocutor between the Americans and Iraqis, explaining each to the other. He told me that he was motivated by a desire to help his country and believed that by helping the Americans he was doing so, though he was often treated as "just a translator" when he tried to provide his opinion about how to do things better. He understood subtle stylistic details that could have real implications in the way things were interpreted by the Iraqis. A brave man, he ignored the many threats directed against him and the pariah status that came with being a "traitor." He lived in an area the troops called Pleasantville because they never had problems there. "They're pro-coalition, or at least not anti-coalition," I was told, probably because most were not local and had come from elsewhere to work in the phosphate plant. Sixty percent of the factory staff was Shia. After the war the ministry appointed a Kurdish manager for the first time.

Muhamad gave the United States credit for fixing the customs checkpoint, improving the formerly very corrupt police, and adding staff to the local hospital. The water plant they built, even though it was very basic, provided the villages outside with treated water for the first time. He told me it was important to understand how things worked in Eastern societies, with corruption and nepotism, to understand how the factory was staffed and how Iraq was run.

Operation Tiger Strike came after Lieutenant Colonel Reilly

decided he had enough "actionable intelligence" to pursue a long list of suspected insurgents. "We have the most concrete set of targetable data in Iraq," he boasted. "We have built this over many months with multiple sources." He had two organizational charts on his wall. One chart was for al Qaeda cells, including safe houses, financiers, and fighters. Reilly and his intelligence staff did not know why the cells were alleged to belong to al Qaeda. "Other sources have said they are al Qaeda" was all that they could say. The other chart was for the resistance led by senior military officers from elite units of the former Iraqi Army. It too contained the names of several high-level officials who coordinated cells of suppliers, trainers, financiers, and trigger pullers. Altogether there were sixty-two names.

On the wall beside the charts were large satellite images of towns with targeted houses marked and numbered. A minimum of twenty-nine locations would be raided, taking out the "nervous system of the area and the guys who actually do the shooting." Reilly slapped the satellite images on the wall. "Everything I have here will be there, two cavalry troops, fourteen tanks, twenty-three Bradleys, fifteen gun trucks, one hundred dismounts, a total of three hundred soldiers." He would also be using all his other human resources, including a paramilitary officer from the OGA, or "Other Government Agency," as the CIA was euphemistically known in Iraq, and a team of ODA, or Operational Detachment Alpha, as the Special Forces were called. In case he needed it, Reilly could call upon an Orion spy plane and an unmanned aerial vehicle, as well as the listening capacities of several different intelligence agencies.

The plan was to target the leaders' homes and the "al Qaeda" safe houses first. This would be a "dynamic operation," he said, meaning they would not be knocking on doors. "We will be successful if we get fifty percent of these people," he told me.

On the afternoon before the mission, Captain Justin Brown, commander of Apache Troop, gathered the key officers and NCOs of his troop's 133 soldiers outside their tactical operations center for the "rehearsal" of Operation Decapitation, as he had called his half of Tiger Strike. Seated on plastic chairs, his men examined a satellite image of the town placed on the floor. They were joined by the CIA special operator.

Brown, a twenty-nine-year-old Texan, reminded his men that "decisions are going to be made at the lowest level . . . We will dominate our battle space. Nothing will move in your area without you having control over it . . . We will bring in every person on this list one way or the other." Brown exhorted them to watch roofs and windows and urged them to drink enough water and make certain their men stayed hydrated. Brown told his men to "maintain momentum, keep adrenaline flowing." Because teams would be operating close to each other, Brown warned them about the risks of friendly fire. Several times in the briefing he discussed precautions to avoid hurting innocent civilians.

Brown had divided the one hundred men in his six platoons into three teams, named Vodka, Scotch, and Bourbon. Each team was then subdivided into an outer cordon, inner cordon, and entry team. One by one the leaders of Vodka, Scotch, and Bourbon briefed Brown and the others present on their operations. A minimum of twenty-seven locations would be raided.

Brown questioned each leader to see if he had considered every detail and prepared for every contingency. "Where will your detainees go? How will you communicate with each other? Talk through movement to subsequent locations? What will you do if a vehicle is disabled? How will you evacuate your wounded? Where would the QRF [quick reaction force] be?" he demanded. Each team would also have an interpreter or army linguist accompanying it.

The Long-Range Surveillance team leader, a staff sergeant, then briefed Apache. LRS, pronounced "lirs," was part of the Fifty-first Infantry Division and was a "gun for hire" called in whenever somebody needed a team. The Polish-born staff sergeant had seven years' experience conducting long-range surveillance operations in locations such as Kosovo and Bosnia.

His small teams had been inserted 300 kilometers behind enemy lines during Operation Iraqi Freedom. They would start before everyone else to get "eyes on" the targets. If they saw guys with guns leaving, they would take them down.

Chief Warrant Officer "Big" Fred Denning sat and took notes. The thirty-year-old Texan piloted a Kiowa Warrior helicopter. He reminded the men of Apache that they would have to rotate "birds" if they ran out of fuel, but because the base was only five minutes away, he could fly back on fumes. Each Kiowa had a crew of two pilots, one flying and the other conducting reconnaissance. Capable of speeds up to 90 knots an hour, he would fly far slower, hovering or circling above the target areas, sometimes five feet off rooftops, usually about 100 feet above. "When we're coming up to the target, all we see is an eight-foot wall," Brown explained. "Nomad tells us if it's four men on the roof, two men in the courtyard, two trucks in front, so when my guys hit the ground running they know all the possible target locations." He added that the mere presence of Nomad, which was also equipped with defensive weapons, was intimidating to the enemy.

I retired to my room on the base to get some rest like all the soldiers. I shared the room with a CIA Special Forces operator as well as a handful of Army Special Forces from what is known as the A team. They had arrived one day in civilian vehicles, a pickup truck and a black Mercedes, with bags full of interesting nonissue guns and silencers, dressed in comfortable slacks and T-shirts. A few seemed older and heavier than I would have expected. "They gave us the B team," was the joke on base. Their hours were erratic. They did not know Arabic, and they were unmistakably white. They spent their time reading gun magazines or comic books, sometimes with the help of flashlights tied around their heads like miners.

WHEN WE FINALLY pulled out on the raid, we first stopped at the test-fire range. Some of Bandit Troop's vehicles got lost and Reilly got on the radio. "We have some roaming elephants," he said in jest. Brown and his driver Sergeant Bentley discussed football. Brown liked the Dallas Cowboys. Suddenly he switched to the subject at hand. "The hardest part of the mission is going in there and pulling some father away from his kids," said Brown. "Yeah, it sucks," Sergeant Bentley averred. "But," continued Brown, "if it's gonna let my men get home safe to see their kids, I'll do it."

Apache's teams drove in black light, using night-vision goggles. After half an hour of bumpy navigating, the convoy approached the first house. The vehicles suddenly went into white light, illuminating the target area just as a tank broke the stone wall. "Fuck yeah!" cheered Sergeant Bentley. "Hi, honey, I'm home!" The teams charged over the rubble from the hole in the wall, breaking through the door with a sledge-hammer, and dragging several men out. The barefoot prisoners, dazed from their slumber, were forcefully marched over rocks and hard ground. One short middle-aged man, clearly injured and limping with painful difficulty, was violently pushed forward in the grip of a Brobdingnagian soldier, who said, "You'll fucking learn how to walk." Each male was asked his name. None of them matched the names on the list. It was the wrong house. One prisoner was asked where the "military officer" lived. "Down the road," he pointed. "Show us!" they demanded. He was shoved ahead, stumbling over the rocky street, terrified that he would be seen as an informer.

He stopped at a house. The soldiers broke through the gate and burst inside. It was a large villa, with grapevines covering the driveway. The women and children were ordered to sit in the garden. The men were pushed to the ground and asked their names. It was the right house. The raiders had found their first high-value target: Major General Abed Hamed Mowhoush, a former commander in the Iraqi Air Force. His son begged the soldiers, "Take me for ten years, but leave my father!" Both were taken. The other children screamed, "Daddy, Daddy!" Women were given Arabic leaflets explaining that the men had been arrested.

House after house met the same fate. Some homes had only women, no men, in which cases the soldiers only broke closets, overturned mattresses, and threw clothes out of drawers. In one house, the CIA commando and soldiers failed to recognize a smiling face in a large picture pasted to a suspect's bedroom dresser: it was Uday, Saddam's notorious son, dressed in tribal clothes. Outside, men were dragged by their legs to be cuffed. A thin ancient sheikh was wrestled to the ground by soldiers who had trouble cuffing his arms. The commando grabbed him and tightly squeezed the old man's arms together, nearly breaking them.

As her husband was taken away, one woman angrily asked Allah to curse the soldiers, calling them "Dogs! Jews!" over and over. When his soldiers left a house, Brown emerged from his Humvee to slap them on the back, like a coach congratulating his players at halftime. In a big compound of several houses the soldiers took all the men, even those not on the list. A sergeant explained that the others would be held for questioning to see if they had any useful information. The men cried out that they had children still in their houses. In several houses soldiers tenderly carried out babies that had been left sleeping in their cribs and handed them to the women. When they were ready to leave each house, the soldiers relaxed and joked, ignoring the trembling and shocked women and children crouched together on the lawns behind them.

Prisoners with duct tape on their eyes and hands behind their backs cuffed with plastic "zip ties" sat in the back of the truck for hours, without water. They moved their heads toward sounds, disoriented and frightened, trying to understand what was happening around them. Anytime a prisoner moved or twitched, a soldier bellowed at him angrily and cursed. Thrown among the tightly crowded men in one truck was a boy no more than fifteen years old, his eyes wide in terror as the duct tape was placed on them. By daylight the whole town could see a large truck full of prisoners. Two men walking to work with their breakfast in a basket were stopped at gunpoint, ordered to the ground, cuffed, and told to "shut the fuck up" as their basket's contents were tossed out and they were questioned about the location of a suspect. The soldier guarding them spoke of the importance of intimidating Iraqis and instilling fear in them. "If they got something to tell us, I'd rather they be scared," he explained. An Iraqi policeman drove by in a white SUV clearly marked "Police." He too was stopped at gunpoint and ordered not to move or talk until the last raid was complete.

From the list of thirty-four names, Apache brought in about sixteen, along with another fifty-four who were neighbors, relatives, or who just happened to be around. By 8:30, Apache was done and started driving back to base. En route, its Psychological Operations vehicle blasted rock music—AC/DC—throughout the neighborhood. "It's good for morale after such a long mission," Captain Brown said. Crowds of children clustered on porches smiling, waving, and giving the passing soldiers little thumbs-up signs. Sergeant Bentley waved back. Neighbors awakened by the noise huddled outside and watched the convoy. One little girl stood before her father and guarded him from the soldiers with her arms outstretched and legs wide.

Bandit Troop handled the other half of Operation Decapitation, aimed at the al Qaeda elements. A baby girl blew a kiss at Bandit Troop's First Sergeant Reiss as his men discovered bin Laden pictures, pictures of a plane going into the World Trade Center, a copy of *Bin Laden: Our Enemy Is America,* and a grease gun and an RPG launcher. In one house a woman ran out carrying several AK-47s and their magazines. Bandit Troop did not return to base until 11:00 A.M. They had arrested thirty-eight men. Six of them were from the list, three others were relatives, and the rest were "military-age males." One man had confronted Bandit Troop, demanding, "Arrest me, I have some information for you." Like many sources, he did not want to be seen as a collaborator.

Coalition officials in Baghdad announced that 112 suspects

had been arrested in a major raid near the Syrian border, including a high-ranking official in the former Republican Guard. "The general officer that they captured, Abed Hamed Mowhoush al-Mahalowi, was reported to have links with Saddam Hussein and was a financier of anti-coalition activities, according to intelligence sources," they said.

That night the prisoners were visible on a large dirt field in a square of concertina wire, beneath immense spotlights near very loud generators. They slept on the ground, guarded by soldiers. Reiss was surprised by the high number of prisoners Apache took. "Did they just arrest every man they found?" he asked, wondering if "we just made another three hundred people hate us." The following day fifty-seven prisoners were transported to a larger base for further interrogation. Three days after the operation, a dozen prisoners could be seen marching in a circle outside the detention center, surrounded by barbed wire. They were shouting "U.S.A., U.S.A.!" over and over. "They were talkin' when we told 'em not to, so we made 'em talk somethin' we liked to hear," said one of the soldiers guarding them, grinning. Another gestured up with his hands, letting them know they had to raise their voices. A sergeant quipped that after such treatment the ones who were not guilty "will be guilty next time."

By the fall of 2003 up to ten thousand Iraqis were detained by American forces and thousands more had gone through the system. Many languished in prisons indefinitely, lost in a system that imposes English-language procedures on Arabic speakers with Arabic names not easily transcribed. Some were termed "security detainees" and held for six months pending a review to determine if they were still a "security risk." Most were innocent. Many were arrested simply because a neighbor did not like them. There was no judicial process for them. If the military were to try them, it would have to be by court-martial, which would imply that the United States was occupying Iraq. Lawyers working for the administration were still debating whether they were occupiers or liberators.

Most of the men arrested were not on any target list, and the lists themselves were suspect. American intelligence was full of errors. One case in point was a man called Ayoub. Acting on intelligence tips, Apache Troop raided Ayoub's home. Tanks, Bradleys, and Humvees squeezed through the neighborhood walls. The CIA operator eyed the rooftops and windows of nearby houses angrily, a silencer on his assault weapon. Soldiers broke through Ayoub's door early in the morning. When he did not immediately respond to their orders, he was shot with nonlethal ordnance, little pellets exploding like buckshot from a launcher. The floor of the house was covered in his blood. He was dragged into a room and interrogated forcefully as his family was pushed back against their garden fence. Ayoub's frail mother, covered in a shawl, with traditional tribal tattoos marking her face, pleaded with a soldier who towered over her to spare her son's life, protesting his innocence. She took the soldier's hand and kissed it repeatedly while on her knees. He pushed her to the grass along with Ayoub's wife, four girls, and two boys, all small. They squatted barefoot, screaming, their eyes wide open in terror, clutching each other as soldiers emerged with bags full of documents, photo albums, and two CDs with Saddam and his cronies on the cover. These CDs, titled *The Crimes of Saddam,* were common on every Iraqi street. As their title suggested, they were not made by Saddam supporters. Yet the soldiers saw only the picture of Saddam and assumed they were proof of guilt.

Ayoub was brought out and pushed onto the truck; he gestured to his shrieking family to remain where they were. He was an avuncular man, small, round, balding, and unshaven, with a hooked nose and slightly pockmarked face. He could not have looked more innocent. He sat frozen, staring numbly ahead as the soldiers ignored him, occasionally glancing down at their prisoner with sneering disdain. The medic looked at Ayoub's injured hand and chuckled to his friends, "It ain't my hand." The truck blasted country music on the way back to the base. Ayoub was thrown in the detainment center. After the operation there were smiles of relief among the soldiers, slaps on the back, and thumbs-up.

Several hours later, U.S. intelligence intercepted a call from the Ayoub they thought they had arrested. "Oh shit," said Captain Ray. "It was the wrong Ayoub." The innocent father of six, the wrong Ayoub, actually worked in the phosphate plant the Americans were running. Yet they could not let him go. If he was released, they risked revealing to the other Ayoub that he was being sought. The night after his arrest a relieved Ayoub could be seen escorted by soldiers to call his family and tell them he was fine but would not be home for a few days. "It was not the wrong guy," Captain Brown said defensively. "We raided the house we were supposed to and arrested the man we were told to."

When the soldiers who had captured Ayoub learned of the mistake, they were not surprised. "Oops," said one. Another one wondered, "What do you tell a guy like that—sorry?" "It's depressing," a third said. "We trashed the wrong guy's house and the guy that's been shooting at us is out there with his house not trashed." The soldier who shot the nonlethal ordnance at Ayoub said, "I'm just glad he didn't do something that made me shoot him" with bullets. Then the soldiers resumed their banter. Lieutenant Colonel Reilly, the squadron commander, acknowledged that he would have to make a big gesture of apology. "I can't just drop him off at home and say, 'Sorry,'" he said. "We embarrassed him in front of his family." Captain Ray did not think compensation was necessary. For him it was enough just to fix Ayoub's broken door.

The tapes of the other Ayoub's conversations were sent for analysis. In them he spoke of proceeding to the next level and obtaining land mines and other weapons. This rightfully alarmed the army's intelligence officers. They were confounded by the meaning of the intercepted conversation until somebody realized it was not a terrorist intent on obtaining weapons. It was a kid playing video games and talking about them with his friend on the phone.

So much spurious information was only helping to create enemies instead of eliminating them. Alfeiri claimed his chief intelligence officer "just hates anything Iraqi," adding that he and his men did not venture off the base or interact with Iraqis or develop any relations with the people they were expected to understand. A lieutenant colonel from the army's Civil Affairs explained that these officers did not read about the soldiers engaging with Iraqis, sharing cigarettes, tea, meals, and conversations. They only read the reports of "incidents" and they viewed Iraqis solely as a security threat.

The day after Tiger Strike, Reilly met with clerical and tribal leaders so that he could explain to them what he had done and why. In previous meetings following operations, community leaders had informed him of innocent men that he had arrested, and he would defer to their judgment and release them.

This time the clerics asked Reilly to release a religious leader. "They said it looked bad to arrest him. They didn't say it was the wrong guy," Reilly explained. The tribal sheikhs also asked for one man to be released because his wife had kidney failure and there was nobody else to take her to Jordan for treatment. The Solomon-like Reilly discussed the issue of paying reparations for the innocent man his soldiers killed by the border checkpoint, a common way of administering justice among Arab tribes of the region.

Reilly seemed concerned about the way Iraqis perceive American troops. "I am responsible for administering justice here for the whole area," he said. "We cannot treat the Iraqis as second-class citizens." He discussed the coming holy month of Ramadan with the clerics, meeting them at the local Islamic school and agreeing to lift the curfew that normally extends from 2300 until 0400 for that month, when Muslims fast during the day but eat and enjoy festivities at night. Three rocket-propelled grenades were shot at the school while they were there. "The clerics were in terror," Reilly said. "They were very angry. It was good for them to feel that terror." It was the third time Reilly had personally been attacked.

On November 26, after two weeks of brutal daily interrogations by military intelligence officers, Special Forces soldiers, and CIA personnel, Major General Abed Hamed Mowhoush died. During his final two days, he had been interrogated and beaten by CIA personnel. The Army's Criminal Investigation Division began looking into Mowhoush's death, although an army news release stated that Mowhoush "didn't feel well and subsequently lost consciousness prior to dying of natural causes." The statement explained that "the soldier questioning him found no pulse and called for medical authorities. A surgeon responded within five minutes to continue advanced cardiac life support techniques, but they were ineffective." On December 2, an army medical examiner's autopsy corrected the record: the general's death was "a homicide by asphyxia." It was not until May 12, 2004, that a death certificate was issued, with homicide listed as the cause.

Two chief warrant officers, Lewis E. Welshofer Jr. and Jeff L. Williams, were initially only reprimanded for suffocating Mowhoush. They had apparently placed him inside a sleeping bag while tying him in what the army called a "stress position" with an electrical cord. Allegedly, they sat on him, covered his mouth, and rolled him across the floor while asking him questions, and then Welshofer held his hand over Mowhoush's mouth until he stopped breathing, then let him recover for a few seconds. "This particular stress position has been used in the past and had rendered one person unconscious," according to military attorneys.

"After that incident, CW3 Welshofer directed that only he and [another soldier] could use the sleeping bag technique." The Army Inspector General's report on the incident accused Welshofer and Williams of having demonstrated "a pattern of abusive interrogations" with the cognizance of the guards. Welshofer and Williams were subsequently charged with negligent homicide and manslaughter. They deny any wrongdoing, saying commanders sanctioned their actions.

I hitched a ride from Al Asad in a civilian truck operated by the American company Kellogg, Brown & Root. We were in a convoy of several such trucks, and as I chatted with my driver, a massive explosion shook us, cracking the windshield and engulfing us in debris. The roadside bomb had detonated a second too early, exploding just in front of us. It was my first brush with death in Iraq.

Already in 2003, I thought the war was lost. The looting of the first few weeks, a massive explosion of violence, and nihilism had unleashed the worst social forces on Iraqi society and created a pervasive atmosphere of lawlessness from which it never recovered. Gangs, mafias, criminals, and weapons filled the power vacuum where armed Islamic fundamentalists did not. The entire Iraqi population was being treated as the enemy by the Americans. Behind the walls in the make-believe land of the Green Zone the occupiers maintained a charade, and perhaps even believed that things were safe and secure, but that charade made no difference to Iraqis living in the rest of the country. Iraq was as alien to most of the occupation staff in the Green Zone as the occupation staff was to Iraqis. The CPA was known by soldiers as "can't produce anything" because, as one army major explained, "it is understaffed, getting funds is a long and drawn-out process, they are out of touch with the reality on the ground, and their mission is unrealistic given their constraints."

INSIDE THE INTELLIGENCE SECTION of the army's civil affairs headquarters in Baghdad, on a bulletin board, I saw an anecdote meant to be didactic. It told of American soldiers suppressing Muslim-Filipino insurgents a century before. They dipped bullets in pig's blood and shot some Muslim rebels to send a warning to the others. A Latino Civil Affairs officer, fed up with Iraqis, explained that the only solution was to shut down Baghdad entirely. Military Civil Affairs is supposed to provide civil administration in the absence of local power structure; minimize friction between the military and civilians, acting as intermediaries between the two; restore normalcy; and empower local institutions. One brigade commander in Tikrit explained to a Civil Affairs major that "I am not here to win hearts and minds; I am here to kill the enemy." He refrained from providing his Civil Affairs team with security, so they could not operate. Not far, in Albu Hishma, a village north of Baghdad cordoned off with barbed wire, the local U.S. commander decided to bulldoze any house that had pro-Saddam graffiti on it. He gave half a dozen families only a few minutes to remove whatever they cared about most before their homes were flattened. In Baquba, two thirteen-year-old girls were killed by a Bradley armored personnel carrier. They were digging through trash. The American rule was that anybody digging on roadsides would be shot. It became common practice for soldiers to arrest the wives and children of suspects as "material witnesses" when the suspects were not captured in raids. In some cases the soldiers left notes for the suspects, letting them know their families would be released should they turn themselves in. Soldiers claim this is a very effective tactic. Soldiers on military vehicles routinely shot at Iraqi cars that approached too fast or too close, and at Iraqis wandering in fields. "They were up to no good," they would explain. Every commander became a law unto himself. A war crime to one was legitimate practice to another. After the Center for Army Lessons Learned sent a team of personnel to Israel to study that country's methods for suppressing an urban anti-occupation insurgency, the army implemented the lessons they learned and initiated house demolitions in Samara and Tikrit, blowing up homes of suspected insurgents. The Fourth Infantry Division was especially notorious in Iraq. Its soldiers in Samara handcuffed two suspects and threw them off a bridge into a river. One of them died. Down south, in Basra, seven Iraqi prisoners were beaten to death by British soldiers. A high-ranking Iraqi police official in Basra identified one of the victims as his son.

"Americans think they can just throw new paint on the walls and it will win people over," said one expert. Their tactics of handing out candy to children during the day and arresting their fathers at night were not winning hearts or minds. It was hard to be patient when mosques were raided, protestors shot, innocent families gunned down at checkpoints or by frightened soldiers in vehicles. It was hard to be patient in hours of traffic jams that Americans caused by closing off so many main roads to guard their facilities or because of "incidents." Their vehicles blocked the roads and they answered no questions, refusing to let any Iraqi approach. Cars were forced to drive "wrong side," as Iraqis called it, nearly killing each other. Iraqis became experts in walking over the concertina wire that divided so much of their cities; first one foot pressed the razor wire down, then the other stepped over. They were experts in driving slowly through lakes and rivers of sewage, at sifting through mountains of garbage for anything that could be re-used.

The fear of death was constantly there when the soldier in a Humvee or armored personnel carrier in front of you aimed his machine gun at you, when the aggressive armed white men in the SUVs raced by, running you off the road, scowling behind their wraparound sunglasses, shooting at any car coming too close, when the soldier at the checkpoint aimed his machine gun at you. Iraqis were reminded at all times who had control over their lives, who could take them with impunity. In the summer of 2003 hundreds of Iraqis would approach the Green Zone, seat of the former dictator and his current replacements, looking for jobs. The American soldiers spoke no Arabic and their Iraqi interlocutors no English. One frustrated American soldier raised his M16 and pointed the barrel at an Iraqi man's face, telling him he was trained in killing people, not career counseling. Elsewhere that summer, an old Iraqi woman approached the gate to Baghdad International Airport, or BIAP, as Saddam International Airport is now known. Draped in a black *ebaya,* she was carrying a picture of her missing son. She did not speak English, and the immense soldier in body armor she asked for help did not speak Arabic.

He shouted at her to "get the fuck away." She did not understand and continued beseeching him. The soldier was joined by another. Together they locked and loaded their machine guns, chambering a round, aiming the guns at the old woman, and shouting at her that if she did not leave "we will kill you."

Morale was low among the soldiers, who had no clear mission and viewed Iraqis as "the enemy" through a prism of "us and them." An officer returning from a fact-finding mission complained of "a lot of damn good individuals who received no guidance, training, or plan and who are operating in a vacuum."

In a bathroom of an important Washington-based and U.S.-funded democratization institute I found in the bidet by the toilet a thick orange book entitled *The Complete Idiot's Guide to the Koran*. It was next to a brochure explaining that Arabic is written from right to left and to a guide to focus groups. It was from these focus group results that the people in the Green Zone learned "what Iraqis want."

4

IRAQ V. IRAQ: Spring 2004

✦ Number of foreign civilians killed in attacks, January–May 2004: 56
✦ Number of attacks against coalition forces, April 10, 2004: 77

THE ROAD WEST from Baghdad toward Falluja was closed for an hour, near the town of Khaldiya, a dusty assortment of small brick structures growing out of the rocky desert hills and then receding back into them. A long convoy of colorful trucks bound for Jordan lined up, shimmering in the sun, their drivers squatting outside in their shadows. Several hundred feet away, a green Bradley armored personnel carrier and two armored Humvees blocked the road, soldiers waving threateningly from behind their turrets at anyone who approached. I heard explosions and exchanges of fire in the distance. Eventually the Bradley swiveled around, throwing sand behind it as it climbed a dune, the Humvees following, allowing traffic to resume. The convoy of waiting trucks and taxis started their engines and resumed driving, huddled together like a herd of tense cattle.

A hundred miles west of Baghdad, a left turn off the highway leads to dirt roads passing through fecund fields fed by the nearby Euphrates. Sheep and cows drink from the riverbank in the shade of towering date palm plantations. I was heading for Sheikh Saad Mushhan Naif al-Hardan's village of Albu Aitha, a collection of family compounds nearly hidden by the thick verdant flora kept fertile by the wide, still waters. I wanted to hear firsthand, from a western Sunni tribal leader, why Iraqis were increasingly attacking each other, not just the Americans. The sheikh was draped in black and gray robes, his face partially concealed by an all-white head scarf, crowned with a black rope. His small keen eyes, thick arching brows, and mustache lay still, waiting for an emotion to animate them. He was joined by his three cousins: a lawyer, a history professor, and a history teacher. Shoes were removed at the entrance to the guest hall. The men lined up to shake hands with and welcome me. I sat on the cushioned benches across from them while a younger man, one of their children, brought a glass of water to be sipped and passed around. The sheikh had recently returned from the Hajj pilgrimage to Mecca.

At first, the sheikh avoided conversation. "Our words will not be true until after we eat," he said. A basin was brought out with soap and water so I could wash my hands. A colorful plastic mat was spread on the floor, upon which was centered a large tin platter of rice and meat surrounded by smaller bowls of sliced vegetables and chicken. Large thin round bread was added as we all sat cross-legged around the mat. A spoon was brought for me out of respect for my inability to eat with my hands like a civilized person, though when I finally plunged my fist into the greasy rice, my hosts were flattered. "Ahhh," they said with pleasure. I was forced to eat well after they had finished. Only when the sheikh decided that he had been sufficiently honored by my appetite, and I by his generosity, did he relent. The washbasin was brought out again for my hands and face. We sat back on benches against the wall as Iraqi tea was brought out, thin glasses that curved inward, filled nearly halfway with sugar and dark tea. The room echoed with the sharp tinkling of spoons mixing the sugar. Only after our third glasses were sipped dry could conversation begin.

Since 1995 the sheikh had led the Aithawi tribe, the largest subtribe (he claimed) of the Dulaimi tribe, one of Iraq's largest tribes (he claimed). Every sheikh in Iraq claims his tribe is the largest. In fact, the western province of Anbar was once named after his tribe in recognition of its regional dominance. The Aithawi trace their tribe to Aitha, who was their first sheikh in Anbar more than two hundred years ago. Sheikh Saad refuses to enumerate his tribe's manpower. It is the tribal equivalent of classified information.

The Dulaimi tribe, whose lands reached from the Saudi border to the Syrian border and up to the outskirts of Baghdad in Abu Ghraib, has been just as recalcitrant in the face of American occupation as it was nearly a century ago during the 1920 uprising against the British, when Sheikh Saad's grandfather took his five brothers and rode south to Kut with all the fighting men his tribe could muster. "The British had more advanced weapons and better tactics," Sheikh Saad said. His relatives are still buried near Kut. Sheikh Saad retreated to his tribal lands fighting all the way. "When the British reached Anbar," Saad continued, "we told them that the only way Anbar would fall and they could occupy us was if they killed or arrested at least two of our sheikhs." The British took their advice, killing Sheikh Sabar of the Albu Nimr tribe and arresting Sheikh Saad, imprisoning him in India for six years. "Then the British occupied the Anbar," Sheikh Saad concluded.

"The British occupiers befriended the tribal leaders," Saad said. "This is the key to winning the people. They understood our traditions, unlike the Americans now. The British did not surround homes and break into them. They consulted sheikhs and respected them, and after they occupied all of Iraq there was no more resistance." The American occupiers, Saad maintained, "push people to the ground and step on their heads. They arrest the relatives and wives of wanted men and hold them hostage. They are holding one hundred thousand Iraqis in their prisons. Iraqis have lost their dignity and for this reason the resistance grows."

Iraqis were incandescent over rumors that their women were being held prisoner by Americans. Sheikh Saad told of three women imprisoned as hostages by the Americans in Khaldiya because their husbands were wanted by the Americans. "I went to speak with the American commander in Falluja who called the commander in Khaldiya. I told the commander, if you don't release these women you should arrest all the men in Anbar because there will be an uprising." Sheikh Saad said that three hours later the women were released and added, "The British never arrested women." The sheikh claimed ignorance about who the resistance was but explained that "for us as the people of Anbar, revenge is an important tradition. If they kill one of our men, we have to kill at least one of their soldiers. An eye for an eye and a tooth for a tooth."

The year before, at seven in the morning on July 20, Sheikh Saad was arrested with eighty-five of his men in an operation that took one hour, using, Sheikh Saad claimed, more than one hundred twenty vehicles and helicopters. Sheikh Saad scoffed, "Like it was a real battle, but they met no resistance from us. Two of the men they arrested were completely handicapped. They accused me of belonging to an organized group called Nur Muhammad [Light of Muhammad] that is leading the resistance with the support and financing of Saddam and bringing in mujahideen from Syria, and they said sixty percent of the attacks in this area originate in Albu Aitha, so I must know about them, but none of it was true. Their method is to arrest many people and hope to at least find something. Until now they have no accurate information about the resistance." Apparently, he did. Sheikh Saad was held for twelve days, but the rest of his men were held for a month, and five were still being held in the Abu Ghraib and Um Qasr prisons. "If Americans had not behaved the way they did, there would be no resistance," he said. "Their behavior and broken promises increase the resistance."

The sheikh paused to contemplate, looking to the side. So far, the conversation had not been surprising—it was typical anti-American rhetoric. Yet hints of a different dynamic now emerged: Sunni-Shia hatred. The sheikh mentioned the 1991 Shia uprising in southern Iraq that followed Saddam's defeat in the first Gulf War. He and his cousins laughed derisively. One cousin was a plump, narrow-eyed professor of Arabic history in a private university in Baghdad. "The target and victim was not the regime," the professor said, believing his own lies. "It was innocent people and they were led by thousands of Iranians. It was not an uprising; it was the destruction of southern cities, houses, schools. They couldn't reach the regime, so they targeted local leaders like police chiefs."

The lawyer cousin added, "It was the second stage of the American war, to continue the American goals." To the paranoid Sunni mind, American devils and Shia traitors worked together.

The sheikh rejoined the revision of Iraqi history, explaining that "under the previous regime we all had equality. We could all study in the university and succeed depending on the degree we achieved. The one exception was the security forces, which went to certain tribes. But I don't want to talk about the previous regime. What's gone is gone.

"Saddam disliked the Dulaimi tribe, and we had nobody in high positions in his government because Saddam feared we would overthrow him. The Americans told me that I am the only sheikh in Anbar who did not visit their bases and work with them. They want me to help them against my people? This won't happen." The lawyer leaned forward, his face long and gaunt, unlike his better-fed relatives, and asserted, "There won't be a civil war, but there might be problems." In such a paranoid state, only one option made sense: to go it alone. The sheikh smiled proudly, lifting his head. "We are an independent tribe. We don't have relations with other parties or the Iraqi Governing Council."

Iraqi-on-Iraqi violence had been present ever since Saddam fell, but in 2004 it became much harder to ignore. In late February, one evening, I was sitting in Sandra, a fresh fruit juice and ice cream joint owned by a Christian family in Baghdad.

It was my favorite sanctuary in Iraq, one of the city's unknown oases of normality, and one I did not share with other journalists. On either side of its wide and brightly lit boulevard good restaurants were open well into the night, the sidewalks crowded with families and even young couples. Expensive cars slowly cruised the street, youth gazing at the crowds of girls in tight clothes. I was sipping a strawberry smoothie with my Iraqi friend Rana, sitting outside. She noted that the scene before us reminded her of the days before the war, when she would go out at night with her sisters, unafraid of the dangers that keep women sequestered in their homes today.

As she was waxing nostalgic about the good old days under Saddam, and I was trying not to roll my eyes, two sharp gunshots cut her words short. Two men walked hurriedly across the street, arms raised and pistols in the air, smiling. "They killed a man!" someone shouted. A man in a suit collapsed on the curb, blood spreading from beneath his head. Not knowing what else to do, I began taking pictures of him.

The crowd grew and cars slowed down as their drivers gazed at the corpse. Soon about fifty men stood around silently, looking around for help, looking at the body, and then looking away guiltily. Someone tried calling the police, but the call did not go through. Two men ran a few hundred meters away to the nearest police checkpoint but were told by the policemen there that it was somebody else's jurisdiction. Two armed security guards from a building across the street returned panting, having failed to find the killers. Someone from a nearby shop covered the body with a rug that failed to conceal the growing pool of blood that had started to coagulate, looking like windswept sand dunes.

Half an hour after the shooting, Iraqi police began arriving, just as the several men in the crowd had turned over the body and were looking through his pockets for identification or a phone. Blue-and-white pickup trucks had brought a dozen police officers with guns drawn, pushing the crowd back and asking witnesses what had happened. They quickly recognized the man: a colonel from their local station. His gun was missing, and they became very tense, raising their guns and pushing the crowd back. They told me to stop photographing. I showed several officers some of the digital pictures I had taken of the body, in the first moments after death. A tall officer with light hair and gray eyes grabbed my camera, telling me I was not allowed to have pictures of dead police on it and I would have to wait for his commander to come before he returned it to me. I grabbed the camera back and we both held it and argued. He waved his gun and held it to my chest, and I let go. We shouted back and forth. He growled that if I did not let it go he would break it and pushed the barrel of his clean new gun into my chest. I relented but followed him around, fearing for my camera.

The station commander arrived in civilian clothes with a worried look. He ordered me to erase my pictures. I pressed various buttons and scowled in mock concentration, pretending to delete them. One of the slain colonel's men arrived and smacked himself in the head when he saw his superior officer's body. He fell to his knees and sobbed, "Sir! Oh Sir! Why did you go out alone?" He rolled in agony, screaming, "It was his first time out alone!"

Rana and I accompanied the body back to the police station. On the way the commander told us that this was the sixth officer from his station who had been assassinated. Another had died in an explosion. An officer commented that the killers were "very organized and systematic. They want to prevent stability."

"Every day we lose another one of our brothers," one policeman said. "Every day I leave my house and kiss my wife and children good-bye not knowing if I will return." Another officer complained that "his family will get nothing. Even in the worst of times under Saddam, the family of a dead police officer received a salary, or a car or a house even. Now they get nothing. If the situation for the police does not improve, we will soon all quit."

On the way home past Fardos Circle I saw an immense sign above a building. It had a picture of a few Iraqi men and women in uniform smiling proudly, and in Arabic was written "Iraqi Security Forces, the New Future." When I returned to my hotel, I told Karim, a photographer, about what I had seen. He asked me if I had heard about the explosion in Falluja. I asked him if he had heard about the deputy chief of police in Mosul getting assassinated. He said, "It's all small news, so you never hear of it. It's all small news, but it's all bad news."

It had been one year since the fall of the regime. The resistance was strengthening, and Sunnis were targeting Shias, as well as anyone who worked with the Americans and the provisional government. One year earlier, Shia pilgrims had been overjoyed during their first walk to Karbala in years. Now, as they prepared for another, they were a target.

Seyid Hasan al-Naji al-Musawi, the leader of a Shia mosque in Baghdad's Sadr City, voiced his fear that Wahhabi Sunni extremists might disrupt the processions. "God willing, it will be peaceful," he said, adding, "but, if you are martyred during Muharram you go directly to heaven."

Moqtada himself seemed determined to achieve martyrdom. In his Friday sermons, given at the Kufah mosque near Najaf, Moqtada derided every decision made by the coalition forces. After the United States gave former president Saddam Hussein prisoner-of-war status, Moqtada and his representatives assailed the decision. "Saddam is a war criminal," Moqtada shouted, "and there are no two people who can argue over this!" Sheikh al-Daraji, a representative of Moqtada's in Baghdad, spoke to thousands in the Muhsin mosque in Sadr City, saying that "at a time when no two people can argue about Saddam's crimes and his crimes against the Iraqi people and other countries, the American leadership declares, according to its arrogant, racist politics, that the infidel Saddam is a prisoner of war." Shias called for a hasty execution.

Moqtada had also been competing with more accommodating Shia clerics such as Ayatollah Ali al-Sistani. On January

16, Moqtada called for a demonstration, to be held on January 20, to protest against Saddam's status as a mere prisoner of war. Sistani called for one on the January 19. The next day, Saturday, January 17, Sistani's office called for a demonstration in support of free elections. Not to be outdone, Moqtada's men took four ambulances with loudspeakers attached and drove through Baghdad's Sadr City on Sunday, January 18, announcing that the demonstration scheduled for January 19 (Sistani's) had been postponed until Tuesday (the day of Moqtada's).

The ploy was not very successful, and on January 19 the Sistani demonstration started in a hospital in Sadr City and proceeded to Mustansiriya. That day and the next, thousands of Moqtada's supporters demonstrated throughout the country, condemning Kurds for seeking a federal system in Iraq, which they blamed for "dividing the country." In Baghdad's Fardos Square they condemned the division of the country and Sadr's representative said that "we are demonstrating against federalism because we saw what happened in Yugoslavia, and federalism is an Israeli plan to divide us!" They held banners saying "No to dictatorship, no to racism, and yes to freedom."

In Karbala thousands of Moqtada supporters demonstrated and Moqtada's representative railed, "We are against Kurdish federalism and we support Sistani's call for general elections." In Najaf thousands of demonstrators shouted, "Down with the U.S.A., yes to Iraq!" They called for elections, opposed federalism, and demanded an Iraqi trial for Saddam Hussein. Moqtada supporters in Kut called for power to be handed over to Iraqis and they demanded a united Iraq as they held anti-occupation banners.

On Friday, January 24, Moqtada rejected UN supervision of elections or participation in them because he claimed the UN had legalized the occupation of Iraq. He added that the Shia clergy was able to supervise the elections, and he called for all Islamic parties to establish an Islamic constitution for Iraq that would guarantee the rights of the Iraqi people.

The interim minister of electricity in Iraq announced that although Iraq would not buy electricity from Israel it might in the future be willing to sell electricity to Israel, adding, however, that it would be "at three times the price. We will extract money from Israel for the benefit of the Iraqi people." Moqtada addressed the minister in his Friday sermon in Kufah: "We won't have any objection at all once we send you and your followers to hell."

In Nasiriya, a demonstration a few days later forced the governor of the Dhiqar province to resign, though he changed his mind after a few days, provoking large protests of thousands, including members of the Mahdi Army, who surrounded his headquarters and called for dissolving the appointed city council and establishing an elected council.

Two weeks later, in Kufah, Moqtada threatened armed opposition to the occupation, claiming that "America came to harm the Iraqis, but it will not be able to destroy Islam." In late February, after a grenade was launched at the shrine of Imam Kadhim one night, Moqtada's associate Seyid al-Daraji spoke angrily, demanding, "We want the tanks to be far from our holy city. The missile did not come from Muslims, it came from the enemy of Islam. We oppose terrorism in Iraq and we think the Americans know the people who did this but they want to hide it. They hide it to make a sectarian war. They should stop playing the sectarian card."

In Baghdad, on February 17, Sadr's representative al-Daraji said that although Moqtada's movement had not yet called for an armed resistance, "it supports a peaceful resistance against the occupation using protests." Al-Daraji refused to comment on armed operations (though he did not condemn them), adding that "only the *marja* is authorized to decide the time of the resistance, and also Shia *marjas* see that at this time resistance is not good because it prolongs the occupation, but American hesitation in handing over power and prolonging the occupation may change the people's position on resistance."

On February 20, in Kufah, Moqtada railed against U.S. administrator Paul Bremer's announcement that Islam would not be the main source of the new Iraqi constitution. "We want to advise everybody," Moqtada said, "that the Iraqi people have the ability to attack their enemies and the revolution of 1920 is the best example and the Shaaban Intifada [the 1991 uprising after the Gulf War] is not far from us and we oppose statements interfering in our internal affairs. Bremer's statement is a declaration of hate against Islam and an attempt to erase the hopes of the Iraqi people to obtain a constitution that is based on Islam. The Iraqi people have an Islamic identity, even if many of them do not apply Islamic rules in their behavior."

On February 23, Moqtada said that "occupying a country is incompatible with the very principle of holding negotiations. We are not hostile to America, but we are the enemy of occupation." He added, "From the very beginning, I believed that the occupiers did not want Iraq to enjoy either the rule of the people or freedom."

Sunnis watched with disdain and increasing concern. In Adhamiya, I visited R.H. inside the immense white walls surrounding his house. A marble courtyard served as a parking lot for his Range Rover and BMW. Glass doors led to a large opulent living room tastefully decorated with expensive Chinese and classical European art, Persian rugs, and an M16 automatic rifle hung carefully on the wall. R.H., a businessman from a wealthy family, and his wife, who donned pants and a T-shirt and did not cover her head, greeted me on their leather sofas beneath crystal chandeliers. A swimming pool lay in the center of their manicured garden. They spoke educated English. In their forties, they look like a wealthy suburban American family. I felt far more at home with them than with the tribal characters I was used to consorting with.

Sunnis like R.H. represented the former elite of the country. Like the white minority that once ruled apartheid South Africa, they felt disenfranchised and they fretted over the fate of their country. "The Americans made a big mistake when they came to Iraq," he said. "Sunnis ruled Iraq for four hundred years. Sunnis always worked in the security and administration of Iraq." After the war most of these Sunnis were dismissed from their positions of authority and received no compensation, he says. "I was never a supporter of Saddam," he was quick to explain. "We hate him because he is the cause of the current situation." He added that Saddam confiscated the successful food processing plant that R.H. owned. "He took it like a piece of cake." Saddam's son Qusay stole R.H.'s ancient gun collection while Saddam's brother-in-law Mudhafar Khairallah imprisoned R.H. for two days on weapons smuggling charges as a pretext. But, he added, "I prefer the old regime to this," gesturing outside to the chaos beyond the walls that guarded his home.

In the beginning, R.H. said, American soldiers visited him often and were very nice. He told his wife to bring a framed plaque from his study. It was a certificate of appreciation for work done between May and September of 2003 given to him by the ODA, or Operational Detachment Alpha (an A team), of the Special Forces Group. R.H. also has a laminated card signed by Detachment Commander Mike L. Pearce, stating that R.H. assisted "U.S. and coalition forces in an effort to capture anti-coalition forces in Baghdad" and that there is "no derogatory information in his background." R.H.'s wife explained that they helped the Americans because "it was as if they came from Mars to help us. Nobody else could have gotten rid of Saddam." When they learned of his collaboration with the occupiers, some friends of the family were furious. He received death threats. His neighborhood was not coalition friendly. The nearby American base was attacked nightly. R.H. worried that his own son Ahmad, twenty-two, "hates the Americans very much."

R.H. showed me his brand-new M16 with its shortened barrel, a scope, and flashlight. He kept it on the wall in his living room in case the Badr Brigade came for him. Like nearly all his neighbors in Adhamiya, R.H. feared the Shias and viewed them with condescension. "Most Shias are simpleminded," he said to justify why this sect, which represents more than 60 percent of Iraq's Arabs, should not be allowed to determine the shape of the new government. "I will kill myself if they rule," he cried out. He blamed the looting that followed the fall of Baghdad on its Shia residents. He claimed with typical Middle Eastern conspiratorial flair that there were five million Iranians who had snuck into Iraq and were seeking citizenship. R.H. and his friends feared that the Shia majority "want to make us like Iran."

R.H. was very pleased with U.S. administrator Paul Bremer's announcement that Iraq would not have an Islamic constitution, a verdict that enraged Shia leaders. "Religion is between you and God," he explained, voicing his hope that Iraq would become a secular monarchy. He rejected Sherif Ali, heir to the throne, as "naïve," preferring instead Prince Hassan of Jordan, brother to the late King Hussein and a onetime favorite of neoconservatives in Washington. "The Shias are all armed and the Sunnis are all armed," he warned. As far as he was concerned, only a king could stop civil war from coming.

As the 2004 pilgrimage to Karbala began, Sunni-Shia tensions simmered dangerously. For the first nine days of Muharram, Shia iconography dominated the streets of Baghdad and southern Iraq, with portraits of Hussain put up in every corner and wall, especially where Saddam's visage had been painted before the war. Red, black, and green flags of mourning and of Hussain and his brother Abbas fluttered from every tower.

In the streets of Kadhimiya in Baghdad and in Karbala the pilgrimage had already started, as had the passion plays and flagellation. Taxi drivers and shop owners played tapes of the wailing songs of mourning. Iranians streamed into Iraq. In the streets of Karbala, Farsi could be heard as often as Arabic. Karbala residents began to complain about the flood of Iranians who were occupying their city, which did not have the infrastructure to handle so many people at once.

Foreign troops were nowhere to be seen, wisely avoiding

provocations that in the past in Iraq and outside had radicalized Shiites. Iraqi security forces had a heavy presence, however, with many checkpoints along the way. A few lonely Polish soldiers working with Iraqi police manned one checkpoint to search vehicles just before Karbala.

As the pilgrims began running to Karbala, some barefoot, they passed a banner quoting Iran's Ayatollah Khomeini, "Every day is Ashura and every place is Karbala," a political message calling for sacrifice and resistance to unjust government. "America and Israel are the Yazid of today," another banner said, comparing both governments to the murderer of Hussain just as Khomeini had compared the Shah of Iran to Yazid. Another poster added that "America and Israel are the enemies of Hussain because they want to kill Hussain's revolution." Yet another banner said that "Hussain's revenge removed Saddam and it will remove the United States's dreams to control the Islamic world."

Pilgrims marched in by the hundreds of thousands, carrying declarations of loyalty and sacrifice to Hussain, and warnings to the Americans. "Death is better than life under tyranny," one said. Another, addressing Bush and Bremer personally, called for Islamic law to be applied in Iraq. One banner, carried by pilgrims from Baghdad's universities, clearly not written by the English department, said, "When the political solution does not benefit for the ambitions of the nation, the Hussain solution is better"—meaning a fight to the death rather than compromise.

A procession organized by Baghdad's College of Engineering called for an Islamic constitution. Its leader, Ali Hadi, explained that "most Iraqis are Muslim, and the *Marjaia* [Shia clergy] should lead us." Other students joined him and said that if America prevented an Islamic constitution, "there will be a second battle of Karbala on this earth," and "the students are the army of the *marjas*; we will give our lives to them."

After the morning prayers on the tenth of Muharram, the day when the Battle of Karbala was believed to have started, trumpets blared and drums beat in a military cadence. *"Haidar! Haidar! Haidar!"* cried out thousands of men dressed in white gowns, calling out to Hussain's father, Ali. They waved their swords in the air, dancing and beating their newly shaved heads, slowly drawing blood that soaked their white garb and splattered anyone around them. Men brought their young sons, some not yet ten, whose heads had been shaved to make the scalp easier to get to. The boys cringed in terror as their fathers held their hands on the sword and drew first blood, proudly congratulating the relieved and bloody children afterward. Some men, their white gowns soaked heavily with shiny red blood, collapsed and were taken to emergency medical treatment centers waiting for them. Others, when finished, stood around smoking and smiling.

It was then, at the bloodiest and busiest moment in Karbala, on March 2, that the bombs exploded, slaughtering close to two hundred and maiming hundreds of others. Suicide bombers, mortars, and hidden explosives went off in Karbala and in Baghdad's Kadhimiya district. The Kadhim shrine contains the tombs of two Shiite saints, Imam Musa Kazem and his grandson Imam Muhammad al-Jawad.

The first bomb went off inside the Bab al-Murad gate of Kadhim, spraying the ceiling and walls with blood. The second bomb went off in the center of the shrine's courtyard, where shoes are placed before the tomb itself is visited. The third bomb exploded outside the shrine in front of the Sharaf Hotel. Ambulances and pickup trucks rushed from Kadhim, carrying the wounded and the dead, and police fired twice at a car driving by. Immediately, loudspeakers in Kadhimiya urged people to donate blood. Several foreign journalists were attacked by angry mobs wielding swords. A Reuters cameraman was reportedly struck on the head.

Shocked people stood outside the Kadhim shrine. Pickup trucks and ambulances carried piles of dead bodies. People were crying and hugging each other. A loudspeaker asked people to leave the shrine. There were many shouts of "Allahu Akbar," or "God is great!" People had their hands on their heads, and some slapped their faces as Iraqi Red Crescent Society ambulances drove by. "The infidels!" somebody shouted as guards with machine guns stood around helplessly. The street was full of empty slippers of the dead and wounded.

"We blame the Americans, let's expel the Americans, let's unite to expel them from Iraq, let's unite as one religion," urged the mosque loudspeakers. Empty bloodstained stretchers were returned to pick up more bodies. Four American Humvees, a truck, two armored personnel carriers, and a medical vehicle clearly marked with a red cross arrived, accompanied by American and Iraqi soldiers on foot patrol. "Throw shoes at them!" somebody shouted. At first, shoes rained down on the soldiers, and then stones, bricks, and branches were hurled at them. They got in their vehicles.

The Americans shot in the air. "There is no God but Allah!" people shouted. A confused soldier on top of a vehicle swung back and forth with his gun, not knowing which way to turn. The Americans retreated two kilometers back to their base as the mob of many thousands chased after them. One cleric shouted, "Go back, this is chaos, don't fight the Americans," but he was ignored. In front of the base, men threw stones at the tanks and Humvees, and the soldiers got inside the tank and reversed into the base. Men picked up bricks from a large pile and strolled casually toward the base, where thousands crowded in front of the gate. They threw stones, bricks, and sticks and tried to pull down the barbed wire. They waved flags over the base walls and danced on top of them, taunting the Americans, waving fists and shouting. Some jumped inside. For ten minutes this continued, until shots were fired and some of the crowd ran away. "The bastard Americans made the explosions!" someone shouted. "By our spirits and by our blood we will sacrifice ourselves for the *hawza!*" others shouted. A voice on the loudspeakers from inside the base called: "I am an Iraqi and your brother. The Americans have told me, 'If your brothers will not leave the base, they will be shot.' Please leave the base. They are serious!"

Hundreds remained, throwing stones. American smoke bombs went off, yellow, purple, and green, hiding the walls and scaring more people off. "It's a miracle," someone shouted, "the Americans shot the gasses at us and God stopped the air so the gas won't come to the demonstrators!"

Unlike some less fortunate journalists, I avoided being attacked by joining the shocked and angry pilgrims and beating my head, calling out to God. On the mosque's loudspeaker a sheikh cried out to the people of Kadhimiya to remain calm. He blamed the attacks on "Jews and Americans" who seek to cause sectarian strife between Sunnis and Shias in Iraq, adding that Iraqis would remain brothers. He warned people to be vigilant because of possible remaining bombs or attackers, and to "keep your eyes open." The floor of the immense Kadhim shrine was covered with blood, and large pools formed near the site of the explosions. Mosque workers covered their hands with plastic bags and carefully walked around, picking up pieces of human remains. A large pile containing hands, scalps, and other bloody parts soon took shape. Shrine guards and workers held each other, crying in silent shock. Guards and caretakers angrily blamed America for the attacks, just as they had blamed American troops for a rocket-propelled grenade shot into the shrine the previous week. The head caretaker explained that the bombings were a warning from America to leading Iraqi cleric Ayatollah Ali al-Sistani to cease calling for direct elections. Other guards and caretakers blamed a coalition of Jews, Americans, and extreme Wahhabi Muslims. None, at first, spoke of seeking revenge against their Sunni neighbors.

The attacks were meant to arouse Shia anger and spark a civil war between Sunnis and Shias. Instead, Sunni leaders reached out to their Shia brethren immediately. The Sunni Iraqi Islamic Party, part of the Iraqi Governing Council (IGC), was quick to condemn the attacks unequivocally, saying that "Iraqi Shias and Sunnis walk hand-in-hand." Other IGC members were also quick to condemn the attacks, and the IGC called for three days of mourning. The attacks also came

one day before the expected signing of Iraq's interim constitution. The IGC came to an agreement on the document
on Monday but decided to wait until after Ashura to hold
the signing ceremony. Even in Falluja, mosque leaders used
loudspeakers to exhort their citizens to donate blood to the
Shia victims of the bombings. Hundreds of youth responded
to the calls and thousands were driven to blood collection
centers.

The next Friday mosques blamed the Americans for the explosions. Moqtada al-Sadr spoke in Kufah. "I call on all the authorities and politicians in Iraq, slogans are not enough. They
have to know that whoever did this belongs to the sinister
triad of Israel, America, and England," he said. "America let
the world stand and not sit again," he said, using an Iraqi
expression to explain how angry the Americans were over the
9/11 attacks, "because of what happened in only the World
Trade Center, but they have to know that our holy shrines
have been attacked and accusing Zarqawi is only a trick. We
will never stay silent again."

In Karbala, Sheikh Abdul Mahdi al-Karbalai, the Sistani
representative, spoke at the shrine of Hussain. He blamed the
occupation forces for failing to prevent the attacks. These terrorism operations benefited the occupation forces, he said,
because they gave an impression that the Iraqi people could
not protect themselves. "These attacks will never scare us, even
if they use atomic bombs or germ warfare," he said. He claimed
that foreigners had set off the bombs, with logistical assistance
from Baathists. He rejected any possibility of civil war. "How
will this happen if all the Shias obey the religious *marja* and
the religious *marja* are advising the people to be wise and not
follow the passions that call on them to seek vengeance on the
other sect?" he asked.

Toward each other, leaders of both sects called for unity
and patience. Ayatollah Ali al-Sistani urged that Iraqis unite.
Dr. Muhammad Bashar al-Faydhi, the spokesman for the
Association of Muslim Scholars, also blamed "foreigners" for

the attacks, adding that "it is impossible for any Muslim to do such a thing. Iraqis could never do this."

Yet this unity and cooperation would not last. Sunni leaders began taking precautions. Armed guards began to man the gate to the Abu Hanifa mosque in Adhamiya. Sheikh Muayad of Abu Hanifa was closely escorted by a bodyguard armed with a small automatic pistol beneath his vest.

Sheikh Muayad himself had visited the Kadhim shrine the morning I went to see him. "Our destiny is one and our enemy is one," Muayad said, describing the enemy as "the one who wants to divide us and make us opposed." He blamed "foreigners" for the attacks, explaining that "sons of the nation would never do this. If they were Muslim it was only in name." The sheikh's assistant, Abdel Hamid, added, "We are expecting an attack at any moment. And if it is our destiny then that is God's will."

A few days after the Ashura bombings, an SUV with masked men shot up a Shia mosque. Several days after that, a thirty-three-year-old Sunni cleric was killed by men in a BMW in a drive-by shooting while walking to his mosque for the evening prayer. Hundreds attended his funeral, which was guarded by anxious armed men. Surrounded by his bodyguards, Sheikh Ahmed Abdel Ghafur al-Samarai of the Association of Muslim Scholars spoke at the funeral, calling on the youth to protect their religious leaders. Samarai blamed the Americans for paying mercenaries to commit murders and cause sectarian strife. More ominously, he also blamed the Americans for favoring the Shias and discriminating against the Sunnis. He criticized them for arming the Kurdish and Shia militias. He called for uniting Sunnis to avoid the threat of other militias taking over and blamed the occupiers and "Zionists" for manipulating Iraq's factions.

Two nights after the Ashura bombings, I received an 11:00 call from a friend in Baghdad's Shaab district, a Shia stronghold. A Sunni mosque near his house had been attacked. "They are Wahhabis," he said. (Iraqi Shiites call all conservative

Sunnis Wahhabis.) Did I want to come? Not a single car was out. Iraqis and prudent journalists left Baghdad streets at night for wild dogs to prowl unopposed. I convinced a taxi driver to take me to Shaab's misty and unlit streets. The road before the mosque was blocked by a truck and about twenty men pointed Kalashnikovs at my car.

They surrounded the taxi and on each side a young man in shabby civilian clothes pointed his barrel in through the windows. They demanded to know who we were and what we wanted. They were very tense. I asked the one on my side who he was, but he ordered me out of the car. The taxi driver explained that I was not an Iraqi. "He's a foreigner!" they shouted to each other. The men swarmed to the car. "They are all Israelis and Jews!" shouted one man in a slurred voice. We tried to explain that I was a journalist, but they had never seen an American passport or a press ID before. Why was I here? What did I want? It was clear from the fear in their eyes and the anger in their voices as they barked orders that they wanted to find somebody to kill. They used none of the polite expressions that color even hostile Arabic conversation. They only gave orders, as if we were their prisoners, their voices echoing against the empty city's buildings.

A man with a slurred voice pointed his Kalashnikov at me and ordered me out of the car in a drunken rage. Not knowing if they were Sunni or Shia, I recited the names of every Iraqi Sunni and Shia leader I could think of and said they were all my friends. I won over two men, who began struggling with the drunken man, who still wanted to shoot me. He would not move the barrel down as they tried to push it. I edged away from its swaying range. The others were undecided and nervously eyed me. One man finally rushed me into the mosque for safety.

More armed guards stood inside. They confirmed that after the last prayer at night, as the devout were emptying onto the street, a car drove by and opened fire. "Praise God, nobody was wounded," they said, pointing to the white gashes in the wall where the bullets had torn off chunks of plaster. They added that only a few months ago the same thing had happened.

In the morning, the neighborhood's streets were busy with children playing amid garbage and sewage pools. Donkeys pulled carts carrying gas for stoves, and boys banged on the containers to announce themselves. American soldiers manned a checkpoint along with fresh Iraqi recruits, searching suspicious cars. A house near the mosque was riddled with bullets and burned. It had belonged to a Wahhabi Muslim killed the previous summer by local Shias.

Sheikh Walid Al-Dulaimi was the leader of the Qiba mosque that had been attacked. He was well liked in the neighborhood for being a friend to the Shias, and locals said he even had problems with Saddam's regime because of this. The mosque caretaker was busy fixing its generator, his hands and robe blackened with grease. He explained that the attackers opened fire from two cars, an Opel sedan and a Nissan pickup, at 7:30 P.M. They were dressed like police. Before they managed to fire an RPG, one of the bystanders grabbed it from them. "They want to create strife between Sunnis and Shias, but it won't happen. I am sixty years old, I have never seen any problems between us. We intermarry and are friends. America is responsible for this." I learned that the drunken man who had been most intent on shooting me the previous night was famous in the neighborhood for his alcohol-inspired belligerence.

Seyid Nasr, the oldest and best-known descendant of the prophet Muhammad in the neighborhood, visited the mosque the day after the attacks. He told the people gathered there that "I am Sunni and I am Shia. We are all Muslims." He was certain that "there will not be any problems between us," and he blamed Zarqawi for the attacks. The sheikh of the mosque was less forthcoming. He peered from behind his locked door and did not unstrap the Kalashnikov from his torso for a moment, afraid of everybody.

Mosque security was higher than ever when I visited Sheikh

Hussein's Maluki mosque in the Amriya district again. Neighborhood boys surrounded it at prayer time, wielding Kalashnikovs unconvincingly. As the men strolled in for the Friday prayer, they were searched for concealed weapons. Slowly, several hundred of the neighborhood men entered, greeting each other and gossiping in the courtyard and then removing their shoes and entering. As the *mu'dhin* finishes his call to prayer, Sheikh Hussein carefully stepped between the closely seated worshippers, making his way to the podium and climbing up the steps. He began with blessings and reminding the people of their God and Prophet. His voice was low and gentle, his arms still. Then he picked up the pace, arms waving faster, raising his voice as he got more excited, until his voice cracked and he was nearly crying, chopping the air in a frenzy, then extending both hands in supplication. His voice exasperated, he slowed down as he answered his own questions, only to begin the cycle again, from the low raspy rumble to the screaming crescendo that woke up those whose heads had sunk into their chests in pious somnambulation.

Sheikh Hussein began by discussing Ali, the fourth caliph or friend of the prophet who succeeded Muhammad in leadership of the Umma, or Muslim nation. Ali is also revered by Shias as the only caliph who should have followed Muhammad, since only he was a relative of the Prophet. "Ali was the first *feday* [fighter willing to sacrifice his life] in Islam," Sheikh Hussein lectured. "He taught the nation how to sacrifice oneself. Be like Ali and sacrifice yourself for Islam. Be like Hassan who tried to unify the people and who compromised with Muawiya for the sake of unity, so that the Muslim world wouldn't be weak, like our situation now.

"Muhammad prophesized when Hassan was a child," Sheikh Hussein explained, "that 'my grandson will one day reconcile between two sects of Islam.' Be like Hassan so that we will be strong." Then it seemed Sheikh Hussain might skip Hassan's more recalcitrant brother, Hussain, who disputed the claim of Muawiya's family after Muawiya and Hassan both died and

Yazid, Muawiya's son, was appointed caliph. "We condemn the attacks in Karbala and Baghdad," the sheikh declared. "The first goal of the enemies of Islam is to make this country weak by causing a sectarian war so people will be busy fighting each other and they can control it and our enemy the Occupier will remain seated on our chests. "

Then he continued, with a surprise, "We have to unify and be like Hussain, the martyr of Karbala, because he sacrificed himself for this country where many warriors were born. Hussain came to Iraq to fight a tyrant because, he said, 'I will not allow a tyrant to rule,' and he did not want oppression. So he came to teach the people that any Muslim should sacrifice himself to prevent the creation of tyranny and Hussain defined the path of martyrdom for the people who followed him and told them to follow it." You didn't hear that often from a Sunni. "We are sorry, Hussain," the sheikh cried out. "We are ashamed to meet you in the next life because Baghdad has fallen." By the end of the sermon, Sheikh Hussein had lost his voice and was too exhausted to talk to me.

Sheikh Hussein knew why tragedy had befallen Iraq. "I swear that everything that is happening in our country is because we strayed from our religion," he said. "We strayed from Islam and took the democracy of the infidels and the freedom of the infidels. There is no solution except Islam, and stability will never come back without it. So insist on Islam. Insist on your religion because the enemies of Islam want to remove this religion."

After prayer was over Sheikh Hussein shook hands with many of his flock. They embraced and kissed in the way Sunnis of western Iraq do, for Sheikh Hussein was from the Dulaimi tribe, whose stronghold is the Anbar province of the west. Sheikh Hussein then retreated to his house inside the mosque, where he feasted with his guests from the nearby town of Abu Ghraib as the sheikh's horde of little boys sat in the corners. American helicopters flew low overhead, shaking the room while Sheikh Hussein and his guests discussed the latest killings of sheikhs and attacks on mosques and grumbled about the Americans.

The reaction to attacks like these, in many mosques, was to urge a return to "purer" Islam. Sunni and Shia imams both did this. Shias were likewise being radicalized. In Baghdad's Kadhim mosque, the Shia faithful began the traditional chorus of "Our god prays for Muhammad and Muhammad's family," but then they continued with a strange innovation, "and speed the appearance of the *Mahdi,* and damn his enemies and make victorious his son Moqtada! Moqtada! Moqtada!" Suddenly, Turkmen Shias were shouting it in demonstrations in front of the Coalition Provisional Authority headquarters, as well as in Kirkuk. Followers of Moqtada began repeating it in their daily prayers.

Private militias flourished. Every major Shia leader had one, including the man who would emerge as the prime minister of the transitional government. Private systems of religious courts began to appear. Worst of all, from the American point of view, Moqtada grew in stature and boldness.

For a year Moqtada al-Sadr had been changing all the rules while confronting the U.S. occupation and rival clerics. The United States and Moqtada had engaged in a game of brinkmanship, with U.S. forces occasionally leaking threats that they would arrest him and Moqtada warning U.S. forces that his people's armed rebellion would soon begin. Moqtada had been winning in this game, gaining experience as a leader as well as admirers of his defiance. His late father's infrastructure remained intact. Although mainstream Shia Islam requires Shias to pick a *marja* and follow his religious verdicts based on his rational interpretation of Islam, it also requires that he be alive. By preserving the office of his slain father, Moqtada has changed yet another rule.

Moqtada and his followers established eight religious courts throughout the country, with two in Baghdad. In Najaf, they initially tried to establish the court within the shrine of Ali, where they already had an office, but they were prevented by the Najaf police. Still, they bullied themselves into prominence.

One local twenty-two-year-old student in the Shia seminary in Najaf, Haidar al-Ma'amar, was praying one day when two men sat beside him and asked him why he opposed praying on Fridays and why he criticized Muhammad Sadiq al-Sadr. Haidar denied both charges. The men said, "So come with us to our court." Haidar felt he had little choice. Four men escorted him forcefully down several alleys. In Moqtada's courts, there are two forms of punishments: fixed or limited punishment for specific crimes, like adultery (one hundred lashes), or stoning and "unlimited" punishments, subject to the judge's discretion.

To the presiding judge, Haidar complained, "This is a very disrespectful way to deal with a seminary student." The judge said nothing, merely gesturing with his finger to the guards that Haidar should be taken away. He was placed in an underground prison where he spent six days and five nights, living on soup and bread.

Haidar was the father of two children and a frail man, with an attenuated body made even smaller by the immense turban he wore that pressed down on his large ears. Wide eyes and a long nose protruded from his long, thin face, made longer by a beard. In Moqtada's prison, he was chained to a column and beaten. He claims he was also tortured with electric shocks. Haidar's forehead is scarred because his keepers bashed it into a column. He claims there were about thirty-five detainees in the prison, including a twelve-year-old accused of homosexuality and a fourteen-year-old who stole money.

Haidar was finally released after his face was broadcast on TV as a missing person and representatives from the seminary pressured Moqtada's office. His true "crime" had been some public statements blaming Moqtada's men for a murder back in April 2003.

Moqtada's men increasingly acted with impunity. Najaf's chief of police was forced to pay over two hundred dollars to release a police officer who was held in their jail. Najaf police fear Moqtada's Mahdi Army, which had even infiltrated their ranks. The Mahdi Army used grenades to blow up over seven DVD shops in Najaf, accusing them of selling pornography. Finally, the Iraqi Governing Council shut down the court in Najaf and released the prisoners. Yet in Baghdad, private courts and prisons continued to operate in the city's Shia bastions, meting out punishments such as whipping for selling immoral movies.

After the Ashura attacks, Moqtada's Mahdi Army increased its presence as a "security" provider. Moqtada compared the attacks to the September 11, 2001, attacks in the United States. He accused the killers of serving the "infamous triangle of Israel, America, and England." He added that "the Quran says you must terrorize the enemy of God, and the Mahdi will terrorize his enemies."

THE U.S.-LED Coalition Provisional Authority decided to lash out at Moqtada in March 2004 by shutting down his organization's newspaper, *Al-Hawza.* It was a foolish move. An ocean of literature was stirring up strife against the occupation, and conflict between Shias and Sunnis.

Yet only Moqtada's newspaper, a radical Shia organ, was closed down on March 28. Singling out Moqtada only gave him a useful grievance. Thousands of Iraqi Shias staged a demonstration in Baghdad's al-Hurriya square to protest the closure. They demanded an apology from the Americans for insulting the Shia seminary and all Iraqis. *Al-Hawza* was published every Thursday and sold throughout Iraq. The text of Moqtada's sermon from the previous Friday was displayed on the front page. News of Moqtada's latest activities, such as an invitation to all his representatives in Iraq to meet him in Najaf or his latest pronouncement, was also on the front page. *Al-Hawza* contained articles obliquely critical of moderate leader Grand Ayatollah Ali al-Sistani. Typical headlines were "Kurdistan Always Belonged to Iraq," "America Kills, Then

Apologizes" (with a picture of Americans abusing an old man), "America Releases Prisoners After the Hawza Threatens Them," "Iraqis of All Religions and Sects Refuse to Watch Half-naked Women on Television."

The American occupying forces closed its offices for sixty days, padlocking and chaining the doors, handing the editor a letter signed by Paul Bremer explaining that the newspaper had violated a ban on fomenting violence. Though the Americans were attempting to silence a vocal and vitriolic critic of their efforts in Iraq, the move played directly into Moqtada's hands. Hamid Bayati, the spokesman for the Supreme Council for the Islamic Revolution in Iraq, confirmed that the move would only "provoke Moqtada al-Sadr's supporters" and confirm Iraqi suspicions that Americans are hypocritical and selective in their application of democracy. (The occupying forces already punished Al Jazeera and Al Arabiya, two Arabic satellite news networks, for broadcasting programs the Americans found distasteful, but no other print publications.)

The punishment of yet another media outlet only confirmed the worst views Iraqis had of Americans and drew parallels with the censorship imposed by the previous government. Shias view themselves as an oppressed and persecuted sect. Moqtada al-Sadr himself often warned of his impending martyrdom. By closing down the newspaper the Americans only supported these fears. *Al-Hawza* had a circulation of only a few tens of thousands. Moqtada reached his supporters through his sermons, CDs of which were sold throughout the country; through statements posted on the walls of his local offices; and through the sermons of his local representatives. Closing *Al-Hawza* did not prevent him from reaching his audience. It was a stupid move.

In Kufah, Moqtada threatened armed opposition to the occupation, and railed against U.S. administrator Paul Bremer's announcement that Islam would not be the main source of the new Iraqi constitution. "We want to advise everybody," Moqtada said, "that the Iraqi people have the ability to attack their enemies." After the interim constitution was signed, Moqtada fumed, comparing it to the British 1917 Balfour Declaration "which sold off Palestine. We are on the way to selling Iraq and Islam. It is a bad omen."

Seyid Hasan Naji al-Musawi, the thirty-eight-year-old leader of Sadr City's Muhsin mosque and commander of Sadr's Army of the Mahdi in Baghdad, said that the final days were approaching in which the Mahdi would return. Shias believe that the twelfth imam, Muhammad al-Mahdi, a descendant of Muhammad, went into an invisible supernatural location when he was a child and has ruled the world from there, but that he will one day return to the corporeal world and restore justice, accompanied by Jesus Christ. Musawi declared that America's real purpose in coming to Iraq was to kill the Mahdi. "Iraq will be the end of America," he said. "The Mahdi will be coming soon and when he comes he will kill the Jewish leadership," which he equated with the Americans. In Shia towns throughout Iraq coalition troops were attacked.

Sheikh Yaqubi of Fudala was also radicalizing, to keep up with Moqtada and in an attempt to participate in the political process as well. In March, Yaqubi, who had promoted himself to ayatollah status, signed a joint document with the Iraqi Dawa Party, the Islamic Accord Movement, the Islamic Action Party, and the Islamic Democratic Current. "The new constitution is disappointing," the document began, "and does not satisfy even the minimum of the Iraqi people's desires because it has many big holes which will lead the country to instability and which will keep the country bound with transitional laws and prevent us from having a permanent constitution because they gave a veto to three governorates which will make them able to reject any permanent constitution chosen by the majority of Iraqi governorates. This will make the transitional stage longer and longer and may lead to pushing the country to political and constitutional problems, and maybe we will not be able to solve these problems peacefully [a reference to civil war]."

The document condemned "the constitution that is written by an unelected council," adding that "we declare that this constitution is illegal, so the elected legislature in the future or now cannot be forced to follow it because it is illegal. . . . We are calling on the Iraqi people to continue peaceful political action."

A YAQUBI ANNOUNCEMENT also made in March warned that "they [Americans] want to make the universities Western. They try to poison the universities with immorality, and they changed the courses and they separated students from the religious leaders and their actual leaders. They thought the universities would fold in their hands and there was no place for Islam there, but the students proved their Islamic awareness and identity in Ashura."

Yaqubi's supporters had been leading Friday prayers in Fardos Circle in central Baghdad, closing the city's main streets and filling them with thousands of faithful in a display that left Iraqis with no doubts as to who controlled the city.

THE CLOSURE OF Moqtada's newspaper on March 28 was a major blunder, only further alienating his followers and adding to Moqtada's following. Arresting Moqtada's influential associate Mustafa al-Yaqubi incensed his supporters (as well as the Spanish troops in Najaf, who did not know about the planned arrest). Moqtada took refuge in his mosque in Kufah, surrounded by his supporters. Before escaping inside his mosque, Moqtada urged his followers to "make your enemy afraid," assuring them that he was with them and would not abandon them. "Your enemy loves terror," he said.

In Shia towns throughout Iraq coalition troops were attacked. So-called moderate cleric Ayatollah Sistani denounced the Americans and voiced his support for Moqtada's cause, in spite of his call for peace, allowing Moqtada's supporters to insist they were fighting for Sistani as well. The Shia sense of persecution and solidarity with their Sunni brethren fighting the Americans was increased by the American siege of Shia holy cities. Internal Shia violence soon increased. In Najaf and elsewhere, Moqtada's men were said to be arresting ten alleged spies a day.

THE COALITION BELIEVED that arresting Moqtada would end the resistance, but the Americans never gave him the martyrdom he sought. Though they had found him guilty of killing their protégé Khoei, and they had sworn to arrest or kill him, the coalition allowed Moqtada to operate unobstructed when the fighting ended. In Iran before the revolution, Ayatollah Khomeini and his supporters condemned the hated Shah as Yazid, the murderer of Hussain, the leader of the Shias whom they mourned during Ashura. In Lebanon, the Shia resistance called the Israeli occupier Yazid. During Ashura, banners in Karbala declared that America was the new Yazid. Other banners warned of Hussain's revenge that would soon remove the Americans. Planners of the war had expected Shias to rejoice at their liberation. The rejection of the Quran as the main source of the constitution began a process of alienation, which led to fighting. How could the Americans have been so stupid to provoke the Shia majority three months before the planned handover of sovereignty back to the Iraqi people? That spring would be the end of the American dream for Iraq, when they lost both the Sunnis and the Shias.

One night that spring, sitting in my room in Baghdad, an immense blast hit me and sent my door flying off its hinges. That's a car bomb, I thought, and I ran to my balcony to see if any nearby buildings had collapsed. Downstairs, I sprinted past Fardus Circle to Andalus Circle, where the Mount Lebanon Hotel no longer existed.

It was dark and hazy, with visibility nearly zero, but a huge orange glow the size of a building shimmered through the smoke and dust. Hundreds of people were running away, hundreds more were running toward it, and still hundreds more were standing in shock, crying, screaming. A woman walked by carrying the inert body of her child. American Humvees and Iraqi police cars pulled up. "There are many dead people," shouted one man, running out of the hotel's wreckage and asking people to help. Terrified and confused U.S. soldiers tried to turn back the crowd of Iraqis who rushed in to respond, swinging their guns in every direction, looking for the enemy. Ambulances arrived, by now well practiced in quick responses to bombs, and carried away the lucky ones who survived, their shredded clothes and bodies drenched with blood. Everywhere there were angry men, stunned, hurt, feeling vulnerable.

Furious survivors attacked cameramen, seeking someone to vent their fury on. Two women in their nightgowns began screaming at an American soldier. Bewildered, not knowing what they were saying, he told them, "Everything's gonna be all right." From atop their Humvees other American soldiers swiveled their machine guns, screaming and cursing at the Iraqis and journalists below them. An Iraqi policeman with his gun drawn pushed me away. All the while, the glowing orange inferno lit the scene as the fire spread to a nearby building.

Journalists moved away to report on their phones in English, Turkish, Italian. Others stood still filming the scene. Arguments broke out between Iraqis who wanted the journalists to film and those who wanted them to leave. More and more bodies were carried out from the gaping wreckage of the flaming hotel building.

That night something felt different to me and other journalists. The Iraqis were hostile to *us.* The crowds and the police were visibly hostile both to the American soldiers and to the press that gathered in front of the blazing building. We were all identified as the foreigners who had brought *faudha,* chaos, to their country. In that spring of 2004, the *faudha* really started, as Shias and Sunnis rose up in mass rebellions throughout Iraq, led by irate clerics.

The only thing that contained Sunni-Shia violence was their common hatred of the United States. In April, Sheikh Harith Suleiman al-Dhari delivered the sermon in the Mother of All

Battles mosque, as the U.S. Marines lay siege to Falluja. The spotless mosque, occupying an immense plot of land, was surrounded by a moat, a parking lot, and many armed guards. Though the Sunni mosque's official name had been changed to Um al-Qura, and a new sign was put outside, locals still used the Saddam-era name. In previous sermons in the Um al-Maarik mosque, Sheikh Samarai, also a member of the Sunni council, had presented a series of discussions about "tyrants," referring to the American occupation. "We ask God to stop the bloodshed and death of women and children and old people," he said in a sermon about "the tyrant's death throes." "The big tyrant here in Iraq is the occupier who wants to start sectarian strife among the Iraqi people, but his efforts have failed, and there will not be a sectarian war because of the good Iraqi people." Samarai added that the failure to provoke a civil war had caused "the occupier" to "lose his mind."

Angrily, he demanded: "Where are the international organizations? This week many Iraqis bled in mosques and places of prayer and many innocents were killed." Al-Samarai told his listeners that "the truth is the occupiers want to start strife so Iraqis will be busy fighting each other and forget the presence of Americans stealing the money of the Iraqi people. Iraqis should be united and they should know the malicious plan and be awake." He concluded by asking Allah to remove the occupation.

Samarai had complained that the occupation forces were favoring Shia Iraqis and called for elections to be held only after the occupiers had left. He explained that ending the occupation was more important than holding elections, which could not be fair otherwise. "How can they protect Iraqis," he asked, when "the Americans are not able to protect themselves?" Dhari was the general secretary of Iraq's Association of Muslim Scholars, Iraq's most important Sunni organization. Dhari had often called for "liberation before elections," explaining that there was no point to holding elections while Iraq was under occupation. He also predicted the failure of

United Nations' intervention and reiterated the oft-heard Sunnis claim that they are the majority. "Sunnis in Iraq are more than half of the population," he said, estimating that they might be up to 60 percent of the population, and adding that the "numbers quoted for the Shia majority in Iraq are a lie which we have not disputed until now for the sake of national unity." Dhari called for a general strike for the next three days to protest the siege of Falluja. More than seven hundred Iraqis had already been killed fighting American Marines.

Thousands of Sunnis were joined by Shiite Iraqis demonstrating their solidarity as Dhari condemned American brutality. Dhari explained that the Sunni council had declared it against Islam to purchase American or British goods, since the money would support the military operations against Iraqis, Arabs, and the Muslim world. Dhari also asked his audience to help in the provision of medical supplies, as well as gas and generators.

"Hai-al al-jihad!" he shouted, calling his listeners to join the battle against the Americans and calling the battle of Falluja a historic moment. Dhari called on Allah to seek revenge for the spilled blood and destroy America and Britain, as well as anybody loyal to them and the infidels. He called on Allah to support the mujahideen, or holy warriors, who were fighting to liberate their country and their religion, and to kill all the occupiers.

"Do not spare any of them!" he said.

He also called for unity, asking Iraqis of all sects to be united and forgive one another "so we can show the world that we are not like the rumors that predict we will kill each other and that the rumors that the U.S. is here to protect us from a civil war are false. Our only protection is our unity."

Dhari's call for a strike was obeyed by Sunnis as well as many Shias. Shops throughout Baghdad were closed. Even the Internet cafés that catered to Western reporters next to the Sheraton and in central Baghdad were closed. Falluja had become a symbol for the plight of the Muslim people, much as the Israeli siege of Jenin in the West Bank, or the Serbian siege of Sarajevo, had previously galvanized them.

After the sermon and prayer had ended, Husham al-Dulaimi, a leader from an important western Sunni tribe, addressed the people using the mosque's microphone, asking them to join the battle. He said that the people of Falluja did not need food or clothes. "We need you and your support," he said, asking them to attack American convoys. The crowd responded with calls of "Jihad! Jihad! Jihad!"

Though Shia and Sunni leaders professed unity against the Americans and following the attacks in Karbala and Kadhimiya, they hated each other. As spring wore on, Sunni and Shia newspapers grew more brazen in their attacks against each other. The only things they agreed on were the need for an Islamic government (though they disagree on what it will look like) and their insistence that the Jews and Americans were to blame for all their woes. The Sunnis were scared, fearing the impending Shia takeover of Iraq if anything resembling a democratic election took place. Shias did not fear the Sunnis; they just disliked them. The Shias also hated the Kurds, blaming them for attempting to divide the country with their calls for federalism and autonomy. Arab Shias began supporting Turkmen in the north, who are often Shias as well, in their bloody clashes with Kurds.

All day and all night, Baghdad shook with explosions from bombs, from rocket-propelled grenades, from artillery, from guns. It was usually impossible to figure out just where the firing occurred, even if one was foolish enough to search after dark. There were systematic assassinations of policemen, translators, local officials, and anybody associated with the American occupiers. The Iraqi police had only handguns and a few AK-47s to use against a foe armed with car bombs and heavy weaponry. The new Iraqi police were hunted at all times in all places, and they were losing every day.

The pace of the violence became so constant, it was almost normal, almost mundane. Unless an explosion was perceptibly close, it was just an echo, and nobody paused in midconver-sation or stopped chewing his kabob. None of the Iraqis in Baghdad really seemed to care much about the American soldiers dying on a daily basis. For many, humiliated by the occupation, American deaths meant a restoration of some self-esteem. And it seemed like few of the American officials cared much about the far greater number of dead Iraqis.

Mosques were attacked every night and clerics killed, lead-ing to retaliations against the opposite sect. Each mosque had an army of young volunteers wielding Kalashnikovs on guard. Neighborhood mosques united to form neighborhood armies, to fight rival mosques or rival neighborhoods. (Even many jour-nalists began traveling with armed bodyguards; in at least one incident they returned fire, making them combatants.) Every-body was armed and scared. It seemed all it would take was a match. "We fear this match," said a leader in the Hudhaifa mosque who did not want to admit to me that his mosque had been shot at, because he did not want the young men to lose patience.

Iraq was becoming increasingly traditional, run by tribal and religious law. In Baghdad's posh Mansur district, religious extremists threatened to bomb the stores of shop owners who did not put the *hijab* on their female mannequins. In Basra, they completely removed the mannequins' heads.

Honor killings—known in Arabic as "washing the shame"—became more and more common. The males who killed their female relatives became heroes. In Baghdad's Seidiya district, Sabah, a twenty-seven-year-old man, dragged his sister in front of their house one day in the summer of 2004. "No one can say shame on me anymore," he said, "this is the shame." He shot his sister in the head.

Not far from there, a thirty-seven-year-old man called Ayad lived in the Maalef district with his family. It was a poor area. Saddam had moved villagers to Maalef but never built them a sewage system. Like so many rural newcomers, they were the peripheral Baghdadis who still maintained their tribal mores.

A tall, muscular man, Ayad sold guns for a living and was of-ten drunk. Once he saw his sister walking in the street with another man. He ran to them, but the man escaped. He beat his sister in the street. Ayad shaved his mustache and swore, like a good Iraqi, "by my mustache," that he would not grow it back until he found the man.

MAALEF HAD A SALAFI MOSQUE and on its walls some-one had written "Kill the Jews." After a sectarian attack angry Shias vented their outrage on the mosque, accusing it of be-longing to the terror group Ansar al-Sunnah. They wrote "Death to Saddam and death to Zarqawi" on its walls. The Sunnis of the mosque later erased Zarqawi's name but left Saddam's. Armed men loyal to Ayatollah Sistani began patrolling the area.

It was just one more area where tensions between Sunnis and Shias were increasing. In July 2004, Sunni mujahideen attacked a taxi, attempting to steal it for use in an operation. They ordered the driver to get out. He began screaming and the neighborhood's men emerged. Many had been sitting in their front yards, since there was no electricity, hoping to catch a breeze and drinking. Ayad and his neighbors rushed to the scene with their Kalashnikovs. "We are not thieves, we are mujahideen," the attackers, some of whom were already wounded by gunshots, explained. "We need this car to make operations to liberate your country." The local Shias beat them up anyway.

Soon the police were on their way and the mujahideen asked the people to release them before the police came. The people refused and the angry mujahideen said, "Your mothers are be-ing fucked by the Americans. The Americans fucked your honor." The locals responded, "But the Americans are fucking your men in Falluja," and beat them some more. One mujahid died from the blows. Another died on the way to the hospital. When the police showed up, they asked why they had kept one alive, rather than killing him as well.

That spring my taxi driver drove by a mosque and saw

Americans in the courtyard. "Look what they're doing!" he shouted hysterically. "They even enter inside mosques! They are dirty Jews. I swear, if I had an RPG [rocket-propelled grenade] now I would shoot them!"

5

THE HEART OF THE RESISTANCE: Falluja, Summer 2004

- ✦ Number of Americans killed, June 2004: 42
- ✦ Number of Americans killed, July 2004: 54
- ✦ Number of Americans killed, August 2004: 66

A DUSTY TOWN EMERGING from the desert thirty-five miles west of Baghdad, Falluja was not a place you would remember unless you were kidnapped or stationed there. With its rigid religious conservatism and strong tribal traditions, however, Falluja came to symbolize the resistance. Fallujans battled five different U.S. commanders brought in to tame the wild western province of the country. I would find myself there at one of the most dangerous times, before the coalition cleared out (i.e., destroyed) the city, while it was still the resistance's great stronghold.

During his reign, Saddam found greater loyalty among the 300,000-strong Fallujans than he did even in his hometown of Tikrit. He never executed Fallujans, though he did kill Tikritis who were his relatives. Fallujans dominated his security and military services. Their proportion of the intelligence services was the highest in the country. After the first Gulf War in 1991 Saddam went to Falluja, not Tikrit, to declare his victory in "the mother of all battles." He was greeted there with genuine love. Also unlike Tikrit, where the tribes are urbanized, based inside the city, the tribes of Falluja are concentrated in the rural areas surrounding the city, and thus have not modernized as much as other parts of the country. The principle of *fiz'a* is very important in Falluja, as it is throughout western Iraq. *Fiz'a* meant that if a tribal or family friend was in trouble, his kinsmen and friends would join in his fight. Throughout the region, there was a deep sense of unity, and Fallujans often addressed each other as *"ibn ami,"* or "my cousin."

Even under Saddam, the sale of alcohol was not permitted in Falluja. The city was famous for having the best kabobs in Iraq and for its importance as a smuggling center. Smugglers working in Syria and Jordan operated with impunity, as long as they bribed the right people.

An American NGO project manager bewilderedly told me about his meeting with a women's group from Falluja that was more radical than the men. "We must be willing to sacrifice our sons to end the occupation," they told him. A story, perhaps apocryphal, holds that in the 1980s the first restaurant opened in Falluja, and people blew it up. Fallujans felt ashamed to have a restaurant, saying, "We have houses for guests." When it was rebuilt, they blew it up a second time. When the first movie theater opened, they blew it up, too, because it went against Islam.

Situated on a strategic point bridging the Euphrates River, Falluja is the center of a fertile region on the outskirts of the desert leading to Saudi Arabia, Jordan, and Syria. Its location also makes it a smuggling center. After the 2003 invasion Falluja did not suffer from the same looting seen in other parts of the country. There was less reason to be hostile to the former regime and its institutions. Religious and tribal leaders appointed their own civil management council even before American troops arrived. Tribes assumed control of the city's institutions and protected government buildings. Religious leaders exhorted the people to respect the law and maintain order. Tight tribal bonds helped preserve stability.

Yet the story of Falluja beginning in April 2003 was hardly a picture of stability. On May 1, 2003, when President Bush declared the mission in Iraq accomplished, there were funeral processions and demonstrations in Falluja. Clerics warned the Americans to get out. The Americans met with clerics and the mayor of Falluja as protestors stood outside. In the mosques, clerics called for a patient jihad, reminding listeners that a million Algerians were martyred to end French colonialism. "Oh, American forces," one said. "Oh America, you have your religion and we have our religion. You have your land and we have our land."

The Americans began driving Humvees around, playing a recorded message: "Allied forces are here to bring peace to Iraq and Falluja and to rebuild Iraq. Do not throw stones. Do not try to hurt them. Thank you for your cooperation."

Meanwhile, soldiers broke down the doors of the Iraqi Islamic Party building and destroyed the ceiling, to see if there were weapons in it. On Friday, May 30, 2003, Sheikh Maki Hussein al-Kubeisi had spoken to hundreds at the Abdel Aziz al-Samarai mosque. Iraqis were not stupid, he told his congregants, and they knew Americans had not come to liberate them. "They came to free the Iraqis from Saddam Hussein. Saddam is gone. Now we need our own government." He warned Fallujans to be prepared to fight American aggression. The day before, local leaders from tribes and mosques had met to complain about the American occupation. Some swore they would continue attacking Americans. Sheikh Abdel Hakim Sabti of the Suheib bin Sinan mosque gave the Americans six months to prove themselves, and if nothing changed, he said, they would declare a jihad.

By June of that year, soldiers from the Third Infantry Division bolstered troops already in Falluja in an attempt to crush the resistance there. Rumors soon spread that the new forces were mercenaries who looted the homes they searched. Graffiti warned the Americans that Falluja would be a fire burning them and praised the mujahideen fighting them. Americans were shot at, and a police station was destroyed. The Americans accidentally killed a member of the mayor's own security team.

That month, the Americans had initiated Operation Spartan Scorpion, hunting for resistance leaders and weapons stockpiles. Loudspeakers on Falluja's mosques announced that the Americans were going to raid the city, and as the Americans approached, Fallujans sounded sirens and flashed lights, sending warnings to each other. Attempting to win over the population, the Americans bulldozed a lot and created a soccer field, and gave the mayor soccer balls to hand out to children. Elsewhere they handed out food, fuel, schoolbooks, medicine, candy, and toys. They might have won over the children in the morning, but handing out candy by day and breaking down their houses to arrest Daddy at night was sending confusing signals.

On July 1, 2003, a letter mysteriously appeared naming thirty-three people as collaborators with the Americans and calling for their deaths. The list included Falluja's governor as well as former high-ranking officers, assembly members, scholars, and civil servants. By then it was clear that the resistance was composed of Falluja's conservative young men, unemployed, most often former military or security servicemen. Unpaid for three months since the security services and military were dissolved, furious at humiliating American house-to-house searches, feeling the Sunni sense of entitlement to rule Iraq, these young men were provoked into action.

Most clerics were still calling for calm. But in September 2003, the Americans accidentally killed eleven Iraqi police officers in the city, on a Friday. The next day at their funeral, as weapons were fired into the air, one sheikh asked listeners to save their bullets for the chests of their enemies—the Americans. A poster on his mosque asked all honorable men in Falluja to take part in the jihad against the men who bring evil into Iraq. He believed the Americans had come to Iraq to convert Iraqis to their religion. As Americans continued to shoot what friends they had left, Falluja's Sheikh Yunis Abdallah, who himself had been imprisoned by Saddam, complained that he could never find people willing to fight Saddam, but the Americans were driving people to embrace jihad.

The cycle of attacks and retaliation had begun. The more the Americans fought, the stronger the resistance became. Things got worse, month by month, until finally, on April 31, 2004, four American contractors were killed and mutilated, their bodies put on display. This was another *sahel,* public lynching, a flesh version of the previous year's triumphant dragging of Saddam's statue in Baghdad. The slayings of the American mercenaries provoked a Stalingrad-like response by the Americans, called Operation Vigilant Resolve. For a month, American forces pushed toward the center of the city, facing fierce resistance. The Fallujan mujahideen were using a key mosque as their headquarters. In May, in a compromise, a former army general under Saddam was given authority over the Falluja Brigade, a local security force created to police the city instead of the American Marines. Americans described it as a success, but Fallujans were clear that they had liberated their city. The arrangement struck with the Americans was simple: leave us alone or we will fight you. The details of the agreement went largely unpublished, but the United States, which only a week before had vowed to take the city by force, had agreed that General Jassim Mohammed Saleh, a former Republican Guard commander, would establish what has been called both the Falluja Brigade and the Falluja Protection Army. After the American-trained Iraqi Army had mutinied, refusing to fight in Falluja on the grounds that they had joined to defend Iraq, not kill Iraqis, General Jassim and his supporters approached Marine commander Lieutenant General James Conway and offered salvation. "It got to the point that we thought there were no options that would preclude an attack," Conway said. Lieutenant Colonel Brennan Byrne described it as "an Iraqi solution to an Iraqi problem." They would crown General Jassim as warlord of Falluja. "The plan is that the whole of Falluja will be under the control of the FPA," Byrne said.

One senior U.S. official explained to the *Washington Post* on April 19, "What we're trying to do is extricate ourselves from Falluja," but Brigadier General Mark Kimmitt, deputy commander of operations for the coalition, maintained that marines were not "withdrawing" but rather were "repositioning" and would remain "in and around Falluja." I saw no marines inside the city, and I was told by Fallujan police and soldiers that they would shoot at Americans if they came in. In defiance of a statement by the commander of U.S. military operations in the Middle East, General John Abizaid, who said, "We want the marines to have freedom of maneuver along with the Iraqi security forces," Kimmitt insisted, "The coalition objectives remain unchanged: to eliminate armed groups, collect and positively control all heavy weapons, and turn over foreign fighters and disarm anti-Iraqi insurgents in Falluja." Yet I found no evidence of such policy. I found the general beholden to the mujahideen leaders, seeking their approval, collaborating with them, and under their command. And though General Jassim was to have been replaced by General Muhammad Latif due to allegations of war crimes committed during Jassim's repression of the 1991 Shia and Kurdish uprising, I found General Jassim still in command.

April 2004 was the worst month yet for the American-led occupation in Iraq, which fought a two-front war in the Sunni Triangle as well as against the Army of the Mahdi, Moqtada's militia. Falluja had become a rallying cry that united Iraq's antagonistic Sunni and Shia against the occupation and solidified the bonds between their militias, creating a popular resistance in Iraq for the first time. The marines began their withdrawal from the city on April 30. Obstinate resistance fighters who rejected the cease-fire killed two of them with a roadside bomb that day.

By May, Marine commander Major General James N. Mattis had forgotten all his demands, including the handover of heavy weapons and the killers of the four American contractors. He could only be satisfied with the mere fact that "nobody shoots," adding that "any day that there is no shooting, it is good."

IN EARLY MAY 2004 I took a taxi from Amman to Baghdad, en route to Falluja. My driver had insisted I wear the traditional Arab dishdasha. After passing through Jordanian customs and approaching their Iraqi counterparts, my driver warned me to remain in the car. The Iraqi resistance had people working for it in the border post, he said, and if they saw my American passport they would contact their friends on the road ahead who would welcome us with rocket-propelled grenades and small-arms fire. I pushed the seat back as he requested and closed my eyes. Soon we were driving east to Baghdad on Iraq's Highway 10, and I had snuck into the country without any American or Iraqi official's cognizance. As we drove past the charred hulls of SUVs whose drivers had been less savvy than mine, and whose passengers had been less lucky than I, I wondered who else was infiltrating Iraq with the same ease I had.

When I got to Baghdad my colleagues were shocked to hear that I had taken the road. Nobody drove into Iraq anymore. The rebellion had virtually severed the western Anbar province from the rest of the country. Thousands of mujahideen manned roadblocks, searching for foreigners to kidnap or kill. At least eighty American military convoys had been attacked. Anybody who could was flying into the country.

I reached Falluja the next day. On the main street, recently renamed Sheikh Ahmad Yassin Street after the leader of Hamas, laborers with scarves protecting their faces from the dust gathered to be picked up for day jobs. It was angry unemployed young men like them, armed only with shovels and pipes, who had dismembered the four contractors after mujahideen had ambushed their vehicles. Nearby, young boys sold bananas and boxes of Kleenex. The boys served as an early warning system, notifying the men if they spotted foreigners. Fair-skinned journalists I knew told of hiding low in their cars to avoid arousing attention, only to have the Kleenex boys spot them and shout,

"American! American!" On a large intersection anti-American graffiti in English was scrawled on the walls as a warning to American soldiers.

The boys gathered around me, and the laborers removed their kaffiyehs from their faces to talk. They had witnessed the attack on the contractors, when two cars had stopped at a red light and mujahideen had opened fire on them from other vehicles. The rear car was hit and the front car sped off and made a U-turn, but it too was hit. A mujahid shouted, "I avenged my brother who was killed by the Americans!" and the assailants left the contractors shot dead. An angry mob on the street mutilated the bodies, burning them and beating them with pipes until they were partially dismembered, a gruesome scene captured on film. I asked one Kleenex sales boy if he had done it. "I would even pull Bush down the street!" He smiled. A laborer said, "God and the mujahideen gave us victory. It will spread to all of Iraq and all the way to Jerusalem."

The bodies were dragged about a mile to the old Falluja Bridge and hung from it. The marines had responded quickly, with brute force, which one American army major regretted. By his lights, it was all because of "a bunch of high-paid dumbass Special Forces types who wanted to get in a firefight because they thought they were bulletproof."

Near the old bridge where the charred bodies were strung up, I found the neighborhood's people sorting through the rubble of their destroyed homes, flattened as if by an earthquake. AC-130 gunships, attack helicopters, and even fighter planes had pummeled the neighborhood. I found one man standing in the center of an immense crater that had been his home, his children playing on the mountains of bricks. Another man sat collapsed in despair in front of the gate leading to his home, which had been crushed as if by a giant foot. He played with his worry beads indolently. One by one the men of the neighborhood asked me to photograph the damage American Marines had inflicted upon them. As I was doing so, a white sedan pulled up and two strong-looking men covering their faces with checkered scarves emerged, demanding to know my identity. They were afraid of spies, they told me, and suspected I was one. I convinced them I was just a journalist and they escorted me to a mosque whose tower had collapsed from an American attack. In the still seething neighborhood, fighters were bitter about the compromise reached with the Americans that ended the fighting and threatened to kill the leaders who had negotiated and approved the settlement.

Down the railroad tracks, on the eastern border of Falluja, the Askari neighborhood suffered a similar fate, its homes eaten by American bullets and shells. American troops manned the Falluja checkpoint alongside Fallujan soldiers, some wearing the uniforms of the former army. Dozens of cars line up there in order to wind slowly around barricades and be searched for weapons and foreign fighters. My driver resented the hour-long wait and took the back roads into Falluja, through a moonscape of sand dunes, past abandoned cement factories with cranes frozen atop them like skeletons. As a city built on smuggling, everyone knew how to sneak around. Trails carved out of the desert lead into the town from every direction, and the main road is ignored by those who know. We drove past a lot in the desert where a dozen rusted trucks were parked, containing Hebrew writing and Israeli license plates, probably stolen in Israel and sold in Jordan. No soldiers or marines regulated traffic in the region, I noticed, as we bumped our way over the dunes.

Falluja's lawlessness was actually threatening the economy by obstructing the essential traffic coming in through Jordan. Iraqi friends who had driven through the western roads described seeing thousands of mujahideen manning checkpoints made of concrete blocks and logs in the middle of the road and demanding identification cards at gunpoint, to search for foreigners. That spring, at least, they had managed to take over the west.

It was quiet in Falluja when I arrived, in part because some mujahideen leaders had left the city. Some had sought refuge in Baghdad. The mujahideen who remained were eyeing the surrounding villages where their tribes were based, and the nearby city of Ramadi. They wanted to "liberate" more territory.

Some neighborhoods were still controlled by irredentist mujahideen, bitter at the cease-fire that betrayed their cause. They were threatening the very radical leaders who had tenuous control of the city. With no clear leader, the people of Falluja were worried about internal power struggles turning bloody.

Supporters of the resistance throughout Iraq had assisted the fight in Falluja, providing food and medicine and smuggling in weapons. All in all, it was a disaster for the American coalition and the soon-to-be "sovereign" Iraqi transitional government.

American Marines had conducted their last patrol into Falluja on May 10. It was a hasty half-hour affair in which a convoy drove up to the headquarters of the new Falluja military force for a brief meeting before they left. At first, the mood on the streets was festive. Thousands of residents came out for a carnival-like victory celebration. Fighters carrying their weapons piled onto pickup trucks and fired shots into the air. Songs were sung and a sheep was slaughtered on the street. Men queued to sign up for a newly formed military unit, collecting the forms from an Iraqi officer wearing the uniform of the disbanded Republican Guard.

On May 11, hundreds of dignitaries gathered under a long tent in Falluja for a poetry celebration, organized by the National Front of Iraqi Intellectuals. It was staged before an unfinished hospital. A podium was placed on top of the rough gray stairs in the hospital's entrance, with the front's emblem and Iraqi flags draped on it. Tall columns and arches framed the background. Graffiti on the walls of the hospital said "Long live the mujahideen and the loved ones of Muhammad," "Victory is Falluja's and defeat for the infidel America," and "The Falluja martyrs are the lights for the way to the complete liberation of Iraq."

Religious clerics wearing turbans, tribal leaders wearing white head scarves, businessmen, military and police officers, and men wearing the old Baathist-style safari open-collar shirt and pants all sat on plastic chairs beneath a long tent shading them from the noon sun. Banners on the tent and walls of the hospital announced that "All of Falluja's neighborhoods bear witness to its heroism, steadfastness, and virtue," "The stand of Falluja is the truest expression of the Iraqi identity," "Falluja, castle of steadfastness and pride," and "The martyrs of Falluja, Najaf, Kufah, and Basra are the pole of the flag that says God is great." Above the podium tough-looking men wearing sunglasses and grimaces looked down upon the crowd. A banner above them described the event as a poetry festival to support Falluja against the occupation. Cans of soda and bottles of water were provided for the honored guests.

"Hey, Falluja," called one poet, "when I wrote my poem, you were the most beautiful verse inside it and without your stand I could not raise my head again." Another poet, with a strong southern Iraqi Shia accent, declared that "Falluja is full of real men." Referring to the great Shia martyr, he continued that just as "Hussain was supported by seventy of his followers, we have to be like his followers and end the internal strife." He led the audience in hand clapping and chants calling for unity between Sunnis and Shias.

A local Sunni recited a poem called "The Falluja Tragedy" in a barely intelligible accent. "Falluja is a tall date palm," he said. "She never accepts anybody touching her dates, she will shoot arrows into the eyes of those who try to taste her, this is Falluja, your bride, oh, Euphrates! She will never fall in love with anyone but you . . . Americans dug in the ground and pulled out the roots of the date palm."

A twelve-year-old boy from Najaf stepped up to the podium. The microphone was lowered to point at his mouth. He wore a pressed white shirt neatly tucked into his jeans, and he waved an arm angrily, pointing a finger at the sky. "I came from Najaf to praise the heroes of Falluja!" he shouted, and ended by calling to God, screaming, "Ya Allah! Ya Allah!" He burst out sobbing. Older men escorted him off as he wiped his tears, and he was embraced and kissed in succession by the dignitaries in the front row. He returned to recite another bellicose poem, this time brandishing a Kalashnikov that was as long as he was tall.

Listening to the hyperbolic poems amid a devastated city, I was reminded of Ma'ruf al-Resafi (1875–1945), nicknamed "the poet of Iraq." A teacher, writer, translator, journalist, historian, and politician, Resafi traveled much of his life and settled in Falluja, from which he fled in 1941 to Baghdad when British troops and mercenaries attacked it. He wrote famous poems in tribute to Falluja, including this one:

> *Oh Englishmen, we will not forget*
> *Your cruelty in the houses of Falluja*
> *Sanctioned by your army, wanting revenge*
> *Its parasites dazzled by Falluja's inhabitants*
> *And on the defenseless you poured a glass*
> *Of blood mixed with betrayal*
> *Is this the civility, and loftiness*
> *Your people claim to ascend to?*

Seated majestically in the center of the crowd, next to the chief of police, Sheikh Dhafer al-Ubeidi, the guest of honor, rose to speak, a white scarf framing his dark bearded face, and a gold-rimmed translucent sheikh's cape draped over his shoulders. "There was never unity in Iraqi history like this," he said, describing the event as "the wedding day for Falluja." Muslims had not felt such joy, he said, "since Saladin liberated Jerusalem." Silencing the enthusiastic crowd, he said, "I don't like clapping, so if I say something you like, then say Allahu Akbar [God is great], which is in accordance with our traditions. Clapping is for poets, not religious leaders." Dhafer warned that Zionists, imperialists, and Masons were leading the occupation and inciting sectarian war. "The meaning of Falluja has

Liberation and recovery: dead bodies discovered in a mass grave from the Saddam era.

The face of the American occupation.

Iraqis sweltering in the line to enter the Green Zone.

The Martyr tradition:
paintings of Hussain on sale in Karbala.

Muharram procession of Shia faithful, flaying themselves with chains
in Baghdad's Shaab district.

Shias commemorating Ashura, the anniversary of the martyrdom of Hussain, by cutting themselves with swords.

Iranian pilgrims at Karbala, weeping for Hussain.

The Red Cross bombing, 2003. While the Shias asserted themselves, insurgents gained strength.

At first, a few moderate Sunni leaders, such as Dr. Kubeisi (here giving his debut sermon at the Abu Hanifa mosque), insisted, "There are no Sunnis . . . There are no Shias," as one banner proclaims.

Even young boys play with Kalashnikovs.

Another young boy recited radical, violent poetry at a festival after the insurgent "liberation" of Falluja.

The American presence was often violent: a man in Falluja's Julan district seated outside his home after the Marines destroyed it.

The terrified family of a man seized by the Americans during a raid.

Male prisoners of America's Operation Decapitation.

The author (center) in Najaf, meeting with Sheikh Haidar (right).

A resistance sniper outside Falluja.

Today in Iraq, every leader has his own militia, and the lines between legitimate authority and thuggishness are hard to distinguish. Here, militia men guard streets and buildings.

become victory," he told them. Falluja was now religiously prohibited for the Americans, he said, "until Judgment Day. Soon,
all of Iraq will be the same." Sheikh Dhafer wished peace upon
the crowd and descended to shouts of "God is great!"

As the tribal leaders seated behind Sheikh Dhafer parted
with one another and lumbered out of the tent, holding their
gowns up slightly with one hand, I stopped one sheikh to ask
him about the event. "It is a victory celebration. We want a
national government that represents the Iraqi people," he
added. "We don't hate democracy, we believe in democracy,
but it should come from the Iraqi people. We have our own
special democracy that takes Iraqi history and culture into
consideration." His companion, a tall gaunt sheikh with a thin
mustache, told me, "We don't want freedom or democracy if
it comes from America!" Another sheikh cut him off, shouting, "How can you tell a foreigner that you don't want freedom or democracy? He will tell the whole world!" The sheikh
did not respond, telling me only that "America should leave
today, before tomorrow!"

I SET OUT TO DISCOVER the reality behind the "Falluja
model." What I found was a city run by the Iraqi resistance,
divided against itself. Fighters looted and meted out vigilante
justice, and strongmen vied for power.

To learn more about the history of Falluja's resistance, I
visited the opulent home of Abu Muhamad, a former brigadier general in the Iraqi military. We sat in his guest hall, decorated with expensive but gaudy art, flowery and uncoordinated,
typical for the region, watching the news about the Iraqi Governing Council president's assassination. His three young boys
were play fighting on a sofa and smiling at me shyly, hoping to
get the attention of the foreigner. Abu Muhamad had a baby
face and dimples, and smiled as much as his frolicking boys.
His current title was left unspecified. He served under General Jassim's command in an intelligence capacity.

Like all members of the previous army, Abu Muhamad had

lost his job when the American occupation dissolved it. He explained that this had only created enemies for the Americans. He spoke of "the massive use of force" and "disrespect for our traditions" that Fallujans experienced, as well as the "media showing American raids and attacks," concluding that "former regime people like me were forced to support revenge."

After the war ended, he said, "we expected things to improve, but everything became worse—electricity, water, sewage, draining—so mosque speakers openly spoke of jihad and encouraged people to join it after a month of occupation." Abu Muhamad explained that the "mosque culture developed against the Americans in this year. The mosques were free. Mosque culture in Falluja centered on jihad. This attracted foreign Arabs who felt constrained by their own regimes and of course there were neighboring countries that supported this financially. Nobody in Falluja opposed the resistance, and many different resistance groups came in. Weapons were very available in Falluja. All soldiers and security personnel took their weapons home and the Baath Party had also distributed weapons."

Abu Muhamad was bewildered by what he called "the stupidity of the Americans," in that "they didn't seize ammunition depots of the army that contained enormous amounts of weapons. The nature of the people here is violent because they grew up with weapons since childhood and weapons become part of our personality. "

Abu Muhamad admitted that "the presence of Al Jazeera's exaggerated pictures and incitement of people led people inside and outside Iraq to sympathize with Falluja." He compared Al Jazeera's Falluja correspondent to a cheerleader. "His broadcasts were like a sports commentator, not a journalist, encouraging people to support one team against the other. And he raised the spirits of fighters."

Yet the resistance was highly unstable. "There is no law in Falluja now," he said. "It's like Afghanistan. Rule of gangs, and mafias, and the Taliban. If they decide somebody is a spy, they will kill him. There is no legal procedure. Imams of mosques who left during the fighting were prevented from returning to their mosques." He feared that soon differences would emerge between different mujahideen groups, leading to further violence.

Abu Muhamad was skeptical about the new Fallujan army that he had joined. "What is the point of this new army? Who does it kill? Who does it defend?" He had been approached by delegates from a leading mosque who brought him the forms and told him he was approved, so he joined.

ACROSS THE TOWN, I visited the headquarters of the Islamic Party. One of the twenty-five parties belonging to the American-appointed Governing Council, now a sovereign government, its controversial leader was Dr. Muhsin Abdel Hamid. He was a radical Sunni who was somehow acceptable to America, though his rhetoric was anti-Shia and militant.

The party offices were located in an old cinema, earning it the name "the cinema party" by Fallujans who viewed it as too cooperative with the Americans. The Islamic Party dominated the city council, but its members were not active during the fighting and some had left the city, earning them the contempt of many Fallujans who divided their community between those who had stayed to fight and those who had left. Boxes of medical supplies were piled high by the doors, and several men in sweatpants were sprawled in front, holding Kalashnikovs. Inside the theater, piled on seats and on the stage, were thousands of boxes containing medical supplies as well as food for the families of "martyrs" and the wounded. The party was sending hundreds of these by truck to Karbala and Najaf, where Shia militias were battling occupation forces. By the door I found a poster advertising an "Islamic music band" called "The Voice of the Right." It showed a bloody heart in the center of Iraq with a hand plunging a spear through it. Another poster showed two pages, one with American soldiers and one with Iraqis and mosques. "With the Prophet's guidance we will unite to turn the page on the occupation." On a table they sold copies of the party's newspaper, *Dar Assalam,* and a radical Sunni magazine called *Nur,* meaning "lights."

I met with Khalid Muhammad, the office director, who insisted on speaking only classical Arabic, an annoying habit akin to speaking Shakespearean English in modern London. It was especially annoying to me because my Iraqi dialect was much stronger than my classical Arabic. Muhammad was worried about groups in the city "who reject the cease-fire and want to turn Falluja into a center to export the rebellion." These differences had emerged during the fighting, he said, "and when we worked on the cease-fire, there were other fighters who want fighting to continue until the occupation ends." Muhammad confirmed to me that General Jassim was not dismissed after all, but was in fact the number-two man in power.

The main competition faced by the Islamic Party, at the time, came from the Association of Muslim Scholars, headquartered in the Abdel Aziz mosque, a battle zone during the siege. The association, long committed to resisting the occupation, had commanded its own mujahideen units during the fighting. The mosque was alleged by Americans to contain mujahideen and was attacked, its green dome speckled with bullet holes and a big hole bitten out of its tower. On the mosque's columns, signs said "God chose for you a group of martyrs from the city of clerics and religious science, and congratulations to them who now live in the stomachs of the green birds," a reference to heaven for martyrs, whose souls are said to reach heaven inside green birds. Abdel Hamid Farhan, the mosque leader, told me his city was not yet free and would not be until the rest of the country was liberated.

Next stop: the Falluja Provisional Council. On the large concrete blocks that guard the council's offices I found the same resistance posters I had seen elsewhere in the city and throughout the west. The resistance had capable graphic designers working for it. "Iraq is the beginning of the end of the occupation" read one poster, showing a fist lunging out of Iraq, waving the flag. On the flag it said, "Congratulations to Falluja's people, jihad, martyrdom, victory." Two armed resistance fighters were on either side, their faces covered by kaffiyehs. An American flag with a Star of David was on fire, its flames burning American soldiers.

Inside, Saad Ala al-Rawi, a lawyer and head of the local provisional council, was receiving petitioners behind his desk. He had a thin mustache and wore the Baathist safari uniform. Referring to the attack on the four mercenaries, Rawi told me, "We are at war, so killing is normal. But mutilating bodies is not acceptable." He added that the Americans used the incident as an excuse to attack Falluja. I asked him if they would shoot at American troops should they reenter the city. "Let me ask you this," he said. "If someone invades your house, will you just stand by?"

On Friday, May 14, I pulled up at the mosque of Sheikh Dhafer, which squats inconspicuously across the street from the hospital that had hosted the poetry festival. Falluja is known as the city of mosques because it has no fewer than eighty of them, but this one was smaller and more modest than most. Its colors were faded, its dome small. But if there was a final authority for the resistance in Iraq, a command and control center, this was it.

I had been warned that Sheikh Dhafer ran the city and to interview people in Falluja I would need his "clearance." Other journalists who had not done so had been held by armed gangs. A writer for a leading American newspaper was caught at a checkpoint, attempting to disguise his face with a woman's black veil. Another writer for a top American magazine was stopped after coming out of the marine base in an armored car, with an armed driver, bulletproof vest, American passport, and a receipt from the Israeli-Jordanian border crossing in his pocket. None of them had been able to report from Falluja. I needed to get a piece of paper from the sheikh that would be, in effect, a license to work in the city.

As I got out of the car in front of the mosque, a big explosion shook the city, and in the distance I could see a large mushroom cloud. The police car in front of the mosque veered off to take a look. On the tall fence lining the mosque, a banner announced "Sunnis and Shias are committed to defeating the Zionist plan." It did not explain the plan; apparently the locals already knew. White paint was peeling off the mosque's rusted gate. A sign above bore the title "Al Hadhra Muhamadia mosque and Madrassa [religious school]." The mosque's tower had been damaged from an American shell.

Leaflets and announcements were taped onto the gate. One said that "the High Fatwa Council asks for pictures and evidence of occupation forces violating human rights and any attack on our values and our Islamic symbols. Please give them to the Council in the Hadhra mosque." Another one contained a long verse dedicated to a man martyred by the Americans. Another instructed people about what documents were needed to receive compensation for martyrs and wounds and damaged vehicles. The council clearly was subsidizing the resistance. A similar one asked the families of martyrs to go to the courts to get a death certificate and then to the hospital to get additional proof of death in order to process their compensation claims.

As an ominous sign of Falluja's internal divisions, an announcement from the "Mujahideen Council" declared that "imams are responsible for their mosques and the mujahideen have no rights to interfere in mosques after today." It added that "some thieves go to markets, confiscating goods and money and consider themselves mujahideen, but they are liars and we ask the people of the city of mosques to catch these people and educate them (forcefully) and the mujahideen will support them to prevent strife in our city."

Past the security guards, a tall palm tree provided a bit of shade on a path to the mosque office. The windows of the building were still crossed with tape to prevent shattering from the fighting. Inside, I found an old acquaintance from Baghdad, Taghlub al-Alusi. He was as gentle and dignified as I remembered him, but with more sharp lines of worry on his face. He was very concerned about the American incursion into Karbala that day. "It's holy for us too," he said. "They are our fore-fathers."

Taghlub had worked with Ahmad Kubeisi's movement for three months, but left even before Kubeisi fled to Dubai because "I found them inefficient." Taghlub's older brother had once led the Hadhra mosque, but after being seriously injured in an assassination attempt, he was confined to a wheelchair and unable even to move it on his own. He had appointed Sheikh Dhafer as his replacement. Taghlub himself was a resistance leader and had led the negotiations for the cease-fire and withdrawal of the marines. Now, he was head of the unofficial Consultative Council that governed Falluja.

A bevy of bony young boys hung around the mosque for no apparent reason but were always available on command to fetch tea or water for guests. The oldest among them, a lanky, grinning seventeen-year-old named Ala, had been part of a delegation sent by Moqtada al-Sadr's militia, the Army of the Mahdi, during the fighting. Ala was from Baghdad's Sadr City and had worked during the fighting in the mosque's infirmary, helping the wounded. I asked him why he had come to Falluja. "It's my country and this is also my city," he said. He was the mosque mascot, a representative of the Shia *muqawama,* or resistance, that had helped Fallujans in the battle, cutting American supply lines near Abu Ghraib. Former and current mujahideen stood by the fence. Muscular young men, some with bandages still covering wounds from the fighting, pulled up on Jawa motorcycles, popular with the former regime's praetorian guard.

After removing my shoes and leaving them by the door, I was escorted into the sparse office and seated on an old sofa. I was offered a glass of water and taffies. A twelve-year-old boy entered the room, to the delight of the mosque's leadership. They introduced him as Saad, a brave boy who had fought as a capable sniper during the battle with the Americans. He was

hugged and kissed by all the men in the room, who congratu-
lated him for being a hero. A scarred scrapper, he smiled proudly
and thanked them in a hoarse voice, with the confidence of a
grown man. He was insolent to the older, bigger boys, who
were scared of him. I was nervous around him too: he reminded me of a rabid pit bull. After prayers I saw him linger-
ing outside the mosque, slinging a Kalashnikov, providing
security.

General Jassim Mohammed Saleh of the Falluja Brigade
walked in wearing a white dishdasha and white scarf. After
exchanging greetings with the guests in the increasingly crowded
office, he briefed them on the latest political events, barking
gruffly in clipped military style, his jowls shaking, his fingers
pushing yellow prayer beads. He defended the need for the
Falluja Army he did or did not command, depending on
whether you listened to Fallujans or Americans. "Everybody
else has militias and it's not called terrorism," he said. "But
when an army defends its city, this is called terrorism?" The
meeting was businesslike but not especially revealing. It was
taken as a given by everyone there that America was their enemy and that the mujahideen were honorable soldiers. Now
that they controlled their city, and the Americans had pulled
out, they were equally absorbed in running the local government and in spreading their success throughout the country.

At his Friday sermon, the sheikh let loose in a raspy voice.
"Everybody hates America now because of the policies of President Bush," he said, "and his own people condemn him, so
what can we do? What can we say? What are the limits of our
response? What are the rights of the Iraqi people?" There was
no action the Iraqis could not take against the Americans, he
answered. "They slaughtered the Geneva accords . . . the gates
of victory for all the Islamic world have been opened in Falluja
and victory will never stop as our Prophet has predicted. All
the world can recognize now that Falluja defeated the United
States."

He condemned mujahideen who "make many checkpoints

in several places and steal cars or kidnap people in those places; they are not mujahideen. It looks like they were educated by our enemies. They went into a neighborhood in our city and they did what the Americans do, forcing people to lie on the ground, spreading their legs and putting their feet on their heads. What religion is this?" Alluding to the extrajudicial killings of alleged informants for the Americans, whom he called "the traitors who sold their religion and their honor and their land," the sheikh reminded his people that "the accused is innocent until proven guilty."

After the noon prayer and sermon ended, I was inundated by invitations to lunch, and joined a businessman with connections to the mujahideen. The men of his family lined up at the entrance of their *diwan* to shake hands and welcome visitors. Glasses of sugar and dark tea were brought out, and we watched the American attacks on Najaf and Karbala on Al Jazeera.

My hosts showed me a leaflet that was circulating throughout the region. A blurry photocollage depicted a giant, spiderlike creature next to a pair of legs that belonged to a man in an American military uniform. The leaflet explained that the creature circles around Falluja, attacking Americans. It could run up to forty kilometers, screaming and biting. I had heard numerous fantastic stories like that. One told of a Kalashnikov that worked for four hours straight without reloading. An armory used by the mujahideen turned into a weapons cornucopia. Dead mujahideen were said to smell pleasantly of musk. "Unnatural things happened," I was told over and over again.

Only later would I manage to get an interview with Sheikh Dhafer. A friend of Dhafer's had described him to me as "the tongue of the mujahideen," meaning he was their voice. Dhafer was the director of the High Council for Fatwas of Falluja. The High Council was an umbrella organization formed after the war to organize the fatwa, or religious verdict, making process. Led by Abdel Qader al Ani in Baghdad, the organization united hundreds of Sufi clerical leaders belonging to a traditionally ascetic sect of Islam made famous by the whirling dervishes. Sheikh Dhafer was not the top man in the local resistance; that honor fell to Falluja's leading cleric, the aging Abdallah al-Janabi, known as the emir of Falluja. As head of the Mujahideen Council, he had given Dhafer authority over the city and its fighters.

In Iraq the normally peaceful Sufis are somewhat more radical. The most famous Iraqi Sufi was Izzat al-Duri, the fugitive former vice president said to be organizing the resistance. On the walls of the Baghdad headquarters graffiti read "Hey, Iraqis, aren't you jealous of Falluja," "Martyrs of Falluja to paradise," "Long live the mujahideen of Falluja," and "Welcome to jihad Falluja." Inside I met the organization's speaker, Dr. Jasim al-Isawi, a political science professor in Baghdad and himself a native of Falluja, who wore the standard Baathist uniform. Isawi had been Kubeisi's spokesman. Falluja was the center of religious thought in Iraq, he told me, and this was why the Americans and Israelis had decided to destroy the city. He showed me the magazine his organization had just published, with a special section on Falluja. A corpse was grimacing on the cover. The caption explained that the martyrs died with smiles on their faces.

Dhafer had a wide nose and long narrow eyes that disappeared whenever he smiled, which was often, behind his round cheeks. When I asked him if he was the real leader of Falluja, Dhafer smiled disingenuously. "I am just a simple member of the city who lived through all the suffering of Falluja," he said. I told him I had heard he was the architect of the victory over the Americans. He grinned proudly and whispered, half jokingly, "Don't mention that, for my security."

Dhafer admitted to me that he belonged to the unofficial city consultative council. He refused to tell me how many members the council had, or who they were, but he did tell me it had a core of about fifty professionals, tribal and religious leaders, and "those who stayed in the city," meaning mujahideen.

He appointed the negotiator who worked with the marines, and he managed their work.

When I pressed him for details about the council, he laughed and squinted at me suspiciously. "What are these intelligence questions you ask me?" The council appointed the team that negotiated with the Americans and ratified the selection of the Baathist officers who were placed in charge of the city's security. During negotiations, Dhafer admitted to me he would meet with the teams and follow events. In reality, all members were appointed with his approval and they returned to him for acceptance of the accord they reached with the marines.

"They must withdraw from all of Falluja including the neighboring villages," he told me. Not satisfied with limiting the liberation to Falluja proper, he sought to extend it to the surrounding villages, several hundred thousand more people and a much wider zone of freedom.

Like all Fallujans, he viewed time as before or after "the events." "Before April 4," he said, "the first day of the siege, all of Falluja was closed by American troops without us knowing about it. The American administration said the siege would not be lifted until we get the people who killed the four contractors." He claimed that "from April 4 until 9:00 A.M. on April 11, the first day of the cease-fire, casualties included 1,200 wounded, 586 martyrs, of which 158 were women and 86 were children." By the time the fighting was over, Falluja hospital officials would claim that up to one thousand people had been killed, mostly women and children. At least five hundred were still buried in the city's two main soccer fields; others were in people's gardens. "Now all people in the world know that the U.S. administration has no honor," he said.

Someone entered the office and whispered in the sheikh's ear that the Americans were approaching the city. He hurriedly left to see what was going on, so I spoke to Colonel Sabar al-Janabi, chief of Falluja's police force, known as the Iraqi Civil Defense Corps, or ICDC, who had come to complain to Sheikh

Dhafer about the problems he was having with the mujahideen and to seek his help. The forty-nine-year-old former military officer had been in the police for the past nine months, but only took control during "the events" of April. The police were involved in defending the city against the Americans, he told me, as well as evacuating the wounded people and preserving law and order. He refused to answer questions about the number of police under his command, and when I pressed him, he smiled and said, "This is an intelligence question," explaining that the Americans did not know but were trying to find out. He would not even provide me with a rough figure, except to say, "We have enough."

The colonel had come to seek Dhafer's assistance with the main problem he was facing. "The people wearing kaffiyehs who are above the law," he said, meaning the mujahideen. They were mistreating his forces. He asked Sheikh Dhafer for his help and support in establishing the authority of his policemen. Outside, his men waited for him in civilian clothing with walkie-talkies and Kalashnikovs. They were new, replacing the old police who had fled.

Though I repeatedly tried to meet with General Jassim in private, I was told he was out of Falluja in a nearby secure village, away from the mujahideen who sought to kill him. I visited General Jassim's headquarters several times and was told every time that he was not present, though I could see his car and driver inside. Outside his headquarters, six of his soldiers languished in a pickup truck with its doors open to let in a breeze. They were listening to an angry cleric sermonizing against the Americans in the tape player. On the walls outside the headquarters someone had written "Allah is great, come to the jihad!"

Instead of meeting the generals, I talked to some of the soldiers under their command, guarding a roundabout near the train tracks. A dozen soldiers were wearing at least half a dozen different types of uniforms from the old army, though none had boots, wearing dusty leather dress shoes instead. They told me that they did not have boots when they served under the previous regime, and some had to buy their own.

One man wore a jungle-patterned uniform belonging to Saddam's special forces; others had several shades of olive and khaki as well as the old Republican Guard uniform. They mocked one man for wearing an American Army–issued uniform with the "chocolate chip" pattern, but he vehemently denied it was American, insisting it was an old Iraqi desert uniform. They were proud of their old uniforms, their lieutenant explaining to me that "we are not Saddam's army. We are soldiers for Islam and for the defense of the city."

Another agreed, explaining, "We did not volunteer for Saddam but for the defense of the city and country." They had all belonged to the army before the occupation, and lost their jobs when U.S. proconsul Paul Bremer dismissed the army in May 2003. They had joined the new Fallujan army when General Jassim had formed it.

I asked them what they would do if Americans crossed the railroad tracks and entered the city. "They won't enter the city," I was told sharply. "We will shoot them," said another. Another man elaborated, "If Americans come inside the city, we will fight them again." The lieutenant explained that "we have direct orders to fight the Americans without referring to our commanders first for permission."

Though they were currently an army belonging to the city of Falluja, they admitted that "if the ministry of defense is formed under the authority of the Iraqi people, we will join it." They saw themselves as a model for the rest of the country. "All the governorates and cities are trying to do what we did," one said to me. "We are an example." They were the first to achieve liberation, they explained, because "Falluja is the mother of mosques and we are committed to our religion and united. Fallujans are used to being independent and dignified. Our dignity is the most important thing to us."

They were also the best-fed army in Iraqi history, with a pile of finished dishes on the grass beside them. Sheikh Dhafer's

Hadhra mosque paid families to cook food for the soldiers and deliver it to them.

The following day, I visited the mosque and found a new man sitting behind the desk. Haji Qasim, a former army intelligence officer, served as Taghlub's representative on the advisory council and was, they told me, "Sheikh Dhafer's right-hand man." Qasim, who received the honorific "haji" after making the pilgrimage to Mecca, was also the founder of Falluja's Center for the Study of Democracy and Human Rights, formed in January 2004, though in my visits I never found him studying, only running the mosque's affairs with his assistant, Muhamad Tarik, the thirty-two-year-old executive director of the center and a member of the town council.

Tarik was a professor in the agriculture department of Anbar University, having received a master's degree in biotechnology from Baghdad University, but everybody in the mosque called him "doctor." Tarik had been present during the fighting, providing an administrative and management role for the fighters and aid workers. He admitted to me that the mosque had been a center for the mujahideen where the defense of the city was organized.

As we were talking, a fit-looking teenager on crutches morosely hobbled in. He wore a soccer uniform, but his training pants had a hole to accommodate the screws coming out of his right thigh. He had come to pick up forms from Haji Qasim to receive compensation. An American helicopter had shot him in his car. When he saw me, a foreigner, he turned incandescent. He demanded to know who I was, and Tarik got up to whisper in his ear. The young man threw his forms down and walked out. The other men apologized uncomfortably, explaining what happened to him while Tarik went to talk to him.

While I was waiting for Tarik to return, eleven policemen stormed in and angrily complained to Haji Qasim about not being paid and about the dismissal of some respected officers. They said they were representing 351 policemen and demanded higher salaries. "Aren't you a journalist?" they shouted at me.

"Record this!" Following them, a man whose car had been confiscated by the mujahideen came to complain. He had come to deliver aid from the Abu Hanifa mosque in Baghdad when it was stolen from him. Haji Qasim made a call and told the man where to go to pick up his car.

Now that I was allowed to report from Falluja, I witnessed the much rougher fate of two other Western journalists. Pulling up to the mosque shortly after the noon prayer was over one Friday, I saw several dozen armed Falluja Brigade soldiers, police, and civilians crowded before the entrance. Some were looking inside an old car. Several more soldiers and police were guarding the gate and there were more inside. One guard I knew greeted me wearing a new black and white kaffiyeh around his head like a bandana. Several police approached and said, "No journalists," but he said, "No, he is a friend," ushered me into the guard room, and made it clear I had to stay there. I noticed several soldiers and policemen standing by the door to Sheikh Dhafer's office. I asked someone what was going on. "Oh, it's nothing," he said, "a simple thing. We arrested two spies; they're British or maybe German."

As I peered through the window trying to see what was going on, armed men rushed about busily. A few minutes later my friend knocked on the door. "Come," he said. I walked across to the office, removed my shoes, and entered. The room was crowded with Iraqi men standing and sitting. At first I did not notice the woman sitting in a corner before tables full of food in Styrofoam containers. She was white, and young. Colonel Sabar was seated across from her, his back to me. He greeted me warmly, a leg of chicken in his hand. I sat down beside them and smiled at her. A middle-aged white man emerged from the bathroom and sat next to her. Taghlub and another man began carefully examining every page of two German passports, turning them around and squinting. Sitting next to the colonel was his son. I took him to be eighteen. He looked just like his father. When he stood up, I saw he had a pistol on the right side of his waist and a walkie-talkie on the other side.

He was only sixteen, he told me. Across, on the other side, sat a short round man with layers of tape covering his nose like a pig's snout. Next to him was a baby-faced man in a tailored suit. "He's the *qaimaqam,*" I was told, the mayor. He was rehearsing a statement asking the elders for approval. An old man sat next to me and nodded toward the German man, saying, "He shouldn't have worn a dishdasha. It was suspicious."

Uwe Sauermann was the German in question: a very tall, pale, fifty-five-year-old freelance journalist. With him was his assistant, twenty-four-year-old Manya Schöche, also very pale. They had driven to Falluja that morning. After being warned not to go to Najaf because it was too dangerous, Uwe obeyed his hotel manager's instructions and took a dishdasha with him and set off with a driver and translator. Upon entering Falluja, Uwe was spotted in the act of donning his dishdasha. He and Manya were stopped at the same checkpoint where the four contractors had been killed. They were forced out at gunpoint by six armed men, one of them in a policeman's uniform. The six accused them of being undercover American soldiers. Soon a mob of hundreds surrounded them, including some of the same laborers who had killed the four contractors. They were beaten with shovels, sticks, and rocks. A plastic bag was placed over Uwe's head. Manya was slapped around and severely handled. Their translator, a Christian from Baghdad, was called a traitor and collaborator. He wore a cross. His nose was broken and he was hit in the back of the neck with a machete.

Just before they were to be doused with gasoline, the police managed to drag them into their nearby station. The mob and mujahideen attacked the station, calling for their prisoners to be returned to them, so the police transferred them to the Hadhra mosque under heavy security. The mob promptly surrounded the mosque with RPGs and Kalashnikovs. One foreign leader of a mujahideen unit marched in with his Kalashnikov, demanding the return of the American spies. The Falluja Brigade and the police nearly engaged the mujahideen in a shootout.

That same day, the committee of leaders in the mosque had decided to confront this particular mujahid, named Abu Abdallah, hoping to disarm his unit or at least subordinate them to their commands. Now, amid rumors of two dead American spies, Falluja went into a state of alert, expecting an American attack. Abu Abdallah's men roamed with their guns. Shortly before I arrived, the two Germans had been brought to the mosque's office and interrogated. Now that the "Committee for the Investigation of Espionage" established that they were indeed two German journalists, they were to receive apologies and food, as I watched.

Manya's face was swollen beneath her eyes and her shirt had blood speckles on it. Uwe's face was spotted with red bruises and he winced when he moved. He had a broken tooth. His hands were trembling. Fear and tension still lingered, and it was contagious. My heart was racing for no reason. The translator was the man with tape on his nose. He was dabbing it continuously, wiping the blood that was dripping from it. He came to sit next to us. The mayor told him, "If you don't eat, I'll be angry." He answered in a nasal voice like someone was pinching his nose, "I can't, I'll throw up." The colonel, with a mouth full of food, commanded Uwe to "eat, eat!" Uwe obeyed.

Uwe and Manya were ordered into a nearby office where local stringers from Al Jazeera and Al Arabiya were preparing their cameras to film the mayor's press statement. They seated the Germans on a sofa on either side of the mayor, who explained that on that morning an old Iraqi car entered the city with two foreigners dressed in Arabic clothing, the man in a dishdasha and the woman in a hijab. "The way they entered was suspicious and illegal," he said, "and they were brought here to the good people of the mosque." He displayed their German passports and urged all the foreign journalists to check in with the mayor's office or the police if they entered the city. "We welcome all foreign press here," he said. "Falluja is a peaceful city, the quietest city in Iraq." The two Germans sat in mute stupor next to him. Uwe was told he could make a statement. "When I saw the pictures of American attacks on Falluja I decided to go to Falluja," he said in a thick German accent, "to take pictures of the city and ask the victims of these attacks what happened to them and how are their lives. In my hotel in Baghdad they advised me to wear a dishdasha because it is better and I will be safer. Somebody shouted *'Amerikaner! Amerikaner!'* and then people came and you know what happened next. Men with guns put a bag on my head like the Americans do and I didn't see anymore. Then I was in an empty house and they interrogated me, and after a while I convinced them I am a German and friend of the Iraqi people, not an American, and they were very friendly. I would like to come again to show the German people what happened in Falluja, so I will try to come tomorrow."

The mayor shook Uwe's hand before the camera and told both Germans they were welcome. Uwe was then ordered to recant his statement comparing the behavior of the mob to the Americans, and he readily complied. "When I said they used a plastic bag," he said, "it doesn't mean that we have to compare you, the people of Falluja, to the Americans. I only meant that the plastic bag itself reminded me of the Americans." Uwe was told to hold his dishdasha for the cameras and then the press conference ended. Saad, the young sniper, was serving refreshments. He asked me if Manya was Uwe's daughter, then his girlfriend. He didn't understand how a woman could be traveling with a man not related to her. "Just give me five minutes alone with her," he told me with a wistful smile.

Under heavy protection, Uwe and Manya were loaded into the mayor's car. A convoy of six vehicles, including two pickup trucks loaded with multicolored Falluja Brigade fighters with their Kalashnikovs at the ready, headed out. Once they exited town the convoy halted and armed men emerged. For a moment I thought they would execute Uwe and Manya. Instead, they reshuffled their men and continued to Baghdad. The Falluja Brigade soldiers returned home.

This incident was only one of many that convinced Sheikh Dhafer's committee that the rogue mujahideen had to be pacified. Dhafer wasn't even safe in his own mosque. Foreign mujahideen were harassing Iraqis for smoking cigarettes and even for drinking water using their left hand, considered impure. They had banned alcohol, Western films, makeup, hairdressers, "behaving like women" (i.e., homosexuality), and even playing dominoes in the coffeehouses. Men found publicly drunk had been flogged. I was told of a dozen men beaten and imprisoned for selling drugs. Islamic courts were being established in association with mujahideen units and mosque leaders. An assistant to the mayor confirmed that there were Islamic courts with their own *qadis,* or judges, who acted independently of the police. He added that they had executed spies, "but before we killed them, we made sure they were spies."

Hijackings and kidnappings continued apace. Two trucks with furniture owned by a foreign company that supplied the Americans were hijacked near Falluja. A man from Falluja came to the company headquarters and told them they could have the trucks back for a ransom, as long as the merchandise was not bound for the Americans. Eventually the trucks were returned for $4,000.

On June 9, twelve members of the Falluja Brigade were killed in a mortar attack on their camp at the edge of town. On June 10, a Lebanese worker and two Iraqi colleagues were captured on the highway near Falluja. Their bodies were found two days later, their throats slit. On June 15, six Shiite truck drivers carrying supplies to the Falluja Brigade were seized by mujahideen, tortured, and brutally murdered. Starting June 19 the Americans initiated a policy of bombing Falluja from the skies every few days, killing scores of civilians in an attempt to target members of Abu Musab al-Zarqawi's network.

The following Friday, hundreds of Fallujan men attended a large demonstration after the noon prayers. They were angry about accusations of harboring Zarqawi and of murdering the six Shia truck drivers. Sheikh Abdallah al-Janabi denied involvement again, blaming it on "those who try to make *fitna* [sectarian strife] between the Iraqis," but he also said that those slain Shias came in on American military vehicles. The crowd and speakers chanted in support of Moqtada al-Sadr in appreciation of his Iraqi nationalism and defiance of the Americans. The crowd denied that Zarqawi was in Falluja, and a young cleric shouted angrily that "we don't need Zarqawi's help in Falluja to defend our mosques and homes" because "the people of Falluja have men that love death like the infidel love life," meaning that they had plenty of men who seek martyrdom fighting the Americans. The crowd erupted in cheers of "Allahu Akbar!" (God is great). Huge banners supporting the Association of Muslim Scholars, which was leading resistance units, were prominently displayed. The mayor of Falluja was interviewed on Al Jazeera; he denied that the six Shias had even been killed in Falluja.

In late July the leadership in Falluja met with foreign fighters in their city and expelled about twenty-five of them, including Syrians, Jordanians, and Saudis. Several resistance groups, including the Army of Muhammad, the Victorious Assad Allah Squadron, Islamic Wrath, and others, issued a joint declaration calling for the blood of Abu Musab al-Zarqawi to be spilled. The declaration also declared their friendship with Iraqi Shias and called for cooperation with the new Iraqi government led by Prime Minister Ayad Allawi. That same day U.S. planes bombed yet another house allegedly used by Zarqawi's network. Fourteen people were killed.

My interest in the foreign mujahideen, in particular Saudis, finally became too dangerous even for me. My contact in Falluja, himself a non-Iraqi seeking to join what he described as "al Qaeda in the northern Anbar," encouraged me to go to the Julan neighborhood, which had been deemed by Sheikh Dhafer's committee off limits to foreigners, to meet Saudi fighters for al Qaeda. He would leave me there to go off "on a job." I began to wonder why al Qaeda would be interested in meeting an American journalist. They were a secretive organization, interested only in reaching out to fellow Muslims for recruitment and in advertising their successes, such as the decapitation of journalist Daniel Pearl. These were the resistance fighters who did not recognize the authority of Sheikh Dhafer and his associates and who threatened their lives for releasing the Germans. An American was much more valuable. That night my contact brought two Iraqis working with the Saudis to meet me in my hotel unannounced. They barely greeted me but looked me up and down with taciturn interest, as if examining the merchandise. I became concerned that if I went to Falluja again I would not return. I was warned that my contact had turned and was being pressured to turn over an American to make up for the lost Germans. I knew that the foreign fighters in Falluja were embittered over the many hostages they had been pressured to release.

Soon after that, an al Qaeda unit in Saudi Arabia calling itself the Falluja Squadron began killing foreigners. The American war in Iraq, meant to democratize the region, had instead radicalized it, creating a united front, with Fallujans fighting for the honor of Palestine and Saudis fighting in the name of Falluja. In 2005, while working in Mogadishu, Somalia, I would see a shop named after Falluja and men wearing "Falluja" T-shirts. In Pakistan I would later purchase an Urdu-language magazine dedicated to the heroes and martyrs of Falluja. A new legend had been created.

6

THE RISE OF ZARQAWI:
Fall 2004

✦ Number of Iraqi police officers killed as of September 2004: 710

✦ Number of Iraqi civilians killed: 3,000

✦ Number of coalition troops in Iraq: 156,000

THOUGH THE MAJORITY of the resistance was Iraqi, the name most associated with anti-American attacks was of the Jordanian Zarqawi. Zarqawi could thank the United States for much of his renown. By blaming every attack on him, they inflated his myth and served as his best recruiters. But Zarqawi did not come out of a vacuum. He was the product of a second al Qaeda, a network of clerics and fighters not associated with Osama bin Laden, based in Jordan, and far more articulate in its ideology.

The Iraqi resistance is not monolithic. Instead there are *resistances* and *insurgencies* and terror *movements*. They differ in location, motivation, and ideology. The majority of anti-coalition fighters in Iraq are part of an indigenous resistance to the American occupation. They are motivated by factors such as nationalism, religion, and a sense of disenfranchisement. They generally avoid civilian targets, and an accord can be reached with them. The Jihadi movement is motivated by an ideology based on Islam, and it justifies its violence by referring to Islam. They are not interested in Iraq per se, but in a war of Muslims against Christians, Jews, and Shia Muslims. The goals of the *muqawama*, or resistance, fundamentally clash with those of the mujahideen, or jihadis. The Iraqi resistance simply wants the Americans out. The jihadis seek the reestablishment of the Muslim caliphate and a Manichean conflict with Jews and Christians to end only at Judgment Day.

TO UNDERSTAND THE IRAQI jihadi movement we must go back to the 1960s, when many Egyptian Islamists moved to the Gulf to teach, influencing generations of students, in particular many Palestinian refugees living in Kuwait, who formed the educated class. Among these Egyptians was the Sheikh Abdel Rahman al-Khaleq, who formed the important Kuwaiti Salafi organization called Jamiyat al Turath al Islami, or the Society of Islamic Heritage. Meanwhile in Jordan, King Hussein rewarded the Muslim Brotherhood for its support against the 1970 Palestinian insurrection called Black September. He gave members of the brotherhood positions in the ministry of education, where they could train future generations in their version of Islam.

Twenty years later nearly 300,000 Palestinians were expelled from Kuwait by the vengeful Kuwaiti government following the end of the Gulf War in 1991. These Palestinians were accepted by Jordan, and most settled in Al Zarqa, a poor city north of Amman. Many were Salafi Muslims, meaning those who want to return to the time of the Prophet and live as his companions lived. They were active in the jihadi movement and their presence made Jordanian society more conservative. Zarqa soon became a center for Salafis in Jordan.

The most important jihadi cleric, polemicist, ideologue, and the mind behind many of the beheadings in Iraq is Isam Taher al Oteibi al-Burqawi, more commonly known as "Abu Mohammed al-Maqdasi," a Palestinian living in Jordan. Maqdasi was a leader of the Palestinian jihadis, having belonged to Jamiyat al Turath al Islami.

Khaleq had come to Kuwait from Egypt in the 1960s. Maqdasi had been in Afghanistan along with his friend Abu Qatada al-Falastini, as Palestinian Sheikh Omar Mahmoud Abu Omar was known, and the two led Jordan's Salafi movement. In Jordan, Maqdasi led Jordanian and Palestinian Salafis who had fought or trained in Afghanistan. Abu Qatada was recently released and rearrested by British authorities intending to expel him to Jordan following the July 7 attacks. Maqdasi called his organization Tawhid (or monotheism) and Jihad, but changed the name to Bayat al Imam.

Abu Hilalah Ahmad Fadil Nazal al-Khalaylah, also known as Abu Musab al-Zarqawi, hailed from Zarqa. The region of Zarqa produced most of the Jordanian jihadis fighting in Iraq. Zarqawi had been a wild young man with no interest in religion. He had a reputation for getting tattoos, drinking alcohol, and getting into fights. Like many disaffected Muslim youth in the 1980s, he was moved to fight in Afghanistan. His journey to Afghanistan was arranged by the Office of Services and Jihad in Pakistan. Somewhere between his rebellious youth and his trip to Afghanistan, Zarqawi had become a devout Salafi. When he returned to Jordan he joined al-Maqdasi's Bayat al Imam organization. Both men were arrested for possessing weapons and for membership in the radical group, though they were released following a general amnesty.

Zarqawi began preaching when he was imprisoned in the Sawaqa prison with Maqdasi. In prison they continued organizing jihadists, especially among thugs from the Jordanian underworld, to which Zarqawi had once belonged. The Jordanian authorities placed all the Islamist prisoners together, in isolation from other prisoners. They formed relationships, exchanged ideas and knowledge, and established trust among one another. Zarqawi was released in an amnesty and left for Pakistan and then Afghanistan in 2000. In 2002, Zarqawi entered Jordan through Syria. He was reportedly in northern Iraq before the war. By the summer of 2003, he had claimed responsibility for the UN headquarters attack.

Maqdasi appointed his protégé Zarqawi the amir of tawhid and jihad. "Amir" comes from the Arabic root *amr,* or to command. An *amir* means a commander, though it has also come to mean a prince. An *amir* was necessary to avoid confusion, and even a group consisting of two people had to have an *amir.* Zarqawi was closely allied with the group Ansar al-Sunnah, which was the reconstituted group Ansar al-Islam, allegedly associated with al Qaeda elements. Zarqawi's second in command was said to be a member of Ansar al-Sunnah. Ansar al-Sunnah was primarily Iraqi, whereas Tawhid was primarily composed of foreigners.

Zarqawi's inner circle was made up of his close friends, none of whom were Iraqi. The movement had stored weapons in secret depots in Iraq. Their goal was to turn Iraq into hell for all its residents, to prevent an elected government from taking power, and to create strife between Shias and Sunnis.

WITHIN IRAQ, the spiritual leader of Zarqawi's group was Abu Anas al-Shami, born Omar Yusef Juma. Shami was another Palestinian who moved to Jordan from Kuwait along with Maqdasi and two other important leaders of Zarqawi's movement.

Shami was born in Salmiya, Kuwait, in 1969 to a family of Jordanian citizenship. He was given a strong education in classical Arabic, and he disliked the dialects, using formal classical Arabic in conversation, even in jokes. He had studied Islamic theology in Saudi Arabia from 1988 to 1991, where he said a pure Islam without any innovation was taught and the importance of jihad was stressed. He was influenced by the work of Egyptian Said Qutb (1906–1966), a leading member of the Muslim Brotherhood, whose book *Signposts on the Road* inspires Muslim revivalists and fundamentalists to this day. Shami claimed he learned from the mistakes the Ikhwan, or brotherhood, had made, when it became institutionalized and reached an accommodation with the state. Shami condemned the modern Ikhwan for changing the judgments and rules of Islam.

In Saudi Arabia, Shami met many former mujahideen who

had fought in Afghanistan. In the summer of 1990, he went to Afghanistan with a Palestinian friend from university. They trained in the Faruq camp for three months, learning basic military skills and receiving weapons training. He swore an oath to the commander of the camp that he would never use his skills against fellow Muslims.

Shami led the Murad mosque in the Sowailih neighborhood of Amman. It was a Salafi mosque and Shami was an important leader of the Salafi movement in Jordan. He still returned to Saudi Arabia often, where he was influenced by the radical clerics Sifr al-Hawali, Salman al-Awda, and Nasser al-Omar, whom he viewed as true Salafi leaders. These men were arrested by Saudi authorities. In Jordan he was a follower of Maqdasi, who believed all Arab regimes were governed by infidels. In the 1990s Shami went to Bosnia, where up to three thousand foreign mujahideen sought martyrdom fighting Serbs and Croats.

Al-Shami lamented the lack of a charismatic leadership, but the September 11 attacks awoke the sleeping hope and motivated youth; new leaders began emerging. He had previously worked for the Islamic Waqf, or Endowment, Institution of Jordan, and had lived in Amman's predominantly Palestinian al-Zuhur neighborhood. His center was shut down by Jordanian authorities. Shami had married a Palestinian woman with Egyptian travel papers who was living in Saudi Arabia with her family, and he sired three children with her. He took a job in the Imam Bokhari Center, which he had cofounded.

In March 2003 he was arrested by Jordanian authorities after he accused that country's ruling family of turning Jordan into an American camp and of taking its orders from the Americans. Shami condemned the American-led war as one against Islam, not against Iraq. After his release from jail he called upon his followers to demand that their government stop assisting the Americans, and he encouraged young people to go to Iraq to fight in the jihad there against the Americans. He soon left for Iraq, arriving in late 2003 and assuming the position of Sharia council manager and spiritual leader for Zarqawi's movement.

Shami's mother recounted that her son had always sought martyrdom. Shami had told his father he was on his way to Saudi Arabia when they last saw each other. Two weeks later he received a message from Shami that he was in fact in Iraq. His wife and children were in Egypt.

According to Maqdasi, democracy was a heretical religion and constituted the rejection of Allah, monotheism, and Islam. It was an innovation, or *bida,* placing something above the word of God and ignoring the laws of Islam. It placed the people, or the tyrant, above Islam, and it was secular, separating religion from the state. Only Allah could legislate laws and Allah's laws had to be applied to the apostates, the fornicators, thieves, alcohol consumers, unveiled women, and the prevention of the obscene. Maqdasi said that democracy was a religion, and God had forbidden choosing a religion other than Islam.

Maqdasi justified the worst atrocities committed by Zarqawi and his men in Iraq. In August 2004, Maqdasi defended the mujahideen against those who accused them of lacking mercy. God sent Muhammad as a messenger of mercy, but Muhammad's mercy could not reach the world without the defeat and decapitation of criminals and leaders of infidelity who obstruct his mercy.

It was with the mercy of the Prophet that they beheaded criminals and aggressors, and it was this mercy that prevented bloodshed of Muslims. The Prophet Muhammad himself killed those who opposed God, and the Prophet beheaded those who had betrayed him. Beheading was the only language that they could use when dealing with those who bombed villages; killed unarmed Muslims; killed the women and children in Gaza, Rafa, Afghanistan, Iraq, Chechnya; and defended all of it by saying, "This is war." He justified burning the bodies of the four Blackwater contractors even though most Muslim leaders had condemned it as un-Islamic. He said the Quran permitted the burning of infidels, explaining: "Punish someone the way he punished you, so if cluster bombs burn bodies, we can burn bodies." Ali burned his enemies (the Kharijites who said he was God), so Muslims could burn their enemies. He explained that jihad was the omitted pillar of the five pillars of Islam and quoted a verse from the Quran justifying the terrorizing of the enemies of Islam.

Zarqawi denounced Muslims who criticized the beheading of the American civilian Nicholas Berg. They were cowards who were not fighting the infidel and did not know how glorious it felt to fight *jahiliya* (pre-Islamic ignorance). Zarqawi lamented that his nation was being tortured in Iraq, Palestine, Afghanistan, Indonesia, and Chechnya. All the Muslim nation could do was weep and protest peacefully. These demonstrations had done nothing for Afghanistan, and now Mullah Omar, leader of the Taliban, was hiding in the mountains. The Muslim nation did nothing to defend the chastity of the women of Sarajevo, Indonesia, Palestine, and Iraq. Zarqawi swore to God that as long as they had dignity and honor, they would not sleep or spend time with their wives while these other Muslim women were under attack.

Belief in Allah could restore the caliphate, he said. It could open the gates of Rome, the White House, the Kremlin, and London to Muslims. God would help them fight the hypocrites, Crusaders, and Jews. Zarqawi prayed to God to give his believers success on earth, to help the mujahideen assemble, to protect them, and to give them victory over the infidels.

In Falluja, Shami lectured his followers and they recorded his sermons. In one sermon he quoted a verse from the Quran warning the believers not to accept the Jews and Christians as authorities and to avoid falling under their evil influence. Shami explained that the state had to be based on the Quran and Sharia, and condemned Arab leaders as blasphemous, tyrannical infidels for creating states that were not. Political parties were against God. The army and police of such a state (he was referring to Iraq's political parties, army, and police) were tools in the hands of the tyrants. Killing them was justified, even if it meant also killing the devout among them. He explained this by analogy. If the Americans tied a Muslim man to their tank and were attacking you, it was justified to destroy the tank even if it meant killing the man tied to it. Jihad was justified even if it caused the deaths of Muslims. It was better that Muslims died in the path of jihad than at the hands of the Americans.

God also ordered the killing of good people if they were in the way and it was necessary. The important thing to remember was that Muslims should not associate with unbelievers. A puritan, Shami warned that believers should separate themselves from nonbelievers in their actions and even their clothes. It was even better to kill a Muslim who had abandoned his religion by helping the Americans than it was to kill an American. These people who served the Americans were "holding the stick in the middle." They were two-faced, telling the Americans they wanted democracy and telling Muslims they supported the mujahideen. But there was no compromise. If you believed in jihad, you had to join the jihad. Those who feared the infidels would beg them for their paltry rewards and they would suffer God's wrath. Those who called for peace, who said it was time to live together, love one another, and prosper, were hypocrites.

In another sermon, Shami reminded his listeners that just as Islam was born a religion under attack, so too it remained. The Western powers used the media as a weapon against Islam. He once more justified killing Muslims who worked with the infidels and spoke of large attacks against the enemy that went unreported, in which hundreds might have been killed, including some Iraqis who collaborated with the enemy by selling them alcohol.

Shami called Shias *rafidha,* or rejectionists, and condemned Shias for worshiping Ali above Allah. He warned that Arab satellite channels were spreading Shiism, which was a greater danger to Muslims than the American occupiers were.

Shami's account of the "battle of al-Ahzab" was made public in July 2004. In the original battle of al-Ahzab, the Jews and enemies of Muhammad surrounded and besieged the young Muslim state in Medina. Abu Anas named the first Falluja battle the al-Ahzab battle, thanking God for their victory and writing a book about it. Success was due to divine intervention rather than a superior military. Street fighting required bravery, which the American soldiers did not possess. Shami recounted that as he wrote down his account of events in Falluja, his body shivered, his heart beat harder, and he was prevented from writing. Falluja was the home of the heroes and mujahideen who sought to raise, or glorify, the name of God and Islam.

When Shami was killed, the information department of the Tawhid and Jihad group made a DVD in honor of him, whom they called the "lion of Mesopotamia." The film opened with an image of a lake and the sun, as a voice called "to do jihad and die on the same day is better than to live for sixty years praying to God." Waterfalls were shown, an image of paradise. A common verse from the Quran was used by the resistance, as it had been used by Saddam when he prepared for battle against the Americans: "Prepare for them as much force as you can, and horses, terrorize the enemies of Islam and your enemies."

When the nascent Muslim community led by the Prophet Muhammad lost the second battle of Islam, the Battle of Uhud, against the forces of Khalid bin Walid (an infidel who later converted to Islam and then brought Islam to Iraq), there was a rumor that Muhammad died, so Muslims began abandoning the cause. Muhammad spoke to his followers. *"Wa muhamadan illa rasul,"* he said. "Muhammad is just a prophet and there were so many prophets before him, and if he dies, will you go back to your old religions? Whoever goes back to his old religion will not affect God, but God will reward those who are grateful to Him." The statement was intended to reassure mujahideen in Iraq that the loss of Shami would not affect the battle.

Maysara al-Ghareeb, the poet of al Tawhid and also a member of its Sharia council, of which Abu Anas had been the head, blessed the companions of Muhammad who beheaded atheism and hypocrisy during their jihad. He called on God to give them victory against the disbelievers and make them martyrs like those who had fought with the Prophet. Jihad was the duty of all Muslims.

Ghareeb viewed conflict and fighting as the natural state of the world. Modern history was a chain of struggles and competition for power, and good intentions or feelings could do nothing to affect power. Power ruled by international affairs and diplomacy was just the language of power hidden by a soft mask. Defeated countries always had to conform to the system the victor imposed on them, and America's current method for dominating the world was through human rights protection. Western civilization was immoral. Its primary motive was money, and it was based on the end justifying the means. In general, infidels had no god but money, and for money they did horrible things. Western civilization was one of looting, genocide, and drug dealing.

Though disagreements among the infidel led to millions of their own dying, when they fought Muslims, they all united, as in the Crusades. Though infidel nations had suffered many natural disasters such as wars, earthquakes, and floods, Muslim countries had not suffered the same afflictions. The infidels were punishing Muslims in every way and in every place, thus Muslims were commanded by God to fight the infidel in their home states. The Muslim world was being dominated and suppressed by a system of divide and conquer. The infidel prevented cooperation between the Muslim countries and supported secular powers. They also established a Jewish state in the heart of the Arab world. They destroyed the economies of the Muslim world by encouraging educated people to emigrate, buying natural resources at low prices, and selling the products back to the Muslim world. They instigated inter-Muslim disputes, selling the weapons needed for the conflicts they started and then taking over reconstruction and profiting from it. They forced poor states to remain in debt, and thus controlled them.

The *rafidha*, or rejectionists, as Salafis and Wahhabis called Shias, had been harming Sunnis from the beginning of Islamic history, said Ghareeb. He provided quotes from Sunni clerics stating that anyone who criticized the companions of the Prophet was an infidel, thus Shias were not Muslims. Instead, they were Jews, Christians, and infidels who formed a group twenty-five years after the death of the Prophet Muhammad. It was forbidden to marry them because they had destroyed Islam.

Ghareeb felt it was important to let Sunnis know about Shias, because many assumed they were actually Muslims. Ghareeb insisted that all Shias were vicious, and once they ruled Iraq they would fight the Sunnis. Democracy was like a sleeping pill given to the Sunnis so when they woke up they would be excluded from Iraq. The Shias were cooperating with the occupiers and assisting the American occupation. They were the slaves of the Americans in Iraq. The Americans were not trying to provoke a civil war in Iraq; rather, they were arming Shias and giving them security jobs in order to lull Sunnis into a false sense of hope. Shias were attacking Sunnis, and hence Zarqawi's movement would attack them. Though innocent people may have died in Zarqawi's operations, many more would have died at the hands of the Americans if they had been left to do as they pleased in Iraq.

Yet even Maqdasi would prove too tame for his pupil Zarqawi. In July 2004, Maqdasi's Web site contained an article providing assistance and advice to Zarqawi. Maqdasi warned against exploding cars, setting off roadside bombs, and firing mortars that caused Muslims to be killed. Jihadi hands had to be clean and free of innocent blood. Maqdasi said that Muslims who worked for the infidels should not be killed unless they helped the infidels harm Muslims. Maqdasi also warned Zarqawi not to attack churches because it would encourage infidels to fight Muslims. Maqdasi's calls for moderation were ignored.

Zarqawi, in turn, condemned the people who "held the stick in the middle." They were not fighting for their nation, they were waiting for the fight to end so they could join the victor. Zarqawi also condemned the Association of Muslim Scholars, cowardly people who accepted humiliation. He mocked Sheikh Harith al-Dhari for speaking out against beheadings.

Although Zarqawi himself avoided Falluja, one of his key lieutenants helped turn it back into a battleground in the late summer of 2004, to the point that that the Americans finally decided to level the entire city, and clean it out, that fall. It began when the Americans decided that the Falluja Brigade was incapable of controlling the insurgents.

In the morning the Americans moved into the Julan district. They were spotted by Abu Khadhab al-Hadhaab, who divided his men into two groups. They were joined by the Egyptian Abu Ibrahim and the Syrian Abu Amaar. Another group, led by Abdul Aziz, had seven fighters of Saudi, Kuwaiti, and Libyan origin who had come from Baghdad to help. The Yemeni Abu al-Murdhia tried to destroy a tank with an RPG. Abu Kudama and his fighters amassed in that same area. Abdul Sattar and Abu Nasser, a Libyan, attacked helicopters.

Meanwhile, in the Nazal district, Abu Hajar and the Syrian Abu Aisha led a group of fighters waiting for the Americans. An old woman fed them breakfast. They sought refuge in an abandoned building, but it was attacked. The Libyan Abu Hafs shot down a helicopter. Some people from the neighborhood asked them to leave so that the Americans would not destroy it, but Abu Hafs told these "low-spirited people" to shut up.

The next day the Americans continued pressing into Julan, and killed twenty civilians. Al Halbusi Raba destroyed a tank, and Abu Husein al-Ansary hit two helicopters. Abu Anas was filming this from a rooftop, and a helicopter shot at him several times. Abu Hafs was shot in the leg, and when Abu Aisha tried to rescue him, he too was shot. A third man tried to help them, and he too was shot, until finally, a local from Falluja threw them all into his car and drove them away. Abu Hafs was hospitalized in Baghdad. There, when a policeman became suspicious, Abu Hafs took the policeman's gun, shot him with it, and escaped.

The Iraqi resistance is both imported and homegrown. If Falluja revealed the strength of the former, Baghdad revealed the endless possibilities for the former. Throughout the fall of 2004, I spent time in many different neighborhoods in the city to get a feel for their sources of insurgent manpower. By then, the mujahideen had established businesses and metastasized from street gangs to professional killers.

Baghdad is divided in two by the Tigris River. West of the river is "the new city," while to the east is "encircled Baghdad," as the walled old city is called. The east side also includes the other older districts of the city as well as most government and university buildings. Eastsiders pride themselves on their pedigree as the original inhabitants of the city. They point to the landmarks, the bookselling neighborhood of Mutanabi Street, the oldest university in Baghdad, the oldest animal market, and classical Arabic markets such as the central Shorja market. At one time the east side housed jewelers and rich merchants, especially Jews, and it was considered the sophisticated side of Baghdad.

The west side, on the other hand, was considered home to the poor and uneducated, its people more prone to color their colloquial Arabic with strong slang. It was known for its fishermen and their traditions. The principle of *shaqi* was important there, and would prove crucial to understanding the growth of the resistance later on. *Shaqi* is an adjective meaning brave or strong, and it meant that the strongest or bravest person in a neighborhood, or the local tough guy, would have a gang controlling his neighborhood. The principle of *shaqi* is still dominant on the west side, and now most of these tough guys have become commanders of the resistance.

Baghdad's Haifa Street was a modern expansion to the old

Karkh neighborhood. It housed many high-ranking Baathists who were given homes there by the former regime. Some of the most expensive apartments in Iraq were to be found there, complete with central air-conditioning and constant electricity. Some of Haifa Street's wealthy residents were not originally Iraqis. They were Palestinians or Syrians who had received Iraqi citizenship from Saddam's regime and married Iraqi women. They and their wives held high-ranking positions before the war. These Baathists took advantage of the anger in their neighborhood after the invasion, supporting the local gang leaders and encouraging them to fight the occupiers, helping them financially and organizationally as well as with arms.

The resistance on Haifa Street was dominated by these *shaqi* men. One important *shaqi* leader was Leith Muafaq, currently a prisoner in the Abu Ghraib jail under suspicion for planting bombs and launching anti-coalition attacks. In truth, using his black Jeep, Leith was transporting missiles such as Katyushas to Haifa Street and selling them to local men who worked as parking attendants there. These men would launch the missiles at night from their car parks and then hide the weapons in nearby apartment buildings. Leith called himself the *amir,* or prince, of Haifa Street. The gang of parking attendants was led by Seyid Hashim, who called himself *amir al umaraa,* or the prince of princes. Leith's family used to live in a ministry compound in today's Green Zone. His mother was the mistress of General Abd Hammud, one of the fifty-five most-wanted former regime members. When Leith was a child other children did not want to play with him because of his mother. Leith worked for a major American magazine for a while, taking its bureau chief to meet members of the resistance.

Saddam often claimed that he was a *shaqi* from the west side, and he recruited local toughs for his security or intelligence services. Others were in the military. These backgrounds helped them plan and carry out attacks against U.S. forces. They used the same networks they had previously established and contacted their friends in other neighborhoods when they needed help. Yet they also merged into Zarqawi's foreign Tawhid and Jihad network. Nationalistic hatred of foreigners disappeared in the face of a common enemy. The insurgent system in Haifa Street was mainly led by Zarqawi's network. Every member of this network in Haifa Street had worked for Saddam in the past.

Another group responsible for launching attacks on Americans in Haifa Street was the Seven Amirs Group, led by Ansar al-Sunnah. Most of the group's members lived in Baghdad's Seidiya neighborhood and in its surrounding areas. They were former bodyguards for Saddam's sons Uday and Qusay and were led by Muhamad Turki (currently in jail). Turki was the oldest son of the sheikh of the Gartan tribe, an extremist Sunni tribe in Baghdad. The Gartan tribe was based in southern Baghdad. The Gartans were predominantly farmers, though many had held important positions in the previous government.

Turki's tribe had large landholdings southwest of Baghdad and in the city proper. During the elections, Muhamad Turki used his vast lands to launch attacks against one of the voting centers in the Maalef neighborhood of Baghdad. His group was also responsible for targeting a Shiite mosque in that same area. The Seven Amirs Group financed itself through local businesses. They opened a video game Internet café in Seidiya. Two brothers, engineers and members of the group, ran the café. The younger brother, Ali al-Salami, was an *amir* in the group. They paid regular salaries to their new members after every operation they conducted. They also profited from robbing trucks delivering supplies to the Americans. Goods looted from the Americans were called *ghanaim,* a religious term for the looting permitted of infidels during a jihad. In one attack they stole one hundred cooking heaters from a Brazilian company. They were also in the car business.

Prior to 2004 they were not especially pious, but that year, when they joined the Seven Amirs, they stopped drinking alcohol and even changed the rings on their mobile phones to Islamic tunes.

Muhamad Turki's group had many houses in Baghdad because its members came from wealthy families. Turki himself had five houses distributed all over the neighborhood, and other members had farms and at least two or three houses each. This allowed them to hide easily.

It would not be until January 2005 that the group was destroyed. While preparing to launch a car bomb, they were shocked by the arrest of Muhamad Turki a few days after the January elections. All of his homes were attacked. The tribe suspected a traitor in their midst but did not know who it might be. Turki's tribe asked Zarqawi's group to investigate the problem. Tawhid and Jihad conducted an investigation, acting like the resistance's FBI, or, as they preferred to see it, the supreme jihad supervisory association. Turki's family trapped his son's associates and captured three of them just two days after Turki was arrested. The captured men were taken to a prison in the Gartan area. They were beaten and interrogated, but none of them admitted anything, and they were released ten days later. The Seven Amirs Group was soon disbanded. Some of the former members kept working for founder Ansar al-Sunnah, others fled to Syria.

In Yarmuk, most of the citizens over the age of forty know each other because they are members of the neighborhood's old families. The Iraqi Islamic Party has its central office in Yarmuk, and is popular among educated or rich Sunnis who are opposed to tribalism. Yarmuk's main mosque, called Al Shawwaf, is controlled by the Iraqi Islamic Party and is full of Baathists. The people who pray at the mosque were all friends when they were young. Many of them were pilots (many of Iraq's pilots live in Yarmuk), and they discuss politics during their prayers in the mosque. When they do not see one of their old friends in attendance, they pressure him to join them and warn that he will face trouble if he does not. There was a known Tawhid and Jihad connection in that mosque. Tawhid members meet in Al Shawwaf mosque.

In Dora, there is a school named Bilat al-Shuhada where

someone wrote on its wall "No Allawi, no Sistani, Yes, yes Zarqawi." Most of the Mo'almien inhabitants are peaceful Christians who were afraid to remove it, but finally in January 2005 someone did and replaced it with a heart upon which was written "USA." That was removed three days later.

In the Bayaa district, the Al Anbar Car Fair is popular with mujahideen who urgently need to replace their cars. It is owned by one of Turki Talal's sons. Leith (the prince of Haifa Street) himself went there to replace his cars after taking part in attacks. Bayaa's industrial district is also an important location for resistance members to purchase cars and turn them into car bombs. Two of the "seven princes" worked as car merchants in Bayaa. Bayaa's Sunni al-Tikriti mosque held a symbolic funeral for Abdul Aziz al-Muqrin, the slain head of al Qaeda in Saudi Arabia. The mourning lasted for three days.

Bayaa's gyms were important meeting places for Tawhid members, who increasingly used them as recruiting centers. One such gym was the Ali Ghani Club. Thair Jasim was one Tawhid member who lived in the Elam district of Seidiya, but went to the gym in Bayaa. His brother was a devout Salafi. Thair joined jihad operations in early 2004 after his brother vouched for him. In increasingly conservative Bayaa, members of the Sunni al-Sadiq al-Amin mosque attacked alcohol and pornography dealers across the street with police support.

On September 11, 2004, Zarqawi addressed the global Muslim "nation." He called for help, lamenting that Muslims were sleeping, not supporting the jihad in Iraq. Though when he had been in Afghanistan Zarqawi had operated independently of Osama bin Laden, in October he swore an oath of allegiance to al Qaeda, renaming his organization al Qaeda in the Land of the Two Rivers. Bin Laden, in turn, announced that Zarqawi was the head of al Qaeda's operations in Iraq. Either bin Laden wanted to co-opt the rival group, or Zarqawi actually needed the Saudi financier's help. Or perhaps both men recognized the power of bin Laden's name to attract more foreign fighters and support.

After Zarqawi renamed his organization al Qaeda in Iraq, its ideology was elaborated by a man called Abu Maysara. Abu Maysara explained that its goals included a renewal of "true" monotheism, purifying it from elements of polytheism; jihad for Allah's sake and for the sake of reconquering Muslim lands from infidels and apostates; the spread of Islam in lands where it does not yet exist; freeing Muslim prisoners; helping Muslims everywhere; and reestablishing the Islamic caliphate so that Muslims are ruled by Muslims.

Though Abu Maysara claimed that they would not spill a drop of Muslim blood unjustly, he explained why they killed Americans and their "collaborators." Iraq was the land of the caliphs, and Allah had ordered jihad to expel those who killed and violated the honor of women. They were not fighting for Iraq as a nation, but for Islam as a nation. Infidels from more than thirty countries had united to fight Muslims, so Muslims from different nations had to unite. Abu Maysara praised the foreign fighters who had left their families and homes to protect Iraqi Muslims from the invaders. After they expelled the Americans from Iraq they would take the fight on to other conquered Muslim lands.

While the jihadists looked to continue their struggle globally, the indigenous Iraqi resistance was increasingly divided. Sheikh Ahmed al-Samarai, vice president of the Association of Muslim Scholars, broke with the president, Harith al-Dhari, over a difference in strategy. Samarai, like most members of the association, wanted to negotiate with the Americans to avoid getting locked out of the future Iraq, as the Shias had been when they boycotted elections under the British occupation of the 1920s. The resulting government had Sunnis and Jews but no Shias. Nearly all the association's members are former high-ranking, power-seeking Baathists.

An angry al-Dhari announced that only he and his son Muthana could speak on behalf of the association. Muthana had arrogated control of the 1920 Revolution Brigades and the Iraqi Islamic Army, as well as smaller cells of the resistance.

Muthana also collected money for the association from the Gulf countries. Some began to cynically refer to the association as the Association of Zawba, in reference to Dhari's hometown. Zawbawis, as Dhari's people were called, had many Salafis among them. Ironically the Zawbawis had collaborated with the British in their occupation.

The Army of Muhammad and the Battalions of the Victorious Saladin are two resistance movements closely allied with those controlled by the association, because they share an ideology of resistance, rather than jihad until martyrdom. Their members also share common experiences as former Baathist members of Saddam's army. In early 2005, a Shia contractor working for the Americans in the Sunni town of Iskandariya in the so-called triangle of death went to Sheikh Harith al-Dhari, head of the Association of Muslim Scholars, to pay protection money. Although Iskandariya is south of Baghdad and Dhari hails from western Iraq, the man paid the $30,000 demanded by Dhari and worked free of any harassment, which was rare in Iraq.

In Al Qaim, attacks became more virulent and the Americans waged a constant war. In November 2004, U.S. Marines raided Sheikh Mudhafar's mosque in Huseiba, in what he called retaliation for his opposition to that month's Falluja offensive. He claimed his mosque had been collecting food and supplies to send to the city and accused the marines who raided his mosque of stealing three million dinars, or a little over two thousand dollars.

Western Iraq is a very traditional place, where tribal mores still govern as much as Islam and the gun. Tribesmen often refer to the foreign fighters as "our Arab guests" and are required to provide them with hospitality, or they are dishonored. These Arab guests also often come well-funded, with cash from the Gulf countries, a further incentive for hospitality. The powerful Albu Nimr tribe had a reputation for independence even under Saddam. Although they provided hospitality for foreign fighters in western Iraq, they also allowed sons of the tribe to join the police force. No sooner had the foreign fighters ensconced themselves among the tribesmen than they attacked the local police force. The enraged tribesmen immediately turned on the foreign fighters. Hospitality has its limits.

Starting around November, when the Americans finally leveled Falluja, a new poem dedicated to Falluja was circulated and much discussed on jihadi Web sites and chat rooms. Written by the Saudi al-Ghamdi in a Bedouin dialect, it addressed the Americans:

> *You who rule countries by their infidels.*
> *You kill with chemicals as though you were killing flies*
> *You who are riding on the fast saddle*
> *By Allah, where are you going to?*
> *If you are going to Falluja*
> *Send my regards to Abu Musab al-Zarqawi*
> *And all the jihadis in his group . . .*

7

ELECTIONS: January 2005

+ Number of Iraqi civilians killed, January 2005: 200
+ Number of Americans killed, January 2005: 107

EIGHT AND A HALF MILLION IRAQIS went to vote on January 30, 2005, amid martial law and an intense police effort, which kept the day's violence at somewhat less than average levels. The elections were said to be another turning point, following the establishment of the IGC, the adoption of an interim constitution, and the handover of sovereignty, and before the next turning point of a draft constitution. If you turned 90 degrees at each such point, would you make progress?

More than 200 parties had applied to compete for the 275 seats on the Transitional National Assembly that would write Iraq's new constitution. These parties would present "lists" of candidates to voters and people would vote for these lists and not for candidates directly. The number of candidates chosen from a list depended on what percentage of the vote each list received. A seat on the assembly required an estimated 40,000 to 50,000 votes, based on the total number of potential voters and the number of seats available. It was essentially the Israeli system, though for reasons that should be obvious, nobody wanted to call it that.

The assembly would in turn elect the president, the prime minister, and several vice presidents. The constitution would then be presented to the Iraqi people in a referendum. There would also be elections for eighteen provisional councils and the Kurdish Regional Government. Altogether there would be three separate elections in nine thousand voting stations.

All the main parties—hundreds of them—were based on local, tribal, ethnic, or religious identity or specific issues. Some parties were based around a family or tribe, some around a city or town, many were led by clerics. Few were liberal or secular, and they didn't matter anyway. None of the parties had any experience with institutions, with outlining plans, with deal making. Some of them had their own powerful militias.

Ninety days before the elections a very late decision was made to include "regime-displaced migrants," as up to 4 million Iraqi exiles were called, regardless of whether they had been displaced or just chosen to move to a new place.

Iraq's election law itself seemed designed to promote civil war. Although the diverse country is divided into eighteen provinces, it had only one electoral district. California, which is roughly the same size as Iraq, has fifty-three. How could a Shia from the southern marshes expect his interests to be represented by a politician from Baghdad, London, or Mosul? Ethnic and religious blocs preferred one district because they were nationally known, and they would be able to avoid challengers who had genuine grassroots support on the local level.

The election took place under martial law because interim Prime Minister Ayad Allawi had declared a state of emergency in November. That month, there were at least 133 car bomb attacks, at least 48 of which were suicide car bombs. There were 35 to 40 "security events" in Iraq per day, down from 67 to 70 a day in August, but still severe.

A random look at classified intelligence reports prepared by the U.S. military and security companies operating in Iraq showed that the war was not at all over. On the four days between December 21 and 24, 2004, there were 89 attacks with improvised explosive devices and an additional 60 unexploded IEDs discovered. There were 71 attacks with small-arms fire. There were 148 attacks on patrols and convoys. There were 29 attacks with grenades. For security reasons the names of the candidates on the lists were not even announced. People would not know who they were voting for. The elections themselves were contrary to the Bush administration's grand vision for Iraq. When the insurgency escalated in the fall of 2003, the Americans faced pressure to hand over "sovereignty" earlier than planned.

Initially the Americans had devised an obscure caucus plan, never very well understood. When Sistani rejected it and demanded immediate elections, the January date was set. Sunni leaders called for a six-month delay, to no avail. Sistani ordered his flock to vote as a religious obligation. Of course, the Shias stood to benefit the most from elections that were strictly proportional and to benefit even more if the Sunni turnout was artificially low due to a boycott or fear of violence.

Clerics throughout Iraq who criticized the elections and the occupation were arrested, including my old acquaintance from Abu Hanifa, Sheikh Muayad. It was hard to escape the impression that anybody who opposed the U.S. occupation would be arrested or killed.

I RETURNED TO KIRKUK in January 2005 to observe the electoral battle unfold. I was stepping into a tinderbox. Kirkuk was the fourth-largest Iraqi city, with a population of 850,000 and the country's second-largest proven oil reserves—40 percent of the total. Kirkuk had once been a cosmopolitan center, where Jews and Sunni and Shia Muslims who were ethnically Arab, Turkmen, Kurds, and Christians lived and worked side by side and attended each other's religious celebrations. As Arab nationalism spread throughout the region, suppressing competing national identities such as the Kurds' and the Jews', the demography of Kirkuk began to change.

Kurds, who are not Arabs, speak a language related to Iranian and inhabit lands mostly in Iraq, Iran, Turkey, and Syria. Though their origins are nebulous, by the time of the Arab conquest in the seventh century the term "Kurd" was used to describe western Iranians in the region of the Zagros Mountains. Kurds believe they have lived in the region for three thousand years, outliving the empires of the Assyrians, Persians, Greeks, Romans, Arabs, Mongols, and finally the Ottoman Turks. By the nineteenth century there was a Kurdish nationalist movement. In 1918 Kurds pinned their hopes on the twelfth point of Woodrow Wilson's fourteen-point program for peace, which stipulated that the nationalities of the collapsing Ottoman Empire should be given autonomy. However, the British discovery of oil in Kirkuk in 1920 led them to attach the Kurdish lands to Iraq, and the rest of the Kurdish lands were divided among the larger countries of the region. Starting in the 1920s Kurds in Iraq, Persia, and Turkey rose up in regular rebellions.

Rivaling the Kurds in their claim for Kirkuk were the Turkmen. There are several competing theories for the origins of Iraq's Turkmen. They are said to be Turkish tribes that stopped in Iraq with the Turkish advance; remnants of the Seljuks who advanced into the region in the twelfth century; Ottomans who remained in Iraq; tribes from the post-Mongol period; and, less proudly, that they are Ottomanized Arabs and Kurds. The most common view among academics is that they are Asiatic migrants and remnants of the Seljuks. Until the fall of the Ottoman Empire and the establishment of the Iraqi monarchy, Turkman nobility ruled Kirkuk and the city's population was majority Turkman.

Some Arabs have also long lived in the region, others came for the jobs that could be found in the oil-producing city. Turkmen looked to their Turkish brothers in the north for help throughout the years, though little was forthcoming. Turkey began expressing more interest in the rights of Iraq's Turkmen following the war, a position viewed cynically as an excuse to

interfere in Iraqi Kurdistan, where an aggressive Kurdish nationalism worried Turkey.

Beginning in 1975 the Baathist regime forcibly removed
hundreds of thousands of Kurds, Turkmen, and Assyrian Christians from Kirkuk, bringing in Arabs to take their place. This
was called Arabization. The government wanted to consolidate its grip on the oil-rich and fertile region and to preempt a
Kurdish takeover of the city. The previous year, the Iraqi government had unilaterally created an autonomous Kurdish zone
in Iraqi Kurdistan. About 250,000 non-Arabs, mostly Kurds,
were expelled. Their former land titles were declared invalid
and ownership was assumed by the government, which rented
the land to Arabs.

In 1987, in retaliation for Kurdish rebellions during the war
with Iran, Saddam launched the infamous Anfal campaign
against the Kurds of the north. About 100,000 Kurds were
killed and at least 4,000 of their villages destroyed in what is
widely called a genocidal war. This only increased Kurdish
militancy, and in 1991, following Saddam's defeat in the first
Gulf War, the Kurds saw an opening and rebelled, much like
Shia Iraqis in the south. The retaliation was swift and brutal
once again. The United States, which had encouraged the rebellion, did nothing. Two million Kurds fled, and the UN estimated that 20,000 Kurds died during this massive exodus.

Finally, the UN established a no-fly zone above the 36th
parallel, and a Kurdish experiment with self-rule began. Two
main parties, the Kurdish Democratic Party (KDP) and the
Patriotic Union of Kurdistan (PUK), divided the region into
two fiefdoms. Although elections were held in 1992, in 1996
they were embroiled in a civil war that cost thousands of lives.
The KDP even invited the hated Saddam to help them.

Meanwhile, in Kirkuk itself, south of the no-fly zone,
Saddam continued to Arabize. In the 1990s the UN estimated
that 805,505 displaced people were living in the Kurdish north.

During the war, U.S. Special Forces stationed in the north
fought alongside Kurdish *peshmerga,* or "those who face death,"

as the Kurdish guerrilla fighters were called. The Special Forces operators expressed admiration for the stamina and skill the often overweight *peshmerga* displayed. Together they descended on Kirkuk on April 9, 2003, and the lack of strong U.S. troop presence allowed vengeful Kurds to rampage, looting many of the city's government buildings and shops. Western observers at the time saw convoys of Kurdish vehicles carrying the booty back to the north. Though thousands of Arabs had fled in advance, those who remained were subject to a campaign of intimidation, and many were warned to abandon their homes, which the Kurdish militias were awarding to *peshmerga* or the families of "martyred" *peshmerga*. The United States eventually established a city council, dividing it evenly among all four groups, much to their mutual consternation, and a tense status quo governed.

As authoritarianism and an atmosphere of fear increased in Kurdistan, it became clear that the KDP and PUK had not learned much in terms of responsible governance. The single electoral district system meant that the many rival parties in Kurdistan would not be able to compete with the powerful PUK and KDP coalition, who would fail to find support in a free election. In order to have their voices heard, Kurds throughout Kurdistan had to act as Kurds, automatically giving their votes to the Kurdish bloc, which is assured 20 percent of the national vote but which had no support outside of Kurdistan.

Driving down from the Turkish border through Kurdistan, in January, I saw no symbols of the Iraqi state. Government buildings displayed only the flag of Kurdistan, as did the shoulders of soldiers. The word *Iraq* was nowhere to be found. Kirkuk was a microcosm of the many civil wars that had already started throughout Iraq, and a likely spark for the disintegration of Iraq, as Sunnis battled Shias, and Kurds battled Arabs and Turkmen.

It was Friday, January 28, the last day of the Iraqi election campaign, with two days left before election day. General Rostam Hamid Rahim, guerrilla war hero and member of the

Kurdish Regional Government's parliament, was determined that every Kurd would vote. Known as Mam Rostam, or "Uncle" Rostam, the fifty-one-year-old had spent most of his life fighting. He still only wore an olive shirt tucked into olive baggy pants, with a sash wrapped around his waist and a khaki vest, the traditional Kurdish garb. A black-and-white checkered scarf that circled his head was moved back every so often so he could scratch at his closely cropped hair. By the time I first caught up with him he had already visited a polling station in the Imam Qasim neighborhood, just around the corner from the headquarters of the PUK, his party, headed by Jalal Talabani. Rostam was the PUK's top field commander. Entering inside the ostensibly neutral territory of the school that served as a polling station, he warmly greeted the staff and campaigned for the Kurdish list.

Rostam's current home in the formerly all-Arab Qadisiya neighborhood had previously been given to Shia Arabs, who had been given incentives to move to Kirkuk. Rostam's wife and four children had been living in Germany since 1987. He visited them for three of every six months, and they occasionally came to see him in Suleimaniya, where he had another home.

Rostam had joined the *peshmerga* in 1968 when he was fifteen. After 1995 he commanded between 1,500 and 2,500 men. "Now if I need five thousand *peshmerga* I can just make a call on the phone and get them," he said with typical bravado. He told me that he and his men had driven down to a Turkman village that Saddam had destroyed and the Turkmen were rebuilding. Out of a population of 1,500, 370 were eligible voters. "They promised to give us all their votes and wouldn't let us leave. They slaughtered fifteen sheep for us.

"Because of the people's love for me in 1992, the PUK nominated me as one of fifty candidates from the movement for the Kurdish parliament. I was a *peshmerga* and I have never been disloyal to the cause and always led from the front. I was injured six times because I have always been a field commander.

I preferred field operations. I don't like paperwork and telephones. I always mixed with the people and never distinguished myself from the simple people. I have never cared about collecting wealth. I never made deals with the regime. I'm expecting to die at any moment, so why do I need wealth?"

He showed off his bullet and shrapnel wounds. "Rambo!" He laughed. "If you make it into a film, people won't believe it. Journalists describe me as a wonder of the world and say it's a miracle I'm still alive." Rostam proudly told me how his men had renamed the Qadisiya neighborhood where he lived the "Rostam neighborhood." Rostam had been involved in a remarkable palace coup that took place within the PUK's inner sanctum in the fall of 2003. Concerned about Talabani's increasing authoritarianism and nepotism, eight of his politburo members and Rostam, who had formed a movement called Islah, or "reform," had confronted Talabani.

"We are a modern party unlike the KDP, which is a monarchy from father to son. The PUK survived attacks and massacres, so why should we be afraid of *Jalal?* We are not having a revolution to remove one dictator only to get another. Every decision was in the hands of *Jalal;* it's not democratic and not acceptable. Politics is like storms, sometimes you have snowstorms, sometimes you have rainstorms. Now is the time of democracy, and you have to be democratic, even in your own home. There are people like us in the KDP who want reform, and maybe in the future we will join to make one party."

Although he attended elementary school, Rostam explained his self-education. "Where there is repression and you want to fight, you learn politics. Revolution is a kind of politics. I learned a lot from the struggles in Laos, Cambodia, Cuba, Vietnam." Rostam had been the enfant terrible of the Kurdish parliament. Before the war he was the only member to have voted against an American troop presence in Kurdistan. He explained that he had done it to show that Kurds were democratic. During the war he was often seen with an entourage of female *peshmerga.*

Mam Rostam's next stop was the Panja Ali refugee camp, next to the Shorja neighborhood, Rostam's own birthplace. Saddam had destroyed the neighborhood with bulldozers in 1991 to punish rebellious Kurds and expel them to the north. Now hundreds of Kurdish families had returned, some living in tents, others in hastily constructed houses. Rostam was seated next to other local Kurdish officials, including the deputy head of security for Kirkuk, who had fought with Rostam against Saddam. They were surrounded by a hundred men from the refugee camp and its nearby polling station. Gesticulating with his broad, thick shoulders and arms for emphasis, Rostam repeated the same message he had been telling Kurds through-out the city: "You have to vote, for the sake of our future." Taking the Kurdish victory for granted, he asked that "when the election results are announced, please don't shoot in the air." Rostam was protected by an entourage of *peshmerga,* though his *peshmerga* were dressed in the Iraqi National Guard uniforms and some wore flak jackets that said "Police."

The convoy of pickup trucks continued to another PUK office, across the street from another polling location. Rostam marched into the office and took a seat behind the director's desk. Tea was brought out. Minor officials greeted him with hugs and kisses on both cheeks. He directed his gaze to the head of the neighborhood committee. "Tell everybody to be quiet and calm on election day and tell people not to shoot in the air when the results come because it will make other ethnic groups nervous," he said. He was certain of their triumph and told the men, "We've done what we have to do. People should just go and vote." Before leaving he added that signs giving people directions to the polling locations should be written in Kurdish, not Arabic.

Already on the 28th, two days before the election, the Kurds had begun their victory celebration. In the PUK office, Kurdish soldiers and policemen in state uniforms, assigned to the Ministry of Oil, lolled about, watching the traffic that had slowed to a stop thanks to the youths sitting on the windows and on top of cars, waving flags, honking their horns, singing, and cheering until dark.

In his home, Rostam went into the kitchen and emerged with bottles of whiskey, ouzo, and beer. He laughed at me when I asked for a Coke. Rostam's usual nightly guests began arriving. General Salar Ahmad Faqi, the rotund and eternally tired chief of the traffic police, settled into a chair, removing his Israeli automatic pistol, a mini Uzi. The chief of security for Qadisiya was there, a handsome man with a freshly shaven visage and permanent smile who refused to give me his name or have his picture taken. They looked like a Kurdish version of the Sopranos, sitting quietly and rolling their eyes as Rostam retold stories they must have heard a thousand times before.

When reports of threats came in through the radio, Rostam, well into his ouzo, began complaining. "Muslims are bad," he said. "Islam is dictatorial. Look at Europe. You can see real democracy, you can see a mosque, a church, and nightclub all together." His friend Adil, deputy chief of security for Kirkuk, dressed in black suit, black shirt, and red tie, added, "I am an example of democracy. I pray, then I drink." As the radio on the table crackled with news of suspicious vehicles, General Faqi responded, "Stop them or shoot at them."

Rostam continued his tirade. "The Arab's religion is all about killing, cutting out tongues, burning. You cannot find the word *love* in the Quran." He tied Islam to Saddam. "The regime killed 182,000 people in the Anfal campaign and destroyed more than five thousand villages and no Muslim cleric said anything." In an oft-heard Kurdish refrain, he mourned the loss of the pre-Islamic pagan religion Kurds had practiced. "Our original religion was Yazidi and they came by the sword to make us Muslims," he said. Watching music videos on his satellite television, he grumbled, "We should replace mosques with discotheques."

Two Kurdish secret service agents entered the house, one with a pistol tucked into his belt and a baby face. The other one, older, clean shaven, with clipped silver hair and gold wire-framed glasses, remained silent, whispering on his cell phone in the corner. Shy young *peshmerga* in green fatigues and with plastic slippers brought in different courses of salad, rice, and meat for Rostam's bevy of well-fed comrades. Cell phones rang often, each one with a different pop melody. Atta, a police commander in Qadisiya, had "Jingle Bells" as his ring.

Rostam recalled negotiations with Saddam in 1984. Kirkuk, because of its oil, proved to be a stumbling block. Foreign minister Tariq Aziz had warned Rostam and the Kurdish negotiators, "You will never get Kirkuk. You can only pass though it and weep for it." Rostam would now have his revenge. "Sixty-five to seventy percent of Kirkuk is Kurdish," he assured me, "so if there was a referendum to join Kurdistan, we could join easily. Kirkuk is part of Kurdistan. When we win we'll make Kirkuk the safest and richest city in the Middle East. We have struggled for more than thirty-five years for Kirkuk. Next year we'll have new elections in Kirkuk and we'll return Kirkuk to Kurdistan."

Though its location on some of the country's main oil fields should have made Kirkuk a wealthy city, it was dilapidated, its roads and buildings crumbling. Traffic crawled around the city's roundabouts. Young men and boys sold boxes of perfumed tissue paper and bananas at intersections. American Humvees with masked gunners rumbled past broken-down Iraqi cars, Arabic signs on the back of the immense vehicles warned other drivers to stay back fifty meters. Cars waited all day on interminable lines for gas, as the flames from oil pipelines sabotaged by resistance bombs lit up the western horizon like monuments to their misfortune.

The city's tallest monument was also to its oil, an immense statue of hands supporting an oil pump. But the streets ran with water, not oil. The winter rains in the days leading up to the election made the city dirtier, washing it with gray dirt and mud. Roads flooded and cars slowly negotiated them, leaving a brown wake as waves crashed over the elevated sidewalks, onto the gates of shops and homes. "We are like Venice now," said my driver. An Arab, he enjoyed listening to Kdhayar Hadi, whose tapes of *mawal,* a traditional combination of chanting, talking, and lamenting set to music, were almost like hip-hop. Hadi complained about the Americans, mocked them, and cursed them for what they had done to his country.

Wires and cables crisscrossed above the city like spiderwebs, blocking the sky, all trying to get what little power was available for a few hours a day. Inside stores and offices Kirkukis of all backgrounds watched Egyptian slapstick comedies and grumbled about having to turn away from them when customers appeared. Every available wall was festooned with posters and banners for the three main party lists competing in Kirkuk: the Kurdish Kirkuk Brotherhood list, the light blue crescent and star of the Iraqi Turkmen Front, and the candle of the United Iraqi Alliance, the "Sistani list," so called because the powerful Shia cleric had given it his blessing. There were few slogans apart from nationalist graffiti.

In the Turkman and Kurdish areas, and in the center of town, a war of signs was being fought. Each party's poster or banner let the target audience know it was meant for them, and then the appropriate number of the party on the ballots was provided, so Kurds would recognize the Kurdish symbols and associate them only with that number, Turkmen would recognize their color and associate it with the right number.

In the Turkman neighborhood called Muhamady I found three Kurds, two wearing American-issue military uniforms and slinging Kalashnikovs, one wearing a suit, putting up ten posters for the Kirkuk Brotherhood list above Turkmen signs. One Kurdish soldier, with extra magazines for his weapon stuffed into his vest on his chest, kicked a large Turkman banner into a ball on the curb with angry conviction, then pushed it into the mud. The other soldier was busy squeezing glue from a tube onto new posters. "Is it normal for political activists to carry Kalashnikovs?" I asked the boy in the suit. "They are just my security," he said of the two soldiers straightening the posters on the wall. I asked him why he had taken down the other group's political banner, and he said it belonged to the Iraqi Turkmen Front. "There are different kinds of Turkmen," he said. "They are the Front. They serve Turkey." Not far away, I found two other Kurdish youth also in American-issue military uniforms with flak jackets and Kalashnikovs, accompanied by a civilian with a pistol and walkie-talkie, putting up more posters on the concrete barriers of the U.S. Army's civil military operations center. In another Turkman neighborhood I was stuck behind a slow-moving convoy of cars covered in Kurdish flags and banners. A loudspeaker on one blasted Kurdish music through the neighborhood, while a man with a microphone in the first car recited a litany of crimes the Kurds had suffered. The cars were full of armed men, hunched over with their Kalashnikov barrels just visible over the windows. An armed policeman stopped my car to hand out leaflets for the Kurdish list. On the road from Kirkuk to Kurdistan and Erbil, Kurdish Iraqi National Guardsmen and *peshmerga* stopped cars to hand out the same leaflets.

The previous Friday, January 21, I visited a Shia mosque in Kirkuk. The inner walls were lined with posters, a Who's Who of radical Shiism: Ayatollah Khomeini of the Iranian revolution; Moqtada al-Sadr, warning the Americans, "Oh infidels, I don't worship what you worship"; another that said of the infidel Americans, "Fight these people by day and by night, secretly and openly, and I call on you to attack them before they attack you." Beneath the posters, on a bulletin board, an announcement declared that Moqtada's movement was boycotting the election. It did not add that he was also secretly fielding candidates to try and get a share of power.

The mosque's sheikh used coded words urging his flock to vote for known followers of Moqtada al-Sadr, telling them to "follow he who deserves to be followed." Inside the mosque's office, Shia tribesmen belonging to the Arabian Tribal Gathering movement came to meet with the local representatives of Moqtada al-Sadr's movement. The three turbaned tribal sheikhs also belonged to the United Arab Front, a party running in the elections. The men of the mosque refused to speak without permission from Moqtada's official agent in Kirkuk, who was not present, and were adamant that the tribal leaders should not talk to me there, lest it appear that their views were endorsed by the Sadriyun, as the followers of Sadr were called. "We the Sadriyun are boycotting the elections," one man said. The prayer leader was willing to say only that "we reject separatism. We are all Muslims and one nation." The angry tribal leaders invited were eager to talk. "They want to chop Iraq into three parts," one said, "nobody would want his home divided."

The next day in the Qadisiya neighborhood that had once been dominated by Baath Party members, I joined six young Arabs for breakfast. Over thin glasses of heavily sweetened tea, a Muhamad told me that he worked as an election box supervisor. He complained that "because we [Arabs] used to work with the old regime or just because we were in the army" they were being targeted. The Kurds were accusing them falsely and telling the Americans to round up Arab men, he said. Afraid of both Kurds and Americans, in the days leading up to the election, he and his friends were staying together in friends' houses. Though he had received many threats, and the Association of Muslim Scholars had ordered Sunnis not to vote, Muhamad, alone among his friends, planned to vote for Ayad Allawi's INA.

Muhamad's friend Ibrahim explained that he would not vote. "Allawi is like Saddam," he said. "What's the difference? He uses the same methods." He added that "none of the candidates cares about Iraq's interests; these elections are fake. They already elected Allawi." Leaflets and posters from the resistance warned the Arabs of the neighborhood against voting. "We are scared for your safety," the signs said, "but we are not responsible for the safety of those who vote." It was a veiled and universally understood message.

A leaflet I found in Kirkuk before the January 2005 elections warned against voting: "Statement about the three-day curfew for the sons of this land: There is no doubt that Allah created his creatures so that they worship Him and not shirk [polytheism] and He helps all the people on the path to success and it is God's work that among his servants there are Muslims and non-Muslims and there is a continuing war between these two until Judgment Day. And now the head of the infidels of this time, America, has started to bear hatred against Islam and the Muslims. This war will not stop, even if the occupation ends, because it is not a matter of occupation but of creating a state [Islamic state]. As we have announced before, our legal verdict about participation in the elections that will take place in Iraq. We warn you against this participation because the polling stations and the people that work in them are a target for the brave soldiers of Allah, so we advise everybody to keep away from any military target, whether it is the crusader American headquarters or their patrols or the Iraqi national guard or the apostate police forces. Because of the continuation of the battle between us and the crusaders and to avoid harming people, we announce a curfew for three days beginning . . . Oh God, we have announced it and You are the witness," concluded the letter signed by the military wing of Ansar al-Sunnah. It was unique in that it provided a theological worldview and a Manichean one at that.

I attempted a visit to the Independent Electoral Commission of Iraq and found it in disarray. The staff did not know what parties were running. They had no lists and were still waiting for their arrival. There was less than a week left before the elections. The following day I returned after hearing rumors of mass resignations from the commission. The head of security and his guards confirmed that the day before, nine people had resigned; several days before that, four people had resigned; and on that day, six people had resigned. The deputy director had quit as well. Their resignations had been refused, however. The director emerged and denied that anybody had resigned, warning the guards not to talk tome.

On January 24, the United Arab Front held a conference.

Several men spent ten minutes struggling to decide how best to place the Iraqi flag against the wall and on which side of the wall it should stand. Finally a man with a hammer ordered them to leave it alone. "Just make sure the 'God is great' is showing," he said. Sheikh Wasfi al-Asi was chain-smoking Marlboro Ultra Lights, a rare sight in Iraq. A city council member and general secretary of the front, he had held that job since it was established, after "the fall of Iraq," he paused, stressing the phrase. I corrected him and asked if he did not mean "the fall of the regime," the usual appellation given to the war. "No," he said, "the fall of Iraq, write it like that because April ninth was not a liberation. Occupation is not liberation. It's not just the fall of Saddam, it's the fall of all institutions in Iraq and the army. April ninth is the date of the occupation of our country, and the first Interim Governing Council declaration was to make it a national holiday, but the national holiday will be when the Americans leave. This doesn't mean we support Saddam or the old regime, but when foreign soldiers remove a dictatorship, they have to just change the system and leave, not stay. They have killed more than Saddam. Iraqi exiles came with the coalition and the focus was on Saddam's mass graves, but the coalition's mass graves are bigger than Saddam's."

Sheikh Wasfi had run a construction and transport company, and had contracts with the old regime to make bus stations and markets. "But I left business since the fall of Iraq," he said, pausing again for stress. He explained that he had called this conference to announce the front's boycott of the election. "We are boycotting the elections because the IECI is not independent. It was pressured by the Kurds to allow the Kurds to register late, and to allow Kurds not from Kirkuk to register." I asked him if his party had offered any specific plans relating to the future shape of Iraq, such as a vision for the economy. "An economic plan is not a priority," he said. "The priority is security. Any words on the economy are ignored by Iraqis. Iraq is looking for security only, so when a man's son goes to school he comes home safely, when his wife goes to the market she comes home safely. If the goal of the elections is just to go and vote, then it's a waste. The goal is to pick representatives for the Iraqi people. In the U.S. when you have an election you pick somebody famous. Iraqis don't know who the candidates are. You can't have elections in this chaos. The elections are too sudden and they have confused Iraqis." Outside, the conference was set to begin, and I received a typed announcement about the withdrawal. Yet immediately after, a rotund man with a Kalashnikov and clips on his chest, his sweatpants stuffed into white socks and muddy loafers, took back the boycott announcement due to a mysterious error.

Outside the Kirkuk government headquarters, two pickup trucks full of masked Iraqi National Guardsmen drove out. Both brown trucks had "ING" written on them. One had a large poster of the Kirkuk Brotherhood list taped onto its hood, the other had a Kurdish flag stuck on its side. The dusty halls were deserted, and my footsteps echoed as I walked past the offices of various council members until I found that of the Sunni Arab I was visiting. He sat behind an immense wooden desk, empty except for a box of tissues and a walkie-talkie. On the sofa there was a Kalashnikov.

Walking past the council's information office, I found several Kurdish men watching Kurdish satellite television. The program was about the plight of the Kurdish refugees and the need to expel all the Arabs from Kirkuk. I walked out, past the guards who spoke only Kurdish, and drove away from the compound, to be stopped by a policeman armed with a machine gun. He was distributing leaflets for the Kirkuk Brotherhood list.

Looking for the chief of police, a half Turkman, half Kurdish moderate, I was first taken to the office of the police Information Department chief, Abdallah Qader Abdallah. A flag of Kurdistan stood on his desk alongside plastic flowers. A map of Kurdistan was on his door, part of a poster for the Kirkuk Brotherhood list. He told me the police force was 40 percent Arab,

40 percent Kurd, and 40 percent Turkman and a few Christians. I did not ask him how that added up to 100 percent.

General Torhan, chief of Kirkuk's police, sat in a room full of plastic flowers. He had served in this position for twenty months. Originally from Kirkuk, he had worked throughout the country as a police officer for twenty-three years. I asked him about the different neighborhoods in town, and if there had been changes in the Arab neighborhoods, and he interrupted me curtly. "There is no Arab neighborhood or Turkman neighborhood in Kirkuk," he said. "Kirkuk is for all Iraqis." Four of his phones rang simultaneously, news of a series of explosions south of Kirkuk, and he picked up three at once, then asked me, "Why do the Americans always say Arab, Kurdish, or Turkman neighborhood?"

Abdallah Qader Abdallah took me to the office of General Sarhat, head of security for all villages outside Kirkuk. Sarhat, originally from Kirkuk but expelled to Erbil in 1980, did not know Arabic and spoke to me in Kurdish. He warned me not to visit the town's Arab neighborhoods because they were dangerous. "These are Arabs Saddam brought," he said. "They should be returned to their homes in the south." The villages outside Kirkuk were 60 percent Kurdish, 65 percent Arab, and 45 percent Turkman, he told me, not exactly doing the math.

After several days of searching I managed to locate the United Iraqi Alliance headquarters in Kirkuk's Wasti neighborhood. It was the organization behind the Sistani list, the largest coalition in the country. Posters of Sistani and Supreme Council for the Islamic Revolution in Iraq (SCIRI) leader Abdel Aziz al-Hakim let me know I had found the house. A sewage pool festered in the yard. Three small middle-aged men were sleeping in a room when I arrived. They hobbled out in a somnambulant daze. One was Omran Abdel Rahman, head of information for the party in Kirkuk. His associate, Ali, had fought for seventeen years in SCIRI's militia, the Badr Brigade, against what he called "Saddam the criminal." Their

Arabic was poor; they were all Turkmen who had spent nearly two decades in Iranian exile. They had fought in the south and northern Iraq. I asked them who their candidates were in Kirkuk. "There are candidates here for the list," said Omran, "but I don't have their names or phone numbers here." He rummaged through the desk until he found the names of their seventeen candidates.

They sent me to a rally at a large concrete mosque, unpainted and new, guarded by a dozen tense armed men on the roof and a dozen more inside and on the street. The roads were blocked off with barriers. They searched me thoroughly. The walls were covered with posters of mass graves and of Saddam's soldiers attacking Najaf. Inside, Seyid Sadiq al-Batat spoke to a room full of 150 men and 50 women, sequestered in the front. He spoke about Islam for ninety minutes, and finally got to the elections. "Elections are an important day for the followers of Ali," he said, referring to the Shias, "and we say to the occupier, no to occupation for a day, for a week, for a year. Sistani refused the American request to postpone the elections. People think that the elections are a gift from the occupier, but they are a trick to let them stay here to use our oil and natural resources.

"They were refusing elections, but we forced them. We won't have a secular constitution. We'll have an Islamic constitution; the majority in this country is Shia. Anybody who wants to liberate Iraq should vote for this list."

The fault lines of the future were already visible. The Shia wanted a much more theocratic state than did the Sunnis, much less the Kurds. Everyone had military power to back them up. When I visited the headquarters of the National Turkman Movement, I recognized a faded picture of a gray wolf baying at the moon. It was a symbol of Turkey's Gray Wolves movement, a fascist organization operating in Turkey since the 1960s, supporting the expansion of a greater Turkey. "We belong to the Turkish Gray Wolves because we believe that anything taken by force will only be taken back by force," the men inside told me. "Kirkuk will never be part of Kurd-istan," they warned.

I stopped by the offices of the Iraqi Turkmen Front's in-nocuous-sounding Humanitarian Aid Society. Walking past Kalashnikov-wielding guards whose uniforms bore an eagle patch that said "Hayat Security Company," I found several young men seated on a couch struggling to clean two Kalash-nikovs and put them back together. Four more Kalashnikovs were leaning against the wall in a corner. A poster of the founder of the modern Turkish state, Mustafa Kemal Ataturk, was on the wall above them, and on several shelves were various im-ages of the Gray Wolves. Omar Khattab, manager of the of-fice, a pistol on his desk, was watching Egyptian comedies. A balding round man whose thin eyes and aquiline beak made him look hawklike, Khattab had his moment of fame when in the previous summer he had led a few dozen protestors who had sewn their lips together and stood for seven hours outside the Green Zone in Baghdad. Seated on the sofa beside the boys still fumbling with their Kalashnikov pieces were two men. One wore a pinstripe suit and a white butterfly collar folded out above his lapel, like a disco star. It was Khattab's head of security. The other man was his assistant. "We are not a politi-cal organization," Khattab explained. "We are a humanitarian organization. We help Kurds and Arabs too." He could not explain what help they provided from his little office full of armed men, except to say that they helped send sick Turkmen abroad for treatment and disburse aid coming in from the Turkman diaspora.

The second time I visited him, Khattab and his armed young men were watching a Jackie Chan movie. His security chief was wearing the same pinstriped outfit. I asked Khattab why he had a small army in his office. "God willing, there will be violence," he said. "We are expecting it. You think we will keep silent about the 108,000 Kurds [registered unfairly]. Civil war has to happen, but we won't start it. Why do you think we were cleaning our weapons? Today there was a demonstration of Kurds, all of them armed, a provocation. Where were the Americans? How can you come here to teach us about democracy and you don't give us freedom?" I asked him what he thought might happen. "Maybe after an hour, after a day, after a week, but civil war has to happen."

Like Saddam before him, the forty-three-year-old Khattab had started out as a violent activist. As a teenager, he was an assassin, shooting at Baathist security men. "We succeeded in assassinating some of them, praise God," he said. He had been jailed eleven times, and in 1979 he was sentenced to be executed but bribed his way out of it by paying 1,000 dinars to change his birth certificate, making him a minor and ineligible for execution. In 1991, he said, the Kurds had jailed him for working with Turkish intelligence. "Every political organization that wants to start begins with leaflets, then begins assassinations so its voice is heard," he explained.

Khattab took me to meet Yawaz Omar Adil, head of the ITF in Kirkuk. His office in the ITF's fortified building was guarded by the same army of private security guards from the Hayat company and was full of plastic flowers. Adil was a former Iraqi Army general, having retired in 1999. When I walked in, Adil was on the phone discussing Sheikh Wasfi, of the United Arab Front, who had announced a boycott of the elections. Khattab leaned closer to me and smiled, whispering, "God willing, maybe we will pull out of elections. It's better because these elections are corrupted." Unshaven and chubby, in sagging baggy jeans and leather jacket, Khattab looked out of place amid the suits in the office.

Adil saw nothing unusual about working with a man like Khattab, who had fought the very same regime he had served. "I was with the army but not in the Baath Party and not serving Saddam. We were with the Iraqi people, we hated Saddam." His party was considering a boycott of the elections, he said, but even though "these elections are fake and corrupt," he thought it would be better to stay because "at least I will have representatives writing the new constitution."

I later spotted several pickup trucks full of masked Hayat security guards shooting into the air, circling around, and screeching to a halt in front of a house. Forty men emerged from the vehicles, which were covered with Turkman symbols and posters for the ITF. They distributed ITF election flyers to local children to hand out in the neighborhood. Some left their face masks on. "We are special guards," they said. I asked if they worked with the ITF, but they denied it, saying, "We are just a private company, we are not involved in politics." The house was the headquarters for the Hayat company. The masked men circling the area with Kalashnikovs told me the company was based in Baghdad and that was where I could find the owner.

Soon a car pulled up with Muhamad Abdel Rahman Ismail, a small wiry man with an equally thin mustache and dark black suit. He was the owner, he explained, and the company was based in Kirkuk. Ismail told me he was a Turkman and a former intelligence officer in the Iraqi Army who had received training abroad in security and investigations. He did have a contract to provide security to the ITF, he said, but his was just a private company and not at all a militia. As he walked past the young perfectly erect guards holding their Kalashnikovs in ceremonial form, one of them saluted and shouted, "I'm ready, sir!"

Ismail, who refused to have his picture taken, asserted that "I am one hundred percent certain there will be violence during the elections. There are many provocations." To prove his vigilance, he told me that only earlier that day he had arrested two young Turkmen who had been firing celebratory shots in the air after he warned them to stop. "I took them into my office and beat them up," he said.

It seemed that only the groups who knew they would win power—the Shia nationally, the Kurds here in Kirkuk—were determined to vote. The Turkmen half expected to lose; the Sunnis were certain of it.

In the Uruba, or Arabdom, neighborhood, constructed by

Saddam to house Arabs he had imported into Kirkuk to replace Kurds he was expelling, the muddy lots and rocky paths
between homes were full of children playing in sewage and
garbage strewn about as goats and herds of sheep picked
through the refuse for scraps of food. Part of a series of slums
constructed by the former regime, which included Nasr, Mam-
duda, and Qadisiya, it was nicknamed "Resistance City" by
U.S. soldiers, who rarely ventured in. Women in purple and
green robes with head scarves squatted in front of their homes
chatting, while others used mops to clean the space in front of
their homes. Men lolled about silently, grimly staring at my
car as it struggled to traverse the pitted and broken streets,
each pothole full of green water. They recognized a new vehicle and new faces.

A trickle of Sunni men, alone or in pairs, slowly made their
way to the al-Tawhid, or monotheism, mosque, whose white
walls and green towers were surrounded with thick sewage.
Donkeys stood outside while children played with birds they
had caught, holding their feet and attacking each other with
the screeching birds spreading their wings.

We parked our car outside to listen to the *khutba,* or Friday
sermon. Three children walked by my car and noticed two
strangers with a notebook. They casually turned around and
circled the car, looking at us, and then as they approached the
mosque they sprinted in. We had been spotted. Two of the
mosque's custodians appeared and glanced at us. I approached
and introduced myself to the suspicious custodians and was
allowed to enter. A hundred men were standing barefoot in
rows on carpets in the outer courtyard because the mosque
was full, their shoes and slippers lined up on the stone floor.
Sheikh Mahmud Husein Ahmad al-Ubeidi began his sermon,
and loudspeakers echoed his shrill fury against the walls of the
neighborhood. "The occupier wants us to participate in these
elections," he said, "but we know they are a fraud." After prayer
was over, I stood in line with other well-wishers, to greet the
sheikh with an embrace and two kisses on the left shoulder, in

the way of traditional Sunni Iraqis, and congratulate the sheikh on his recent return from the Hajj pilgrimage to Saudi Arabia, wishing him a blessed Hajj and expressing the hope that his sins would be buried. The sheikh invited me for lunch and we drove to his nearby home, where twenty men were seated in his dark guest room. Paint peeled off the walls against which boys and old men in dishdasha robes were leaning, perched upon thin mattresses. I explained that I was interested in learning more about Kirkuk. "We fear Iraq will have a sectarian war," he said, and was interrupted by his three-year-old son Osama running to embrace his father. "I named him Osama after bin Laden. Bin Laden is a good man." The sheikh smiled.

"We are not ready to be treated like the Baathists treated us," he said, explaining that he had been paid only five dollars a month under Saddam's regime and admitting that since the war the government now paid him 120 dollars a month. Sheikh Mahmud admitted he was a member of the Association of Muslim Scholars, the radical coalition of sheikhs that supported the resistance and opposed both the occupation and the elections vehemently. Though they did not have an office in Kirkuk as they did in most Sunni areas, Sheikh Mahmud represented them there and relayed their orders from Baghdad. "The Association said we should not participate in the elections," he said. "We should have the elections after the occupation is over, otherwise the Americans will install whoever they want and the elections will fail." He repeated propaganda heard in Sunni areas from Falluja to Mosul. "We heard that seven hundred thousand Iranians were brought into the south, and here foreign Kurds were brought in." Sheikh Mahmud and his seated supporters did not think Sunnis would be weakened by their intended boycott. "If we support the elections, we have to accept the results," he said. "But if we reject them, we stay strong."

That night I told Mam Rostam about Sheikh Mahmud's anti-election sermon in the Tawhid mosque. He laughed and slapped his thighs. "This is great for us!" he said. He laughed in protest when I told him how I had cautioned the sheikh that Sunnis would lose out if they did not vote. "No, you should have told them, 'You're right, don't vote, it's for the infidels.'" I told him that the Arabs in Kirkuk seemed intimidated by Kurdish actions. "That's the nature of an occupying man," he said. "The occupier never enjoys the land; he is always scared of your return."

On the morning before election day Mam Rostam awoke and switched on the Kurdish satellite channel, where music videos from Suleimaniya were playing. "Isn't this better than praying at a mosque?" he asked me. He was full of advice. "Arabs are all bad, and the Americans are all stupid. They make so many mistakes. Arabs working with the Americans inform the resistance. America has no friends in the Middle East except Kurds and Israel." I asked him what some of the worst American mistakes were. "The Iraqi National Guard shouldn't be ethnically mixed," he said. "I cannot give useful advice to Americans when their translator is an Arab or Turkman." Rostam was personally replacing the police protecting polling stations with Kurdish police. "Just by their look you can tell who is loyal to the cause," he said. Rostam had put his *peshmerga* into Iraqi National Guard uniforms but maintained the same officers and chain of command. "We just put them in the ING for training," he said.

Rostam had an angry conversation on his radio, wincing and slapping his leg in anger, then he went out to shout at his fighters. "Whoever I arrest for terror, in my opinion, I should kill him on the spot. A terrorist cannot be reformed," he explained. "So I told my men to kill anybody they arrest." Rostam was furious that they had arrested an Arab man and handed him over to the police and not simply killed him. "If he was under my hand you could see his dead body now. They have been brainwashed." Rostam sent his men to hunt for "Arabs," which he saw as synonymous with "terrorists," in the neighborhood, to kill them. "Anybody who is against democracy should not be burned, he should be put in acid!"

Rostam's police commander for Qadisiya, the wiry colonel

Atta, was a *peshmerga* who had fought with Rostam and was unusually skinny for an old *peshmerga,* unlike Rostam's other portly group of aging fighters. He announced that in the past twenty-four hours he had arrested five Arabs, all Shias from the south. This made it highly unlikely that they were part of the resistance, which was typically all Sunni Arab, I thought to myself. "If Arabs weren't in the police force in Kirkuk, we wouldn't have any problems," Atta complained. "The Arabs give the terrorists information."

Atta offered to take me along with him and his men on their nightly patrols in search of terrorists, presumably to put them in acid. In the distance, .50-caliber fire from U.S. Humvees and helicopters could be heard in a steady chatter. Three pickup trucks full of Kurdish *peshmerga* dressed in police and ING uniforms drove slowly through Qadisiya and the adjacent Arab neighborhoods late at night, their sirens blaring. An eager *peshmerga* who never removed his sunglasses, a gift from the Americans, manned the heavy machine gun on top of the roof and asked us to convince Atta to let him shoot at something. After circling for an hour and waking every household in the area, Atta ordered his men to shoot above the houses and fields in the area, at nothing in particular.

The day before the elections I found Chief of Police General Torhan in his office, a digital fish tank on his television. I told him I had spent the night at Rostam's house. "Why are you staying with Mam Rostam?" he asked. "Do you work for the PUK?" A sudden distant explosion shook the city. Torhan looked up, grinned, and raised his eyebrows. He picked up the phone to ask what had happened. That morning Torhan had received a letter from the Election Commission requesting that his police secure thirty-five new voting locations, all in Kurdish neighborhoods. "It's the Iraqi way," he said. "Every time, there is a surprise."

In the deserted KDP headquarters I found Muhamad Kamal Saleh, deputy director of the KDP office in Kirkuk. Only the flag of Kurdistan was on his desk. Above him were posters of both Mustafa and Masud Barzani. His cell phone rang constantly with a Kurdish national song. Number two on the Kirkuk slate, he was guaranteed a position after the elections. "We hope to have more Kurds on the council after the elections, more than half. Kurds are forty-seven or forty-eight percent of Kirkuk. It's low because the imported Arabs have not yet been returned to the south."

He was confident that the unwanted Arabs would leave. "They came for their personal interest, so if you offer them incentive they will go. About three hundred thousand Arabs should go. About fifty thousand have already left Kirkuk. Ninety percent of them are only waiting to receive incentive to leave. They will be given jobs, transportation, land, homes in [the] south." He expected Kirkuk's oil revenues to pay for their transfer. Saleh's responsibility had been education. He complained of logistical problems turning Arab schools into Kurdish ones.

In front of the independent electoral commission of Iraq, new barriers had been placed. Four pickup trucks full of twenty bantering Kurdish Iraqi National Guardsmen, some of them masked, stood waiting. On their trucks, which bore the initials ING, were flags of Kurdistan and nationalist stickers.

Rostam was a good example of the principle that democracy is more than just a formal process, it is a culture—and Iraq is a long way from having a democratic culture.

In Uruba and the nearby Arab neighborhoods I visited polling locations that had been attacked the previous night. Shots had been fired at one school, a bomb had exploded harmlessly outside another, another had been shot at, and an RPG had hit the wall of a fourth.

The culture of Kirkuk was far more one of ethnic cleansing than plural tolerance. Assistant Governor Hasib Rozbayani was a good example. He casually carries a pistol and travels with security guards. Rozbayani had long curly hair with glasses balanced on top of it. A pet gazelle lives in his yard, alongside pheasants. Rozbayani explains that for Kirkuk, normalization means "a return of all Kurds kicked out by the Baathists, the Arabization Arabs should return to their original governorates. They should prefer to live in peace, not be in conflict every day. Their presence leads to conflict." Rozbayani had served as assistant governor for resettlement and compensation since June 2003, after returning from a long exile in Sweden.

Rozbayani was not officially affiliated with any party, though he was known to be close with the KDP. A longtime Iraq expert working for a Western NGO warned me that Rozbayani was a "real fascist." "More than fifty thousand Kurdish families were kicked out of Kirkuk," he said. "They should come back and all the Arabs should leave." Outside in his yard, I found a punching bag. He had studied Zen, he told me, and translated the first book on Zen into Kurdish. "People in this region need to learn Zen," he said. Perhaps he could write *Zen and the Art of Ethnic Cleansing*.

On election day, a school near Rostam's house served as one of the city's 109 voting centers. Men and women lined up in the hundreds on opposite sides of the school, squeezed between walls and barbed wire. The sounds of nearby heavy gunfire cut through the chatter. People came early, starting at 7:00 A.M., as Blackhawk helicopters circled above. Children held their mothers' hands; many of the women wore shiny new clothes, their finest, full of color and glitter. People came holding sample ballots and their registration cards. A sign at the entrance read "Vote for who you want and only who you want." The school was decorated with Kurdish colors on ribbons.

After their bodies were searched and their cell phones left at the entrance, voting was a five-step process. An even number of men and women stood in lines to enter the voting rooms. They studied sample ballots to make certain they knew what number they were going to mark. Their names were checked, and they were handed ballots. They were led to the cardboard voting booth where they marked the box of their choice, struggled to fold the ballot, and stuffed it into the box. Finally, they dipped their fingers in indelible ink, made famous in

photographs around the world. It was to prevent multiple voting. The air was exciting, and people moved quickly and in
remarkable order compared to the usual chaos that resulted
whenever crowds of Iraqis gathered. Everyone seemed eager
to vote, smiling as they walked out of booths.

Rostam's convoy set out for his childhood neighborhood,
Shorja, where voting was held at the Germian school. He was
accompanied by two dozen *peshmerga* and his personal cameraman. Thousands of people were on the street. Rostam
circumvented the entire line and its security procedures and
entered with his entourage. Other voters were made to wait as
Rostam put on his reading glasses and made a show of carefully studying the ballot. He was shown how to fold it, and
the staff were very impressed as he did so, or they made a
point of being so. Outside, men beat drums, sang, and danced,
some with the flag of Kurdistan. There was no symbol of Iraq
in sight. It was a celebration of Kurdish national identity, not
Iraqi identity, as men and women in traditional Kurdish garb
danced to Kurdish music and waved flags of the state they
hoped to have.

Elsewhere the mood was very different. Driving through
deserted Arab slums, I could find no evidence of the election.
No posters, no banners, no prominent voting locations bustling with people. When I finally found several men on the
street, they could not point me in the direction of a voting
location; they did not know where any would be found. Nor
could they name any Arab political parties. I finally found not
a poll but a checkpoint, complete with warning fire from the
national guardsmen. At last I stopped a group of men on the
street and found one who had ink on his finger from voting.
He pointed me in the direction of a nearby school. Meanwhile, several young men approached hastily, their arms behind their backs, glaring at me. They warned me that I was
lucky to be talking to the man I was with and maintained their
hostile stares as I drove away. As our car slowly searched the
narrow streets for the school, a small Volkswagen approached

from the side, driven by a young male who was scanning the streets. There was no sticker on his windshield. He was unauthorized to be driving. My driver stopped, and I was convinced we were about to get blown up. "Go! Go!" I shouted. It was that familiar feeling in Iraq, nerves burning, skin tingling, helpless fear, expecting to die.

One hundred meters from the barriers erected in front of the school, I heard shots fired from machine guns and pistols, and I realized the Iraqi policemen were firing at us. We stopped and reversed and they ran after us, continuing to fire. We were quickly surrounded. A short heavyset cop with a ski mask knelt on the street, aiming his machine gun at my door. I opened the door, screaming that I was a journalist, and for some reason threw out my notebook and pen to prove it. Then I panicked, realizing that I had lost my most valuable possession. I put both arms straight out as they dragged us out of the car at gunpoint and searched us, placing both my hands on the car's trunk, spreading my legs, pointing a gun on my body. Finally they realized we really were only journalists. They had not recognized the large sticker on our windshield that the U.S. Army had given to us. Six policemen were on the rooftop of the polling site, one with a .50-caliber gun. The others watched every corner and eyed the neighborhood's roofs. They explained that there were many snipers at night, and for the past five nights they had not slept because they had been guarding the school and had faced constant attacks. "The resistance is very strong here." An occasional trickle of one or two people strolled into the school to vote. Inside, some of the staff wore masks to avoid reprisals as collaborators.

The lonely voters and grim staff were silent, and the mood was funereal. Hala Wahid Ali, the center's director, admitted having received threats but added, "If we don't do this, then who will?" A middle-aged man in a head scarf emerged from the voting room. He explained that most Arabs in the neighborhood did not know who to vote for. He had voted for the Islamic Party, not realizing that they were boycotting the elections.

His companion showed me his clean fingers. "I didn't vote," he said defiantly. Another voter said he supported party number 199, but he could not remember its name.

Rostam was in a jovial mood that night. He and his friends were already celebrating their victory with a glass of Jack Daniels. Rostam reported that the returns meant a 70 percent victory for Kurds in Kirkuk. "Arabs by nature are hateful people," Rostam began again. "They don't like us having nails on our thumbs to scratch our heads and they hate our freedom. The world must know how democracy-loving the Kurds are. We were taking our disabled people on our backs to vote, and the Arabs and Sunnis were shooting at their people going to vote."

Across the country, Shia and Kurdish turnout approached 80 percent, while most Sunnis boycotted. In Samara, a Sunni city of 300,000 north of Baghdad, only 1,400 people voted, and they probably belonged to the city's tiny Shia minority. The new prime minister, Ibrahim al-Jafaari, announced his commitment to a strengthened program of de-Baathification. It was not a warm invitation for Sunnis to participate in Iraqi politics. The Kurds planned for secession, at least in private. "Across Iraq today," said President Bush, "men and women have taken rightful control of their country's destiny, and they have chosen a future of peace and freedom." The resistance knew that it would be too difficult to launch attacks on that day, so they treated it like any other day, striking where they could, killing "only" about one hundred people. Soon after, they resumed their bloodletting.

Nothing really changed for the Iraqis. Three months after the elections an incomplete Iraqi government was sworn in. The Bush administration touted Iraq's Pyrrhic success in adhering to an arbitrary timeline, but the entire American project had long since lost its credibility.

In February, immediately after the election, attacks were back up to sixty a day. Iraqis continued to suffer from gas, benzene, and power shortages, and they continued to live in insecurity.

On Friday, May 6, sixty-seven Iraqis were killed by suicide bombs. Zarqawi's group claimed responsibility. In that first week of May, all told, three hundred Iraqis were killed in attacks.

Police, soldiers, and officials working for or with the new government continued to be assassinated. No one was safe anywhere. The Americans controlled only the spaces where they had soldiers, effectively only the Green Zone (renamed the International Zone) and the military bases scattered throughout the country. Otherwise Iraq belonged to militias, the resistance, terrorists, any man with a gun. The roads leading to Baghdad were a terror zone. The streets of Baghdad were war zones. Two years after the conquest of Iraq, after so many turning points, Iraqis continued to live in a republic of fear.

8

REPUBLIC OF FEAR

- ✦ Approximate number of Iraqis imprisoned by American-led forces, March 2003–January 2006: 50,000
- ✦ Percent of detainees convicted of a crime as of January 2006: less than 2
- ✦ Approximate number of attacks against foreign and Iraqi security forces or Iraqi civilians, 2005: 34,000
- ✦ Total number of such attacks in 2004: 26,496

THE AMERICANS CAME FOR SABAH one Friday night in September. His house in Radwaniya, on the western outskirts of Baghdad, stood in a dry yellow field—a few shrubs and small palm trees growing in an empty yard surrounded by brick walls. I came to visit shortly after the raid, during which the Americans had shot him three times. It was the month of Ramadan, and our mouths were as dry as his yard. The resistance was very active in Radwaniya, and we drove through fields and dry canals to avoid any checkpoints that might reveal to locals that there was a foreigner in their area. Journalists were targets now, as well.

The Americans had come maybe twenty times before, to search for weapons in the house where Sabah lived with his brothers Walid and Hussein, their wives, and their six children. They had always been polite and had thanked them as they were leaving after each search. The family kept the single Kalashnikov it was permitted to own in the living room, and when the Americans came, they knew where to look. "This day they didn't act normally," said Hussein, round and slightly balding and looking very tired. "They were running from all sides of the house. They kicked open the doors. They didn't wait for us to open the doors." There were up to two dozen Americans with more Iraqi National Guardsmen waiting outside. As soon as the Americans came in they hit the brothers with their rifle butts. There were five soldiers on each man. They beat them and kicked them on the floor. Sabah's nose was broken. Walid lay on the floor with a rifle barrel in his mouth. The Iraqi translator who accompanied the Americans told them to pull the trigger and kill Walid, but instead they ripped the gun back out of his mouth, tearing his lips. The family was ordered out. As they walked out of the living room they saw Sabah with his hand on his nose and Walid with blood coming out of his mouth. The Americans had not yet searched the house. The Iraqi translator asked the brothers where "the others" were and cursed at them, threatening to fuck their sisters.

As the terrified family waited outside on the road, they heard three shots from inside. They then heard a scuffle and the soldiers shouting at each other. The Iraqi National Guardsmen attempted to enter the house, but the translator cursed and shouted at them, "Who told you to come in?" Thirty minutes later Walid was dragged into the street and the translator emerged with a picture of Sabah. He asked the huddled family for Sabah's wife and told her, "Your husband was killed by the Americans and he deserved to die." At that he tore the picture before her face.

The family found Sabah's body inside. His bloody shirt showed three bullet holes that went through his chest. Two bullets had come out his back, and they had lodged into the wall behind him. The family also found several pairs of plastic handcuffs. The house had been ransacked. Sofas and beds were overturned and torn apart, the contents of closets were jumbled, tables and vases with their plastic flowers were broken and tossed around. Even the cars had been searched and vandalized. Sabah's pictures had been torn up and his identification card confiscated. One picture remained on his wife's bureau, of Sabah standing proudly in front of his Mercedes.

The next day Radwaniya's men gathered in front of the family's house. Most wore dishdashas and kaffiyehs. Some had brought their children with them. Sabah's lifeless body lay on a carpet, his face and chest lined with crusted blood. He wore sweatpants that matched his bloody shirt. He was partly bald with a thick mustache and a couple of days' growth of beard, his feet were bare and his belly soft. The men rolled him over. Some smoked. They carefully wrapped his body in a blanket. Finally, several of his male relatives began to sob, screeching and wailing, while the other men looked around in uncomfortable silence. One of Sabah's brothers caressed the blanket covering his body. A wooden coffin was brought in and the men put the blanket in it and lifted Sabah's body into it. Ten men carried the coffin out, shouting, *La ilaha il Allah!*—There is no god but Allah—over and over again. They led a procession of hundreds marching through the main road in the bright sun. Relatives kissed the coffin and hit themselves. The coffin was placed in a blue pickup truck and relatives and neighbors sat beside it silently in the truck's bed, the wind blowing their scarves and shirts as they led a convoy of dozens of cars to the Karkh Islamic cemetery, where Sabah's body was buried unwashed, as a martyr's.

Sabah's brother Hussein told me that the day Sabah was killed a roadside bomb had killed several American soldiers. "Why should we pay for this?" he wondered. The family did not want compensation, he told me. "Human life cannot be replaced," he said. "I just want to know the reason. We want an investigation and punishment of the men who did this. Sabah was not a member of the Baath Party or the military. He knew nothing about weapons. He had a shop for construction materials. His life was from here to the shop and from the shop to here. He was in the shop until night every day." Their family was relatively affluent, he said, buying and selling cars. "You know the Iraqi nature," said Hussein, "when you have a wealthy family people hate them, so we think somebody in the neighborhood said we were in the resistance." The family made a filmed report of the incident, documenting Sabah's body and the testimony of witnesses, demanding justice. I asked Hussein if he wanted revenge. "We are Muslim, praise God, and we do not want revenge. He was innocent and he was killed, so he is a martyr."

Two and a half years after the invasion, as another round of elections approached and there was talk in Washington of drawing down U.S. forces, Iraq remained bloody, and the Americans were detested to different degrees by nearly everyone. I was in the country for one last trip prior to the December voting. American forces, with the support of some Iraqi troops, were sweeping the region near the Syrian border yet again. I was in Baghdad, where IED attacks and car bombs remained a daily occurrence.

Hussein's neighbor, several houses down, lived in a smaller house with dry overgrown plants around it. Although it was Ramadan, we all drank tea. Twenty-three-year-old Haidar was an officer in the intelligence section of the Iraqi Ministry of Interior's *marawir*, the SWAT team. Haidar was so thin he looked moribund. His voice and mannerism seemed too gentle for a police officer, especially one dealing in counterterrorism. Haidar had completed the military academy before the war. "After the war they called and said we want the youths to join the intelligence," he said. He had received ten months of training by the U.S. Marines and a South African trainer and since then had participated in numerous operations against terrorists and criminal gangs. I asked him if he was not worried about his safety, since security officers were regularly assassinated. "If we all start worrying about threats nobody will work," he said.

Because of Iraq's history of army-led coups and takeovers, a decision had been made early on to establish a small and weak army and to place the onus of the counterinsurgency battle on the police, who were given a paramilitary capacity. Haidar told me that members of his intelligence unit had infiltrated resistance groups, praying with them and participating in their planning. "Some of the resistance are organized gangs like mafias," he said, who receive money for their operations from outside the country. "They use religion and claim they are the resistance." Haidar stressed that "some of the resistance has good goals. The real resistance won't kill Iraqis. They attack the occupier and they attack them in remote places and don't use civilians as cover." Haidar had commanded a prison for terrorists briefly. Most of his prisoners had been Iraqis and many were from Samara or Mosul. A minority had been foreign. He saw one seventeen-year-old from Yemen who had been captured in Samara after destroying several American Hummers. He also reported that the mosque in Baghdad's Al Nahrain University had been used as a center for kidnappings and killings.

As in the past, and in other Arab countries, the word *dhakhiliya,* or "interior," had come to mean fear for many Iraqis. This time it was mainly for Sunnis, however. I asked Haidar if rumors I had heard about the Ministry of Interior being infiltrated and dominated by members of the Supreme Council for Islamic Revolution in Iraq's Badr Organization militia were true. He agreed and added that Ministry of Interior members affiliated with Badr were assassinating Sunnis throughout Iraq. He added that Sunni officers were being removed and replaced by unknown Shias.

Haidar hoped for an Iraq with no militia above the law and only an official police and army. "The Americans should stay for two years," he told me. "If they leave, there will be a civil war." Unfortunately, a civil war was already raging.

My Iraqi friends were terrified for my safety. They ordered me to avoid anything that was *shash,* slang for something that attracts attention. I traded in my clothes from New York for clothes purchased on Baghdad's Karrada Street. They took me for a haircut and a shave and gave the barber more specific instructions than my wife ever had. "Eat as you like, dress as the people like," as the Iraqi proverb says.

The violence had not improved as the killings continued—ten on one day, one hundred the next day. There were some signs of hope, however. Observing the composition of the new government and the constitutional committee, some Sunni leaders had begun to realize that they might be locking themselves out of Iraq's future. In late March Sheikh Dr. Ahmad Abdul Ghafur al-Samarai, director general of the Sunni Endowment and a former top official in the Association of Muslim Scholars, gave a sermon calling on Iraqi Sunnis to join the military and police as long as they supported their nation and not the occupiers of Iraq. If the "honest and loyal elements" of Iraq, meaning its Sunnis, did not participate, then those who sought to harm the security of the nation, meaning Shias, would dominate the security forces. Al-Samarai later explained that the "real resistance" understood the importance of such a move because they did not want militias ruling Iraq. Sixty-four high-ranking Sunni clerics from throughout the country signed on to al-Samarai's fatwa. When Abu Musab al-Zarqawi later declared war on Shias in a speech, Iraq's radical Sunni leadership reacted quickly to condemn the idea. Five resistance groups—the Army of Muhammad, the al Qaqa Battalions, the Islamic Army of Iraq, the Army of Mujahideen, and the Salehdin Brigades—condemned Zarqawi's statements as well, calling them a "fire burning the Iraqi people" and explaining that the resistance attacked only the occupiers and those who assisted them, and did not base their attacks on sectarian or ethnic criteria.

The problems remained, however. It does not take many violent men to destabilize a large mass of more peaceful people. After these incidents, al Qaeda in Iraq appeared to become more Iraqi. It reconciled with the Association of Muslim Scholars and appointed Iraqis as Zarqawi's deputy, as his spokesman, and as head of the group's fatwa committee.

Militias were everywhere, overlapping with government

forces and controlling the lion's share of Iraqi arms. When Sheikh Muayad of the Abu Hanifa mosque, who had so vehemently condemned the Americans from his pulpit, announced his membership in the Islamic Party and his support for the new Iraqi constitution, he became a wanted man, viewed as a traitor by the resistance and the people of his neighborhood. Protected by the Iraqi National Guard, he left his mosque and moved out of his home.

There were more concrete blast walls and hexon sand boxes than ever in Baghdad. What I noticed first was the increased presence of Iraqi policemen and National Guardsmen on the roads. Many still wore masks to conceal their faces. Often they were laden with armor like their American instructors, and from a distance I had trouble distinguishing them from the Americans. Iraqis had trouble distinguishing them in their behavior as well. Iraqi security forces drove white SUVs and pickup trucks, blasting through traffic, firing warning shots above or at cars in their way, hanging out of the windows aiming their Kalashnikovs menacingly at the population they were meant to protect. No longer were they the docile security forces I had known, content to suffer one suicide attack after another. They had taken the war to the enemy, and the enemy, it often seemed, was the population. I was as scared of them as I had been of the western private security contractors who had trained them to shoot first and ask questions later. They stood in intersections with guns drawn, waiting for an unseen enemy.

The once-aggressive Sunnis of Iraq now felt besieged, on the defensive. For the first time parties had been established that explicitly spoke in the name of a sect. The precedent was set by Adnan al-Dulaymi's Conference of Iraqi Sunnis. Dulaymi was a dean who had taught in Jordan's Al Zarqa University from 1994 until 2002. Zarqa gained renown as the center of Jordan's Salafi movement and the hometown of terrorist al-Zarqawi. Dulaymi returned to Iraq a week after the fall of Baghdad. He was appointed head of the Sunni Religious Endowment but was removed for what he claimed were political reasons, because he was "defending the Sunnis." He formed the Conference of Iraqi Sunnis and was appointed religious advisor to President Jalal Talabani. Dulaymi's Conference described the Iraqi constitution as illegitimate because it sought to partition Iraq. The elderly cleric, who always wore a trademark hat that looked like a black sailor's cap, warned of plots to destroy Iraq and provoke sectarian conflict, coded language for giving Shias and Kurds too much power at the expense of Sunnis. Dulaymi attributed much of the violence to Iraq's neighbors but also blamed the Iraqi state, meaning the Shias who controlled it.

In the past Dulaymi had distinguished between resistance and terrorism. Terrorists shed the blood of innocents, he said, and conducted "unjustified violence and mass killing." Resistance to occupation was legitimate, however, and he criticized the American occupier for targeting Sunni cities, with the support of Shias, in order to prevent the political participation of Sunnis. Dulaymi repeatedly warned of malice directed against Iraq's Sunnis, who he claimed were 60 percent of the population.

Dulaymi had formed his conference to unite Sunnis under "one umbrella" and encourage their political participation. His party established a newspaper called *Al I'tisam,* which means "holding fast." I met with Dulaymi's deputy, Sheikh Imad Muhamad Ali, who had been working with Dulaymi since September 2004. Sheikh Imad was originally from Diyala and had a master's degree in Islamic law. He had formerly led the Salafi Tawhid Mosque in Baghdad's Dora district and was a member of the Association of Muslim Scholars. He explained to me that although the AMS was not participating in the December elections, they were also not proscribing participation. "The people should participate in the elections in full," he told me. "The Iraqi situation is very difficult and the only way to solve it is through political participation." I asked him what specific steps could be taken to establish peace and security in Iraq. "First, end the occupation," he said; "second, establish the former Iraqi Army; third, dissolve the militias; fourth, close all borders and maintain them, especially with Iran and Syria."

I asked the sheikh if he wanted an immediate American withdrawal. "The occupation should not end today," he said. "They should leave with a schedule. Before they withdraw they should reestablish the original Iraqi Army. The new army is just militias and should return to their parties. The American Army should leave the cities and move to bases outside the cities, and during this period the Iraqi army should be given new arms and equipment and an agreement should be made for gradual withdrawal. It should take a year and a half. This depends on the presence of a strong government with full sovereignty, not a government whose members have to enter the Green Zone with IDs from the Americans granting them permission. If this does not happen, then there must be negotiations between the resistance and the Americans."

I asked him how the Americans could find resistance leaders to negotiate with. "The resistance is here," he said with a smile. "They are not ghosts. They are Iraqi and they are heroes. My advice to the resistance is that they should consider negotiating with the Americans." I pressed him again on who the Americans should negotiate with. "They have representatives," he said. "Who? You?" I asked. He smiled and laughed, nearly winking at me. "Do you want me to have trouble? I'll have to run away if I say that!" I asked if he thought the resistance would consent to negotiations. "I hope the resistance will agree," he said and then smiled. "If I was a resister, I would agree." He added, "The Iraqi resistance wants a free Iraq and to return security to Iraq, but there must be a day that the Americans plan on leaving Iraq and the resistance should consider negotiations." Before he walked me to my car and warned my driver to take care of me, because these were dangerous times, Sheikh Imad again asked me not to write that he was the resistance's representative, because he feared the Americans would come and get him to "negotiate."

I returned to Sadr City to see just who was still influential there. A few days before an Irish journalist writing for the British newspaper *The Guardian* was kidnapped in Sadr City by members of Moqtada's Mahdi Army militia who hoped to trade him for the release of their militiamen held in the south by the British. I arranged to meet Fatah Abu Yaqin al-Sheikh, editor of the Sadrist newspaper *Ishraqat al-Sadr* and a member of the National Assembly representing Sadr City, in his office in the entrance to the Shia bastion. Downstairs in the broken-down three-story building men were hard at work welding immense signs for Moqtada's movement. One sign showed the shrine of Imam Kadhim with Moqtada and his father and uncle (the First and Second Martyrs). Black-clad and masked soldiers of the Army of the Mahdi marched, looking eerily like Saddam's Fedayeen, and Iraqis were shown screaming and crying. "God accept this sacrifice from us and protect Iraq and its people," it said.

Fatah showed up with two pickup trucks full of militiamen protecting him. Some had little swords hanging from their guns, representing Dhulfiqar, the fabled sword of Ali. Fatah was widely rumored in Sadr City to be a former Baathist agent himself. He had owned a haberdashery before the war and remained fastidiously shaved and groomed. After the war he had established a newspaper that spoke for Moqtada, and by 2004 he had become the strongman for Sadr City, charging journalists entry fees and intimidating those who refused. Fatah had run as an unofficial candidate in the January elections that Moqtada had refused to boycott or support, and the seat he won represented thirty thousand Iraqis. Fatah had named his two-year-old son Moqtada, and his sparse office was decorated with pictures of himself with the radical cleric as well as the ubiquitous plastic flowers. "Oh infidels, I don't worship what you worship" read one poster of Moqtada, who was waving a finger as armed fighters stood beside him. Behind him on the wall was an Iraqi flag. Moqtada had recently appointed him as his representative for the Anbar province.

Soon after his election Fatah had gotten into a scuffle with

American soldiers guarding the Green Zone, and he had used it for its publicity value. Still, he too did not want an immediate U.S. withdrawal. "I reject their military presence, but we need their expertise," he said. "We have to end the occupation, but they have to leave gradually, not all at once. When the Iraqis build a battalion the Americans should withdraw a battalion. If they leave all at once we will be back to April ninth [i.e., postwar chaos and looting]." Fatah was proud of the anti-American stance the Sadriyun had taken. "People expected Shias to welcome the Americans," he said, but the "two famous intifadas," as he referred to the Sadr uprisings of the spring and summer of 2004, proved them wrong.

Like all Sadrists, Fatah was suspicious of Iran. "Iran is a threat to the whole area, not only Iraq. Iran and America are now fighting over Iraq. If America leaves, then Iran will occupy Iraq."

Unlike other clerical Sadrists I had met, Fatah was not interested in a government run by the clergy. "The government has to provide justice for the Iraqi people," he said. "It doesn't have to have men with beards or turbans. I am with the government that provides justice, even if it is secular, and against an unjust government, even if it is Islamic. Seyid Sadr wants to preserve Islam and preserve it from the dirty details of parliament. A government of justice is most important. There is no Islamic government in the world today. People say Iran is an Islamic government, but no government until now can say they are. Only the Imam Mahdi will make the Islamic government. The Imam Mahdi is the leader of the Army of the Mahdi, not Moqtada."

Fatah gave me copies of his newspaper, which was now far more professional than when I had first purchased it eighteen months before. I found a news item with his picture on it on the front page of nearly every issue. "I'm like a new dictator," he laughed. I looked at the headlines of *Ishraqat,* which means "sunrises." "Revenge . . . Revenge," said one. "Every nation's blood is from the tears of the martyrs of the Mujahid Sadr

City." Another headline quoted Moqtada: "America fights Islam and nothing else. I don't believe the occupier will leave," and the story explained that "His eminence said this during an open speech with the sons of Iraq and Iraqi government officials and members of a grouping of Iraqi nationalists. He confirmed that America came to combat Islam and that the Iraqi people reject the occupation and dictatorship."

Fatah took me to Moqtada's local office in Sadr City, which had taken over the Friday prayers from the Muhsin mosque. Tens of thousands still filled the streets every day in an ocean of people rising and bowing in unison.

On the walls of the Sadr office I found announcements exhorting the people to support the Shias, plant trees, and preserve the grass. A nearby shop sold stickers for children's schoolbooks with spaces for the child's name, class, school, and address. They had bright colors and flowers and each depicted Moqtada in a way I had previously not seen. He was smiling, friendly, even embracing children. Each sticker contained one of Moqtada's aphorisms, such as "If the teacher is good, then certainly the student will be good." The shop also sold keychains with Moqtada, his father, and his uncle framed by hearts. Stickers for cars depicted Moqtada and his fighters in various natural settings. Some were in the deserts of the American Southwest, others in lush jungle paradises, and one was on an ocean, with two crescent moons in the sky (perhaps Moqtada was on a different planet). Locals with expensive mobile phones could watch a film entitled *They Should Face Us If They Have the Courage,* which depicts the Army of the Mahdi in various battles during the Sadr uprisings. As I parted from him Fatah asked my driver if he wanted to take a pistol or Kalashnikov for my safety, and offered to arrange a weapons license for me. He was very concerned for my safety, but the only danger on the street were the ubiquitous little boys playing with large toy Kalashnikovs that shoot small plastic pellets. Throughout my time in Baghdad I did not see a single Iraqi boy on the streets who did not own one of these rifles.

I saw boys scampering through the streets of Amriya wielding these same toy Kalashnikovs when I joined a friend for *iftar,* the meal to break the Ramadan fast, and waited for Sheikh Hussein of the Maluki mosque to arrive. Amriya had been the location of many sectarian killings in recent months, 150 according to locals, and most of the victims had been Shias. Shias had been warned to leave the neighborhood. Sitting with my friend Hassan and his father, Abu Mustafa, they recounted how Hassan had been shot in the belly for working with the Ministry of Defense. Hassan's long-time Shia neighbor had been shot on the street near the neighborhood school by men bearing Kalashnikovs in a drive-by shooting. There was no apparent motive other than to intimidate local Shias. Sunni groups had been established specifically to kill Shias, and they had been successful throughout the country. They had targeted a bus-and-taxi depot taking people to Amarra and Nasiriya, Shia towns in the south. They had exploded car bombs in the predominantly Shia-owned shops of the Karada neighborhood. In Amriya, their attacks had also gone astray, and in a nearby house nine of Hassan's neighbors had been killed when a mortar shot by the resistance missed the military base it was targeting and landed on them instead.

Unlike Sunni assassins who targeted the general Shia population, gangs of Shia killers, suspected to belong to the Badr organization or the Army of the Mahdi, most often targeted radical Sunni clerics or former Baathists suspected of supporting the resistance. My old friend Sheikh Hussein, a Salafi himself with clear links to the resistance that dominated Amriya— even manning checkpoints—had nearly been assassinated by Shia Badr militiamen belonging to the Ministry of Interior who had arrived at his home in a police car. He had narrowly avoided them by hiding, and only recently had emerged. I noticed that his significant girth had increased and assumed he was well fed while in hiding. He said, "We are all targets today." Sheikh Hussein supported Sunni participation in the upcoming elections.

Sheikh Hussein was also a member of the Association of Muslim Scholars, and like many of its members, his attitude toward political participation appeared to have become markedly more flexible. On Friday, October 15, I drove into the association's headquarters, the Um al Qura Mosque, past a shepherd tending his large flock of sheep; past the Iraqi National Guardsmen, who were Shia, lazily watching the mosque; and past the many armed security men protecting its gates. We were patted down as we entered the mosque.

That day hundreds of men strolled in to pray and hear Dr. Mahmud al-Sumaidai's sermon. Sumaidai was one of the association's spokesmen. He warned of following clerics who were too radical. "People manipulate the meaning of the Quran as they want," he said, "and we suffer from this now. We should follow our imams and listen to their sermons, but we should not be against the religion. There is no obedience to a leader who leads to sin." It was all very oblique, but the audience understood what he meant clearly. "I am now talking to the people who want to lead this country," he continued. "They should put Islam in front of their eyes. They should put Iraq in front of their eyes. The policies of sectarianism and exclusion of parts of the Iraqi people have failed." He meant that Sunnis had been excluded from Iraqi politics, but he failed to mention that they had excluded themselves, so that he could later on urge them to participate. "They should not distinguish between one sect and another," he continued. "You should participate in the elections. A full participation so we can preserve Iraq's mosques and our scholars and our families." He added that this would prevent any one Iraqi sect, and he meant the Shias, from controlling the others, meaning the Sunnis. He continued that "all Iraqis should stand against our enemies, telling them to go out of our country! Go out of our country!" He addressed the American enemies, telling them, "You remained here with the agreement of your 'tails' in this country," an insult directed at the Shias, and continued, "For all my brothers, the Iraqi Muslims, your vote is very important, so you should be careful in giving it to a man who has integrity. He believes in Islam; he should be a patriot and just, and you should not vote for a man who wants to give the government to a certain sect. If you vote for a man, and this man destroys the country and spreads corruption, then you will be his partner in all of this. So I will see you, my brothers, on election day, gathering and giving your vote to the person who deserves it." Sumaidai asked God to stop the oppression and the people who are making it, and to defeat the infidels and terminate the killers. He asked God to provide them with trustworthy people and believers to lead the country and to find a man who would lead them on "the road of belief and the road of Muhammad and lead us to safety after destruction and instability."

It was the first Friday after Ramadan, and Sumaidai had spent most of his sermon urging his flock not to be devout merely on Ramadan, but to continue on the path of piety all year long. It was time to celebrate Eid, the end of Ramadan. I was tired of my friends restricting our excursions out of fear for my safety, and demanded that we return to al-Rubai Street, where eighteen months earlier a police officer had been assassinated in front of me. The street was now closed so that families could congregate in its shops and stroll undisturbed. Hundreds of policemen stood guard and mingled with the crowds. They found a child who had been separated from his parents and had them paged on loudspeakers. Children squealed in an ancient amusement park. Young boys with drums danced and sang. They set off loud firecrackers, and I winced with each burst, uncertain of what would follow.

The United Iraqi Alliance (UIA), the dominant Shia list known as 555 for its number on the ballot, swept Iraqi elections on December 15, 2005, but still needed to ally with either Sunni or Kurdish parties to form an absolute majority that would allow it to establish a government. SCIRI favored an alliance with the federalist Kurds, opposing any deals with the Sunnis, and offered one of its own for the position of prime minister. Moqtada supported the incumbent prime minister, Jafaari of Dawa, for the position, and also favored an alliance with the Sunni Islamist parties. He opposed the more secular, former Baathist parties, calling the participation of Ayad Allawi a deal breaker. Moqtada even criticized SCIRI for negotiating with the Kurds, but at least for now the battles were still political. Allawi and his party were hated by Moqtada's men both for having former Baathists in their ranks and because Allawi had asked the Americans to battle Moqtada in the spring and summer of 2004. Moqtada preferred talking with the Sunni Iraqi Islamic Party and the Iraqi Accord Front.

Other divisions in the UIA began to show when SCIRI's Abdel Aziz al-Hakim publicly ruled out making changes to the constitution, infuriating the Sunnis and increasing sectarian tensions. Moqtada, a dangerous thug, was now the only bridge between Iraq's Shias and Sunnis. He may have opposed the Baathists, but he had established an excellent working relationship with radical Sunnis since the fall of Baghdad, and like them he demanded a centralized Iraq, perhaps in part because he had so much support in Baghdad. Once the most divisive figure in Iraqi politics, Moqtada had become the only one capable of halting the civil war. The choice seemed to be between civil war and a government of radical Islamists.

Iraq's Shias were triumphant, knowing that Iraq was now theirs and could not be taken away from them (except by the Americans). There was no threat of Sunnis retaking the country, because they had never taken it before; they had been given it, first by the Ottomans and then by the British. Iraq's Sunnis view all Shias as Iranians or Persians and refuse to recognize that Shias are the majority or that Shias had been singled out for persecution under Saddam.

Attacks against Shia civilians have done nothing to weaken their increasing power in Iraq, validated by the January 2005 elections. Throughout the region sectarian tensions have begun to increase. Sunnis in Jordan and Saudi Arabia are threatened by the Shia renaissance in Iraq. In December 2004,

Jordan's King Abdallah warned of a "Shia crescent" from Lebanon to Iraq to Iran that would destabilize the entire region. Iraq's Shias, in turn, have demonstrated against Jordan, condemning that country for the steady trickle of suicide bombers who cross into Iraq and commit atrocities against Shia civilians.

In September 2005, Saudi Foreign Minister Saud al-Faisal warned that a civil war in Iraq would destabilize the entire region and complained that the Americans had handed Iraq over to Iran for no reason. In response, Bayan Jabr, Iraq's interior minister, called the Saudi foreign minister a "Bedouin riding a camel" and described Saudi Arabia as a one-family dictatorship. Jabr, who had commanded the Badr Corps, also condemned Saudi human rights abuses, particularly the repression of Saudi Arabia's approximately 2 million Shias and Saudi Arabia's treatment of its women.

In Saudi Arabia, home of Wahhabi Islam, Shias are known as *rafida,* or "rejectionists." A highly pejorative term, it means that Shias are outside Islam. To Shias it is the equivalent of being called "nigger." Zarqawi uses the word to describe Shias, as do many other Sunni radicals in the region. Saudi Arabia's Shias have been persecuted, prevented from celebrating their festivals, and occasionally threatened with extermination. Saudi Arabia is also the main exporter of foreign fighters to the Iraqi jihad to fight both the Americans and the Shia "collaborators."

As in the Iran-Iraq War of the 1980s, a regional sectarian war is being fought in Iraq, with Jordan and Saudi Arabia providing support for Sunni violence in order to give Iraq's Sunnis more political leverage. Iran, of course, is supporting its client SCIRI, perhaps even funding it, as SCIRI wages war against Sunnis.

It is all to Moqtada's advantage. He was invited by SCIRI to join the UIA in the December 15, 2005, elections for the National Assembly. Moqtada was thereby granted equal status with other parties. He is legitimate now, no longer on the outside. Moqtada and his followers were already fierce enemies of the Kurds, condemning their autonomy and clashing with them in the north, where many Shia Turkmen were aligned with Moqtada. There can be no peace with men like this in positions of power in Iraq.

My last night I sat with my friends in Sandra, my favorite fresh fruit juice and ice cream place, happy that the owner still recognized me and remembered my usual drink, a strawberry and banana milkshake. One friend, a Sunni, confided to me that things had been much better under Saddam. Another friend was annoyed that Iraqis could be celebrating Eid and ignoring the horror around them. Yet, he said, "They could level all of Baghdad and it would still be better than Saddam. At least we have hope."

A few weeks later the same friend e-mailed me in despair: "I'm living here in the middle of shit, a civil war will happen I'm sure of it. . . . You can't be comfortable talking with a man until you know if he is Shia or Sunni. . . . People don't trust each other. . . . To be clear, now Shia are Iranians for the Sunni, and Sunni are Salafi terrorists for the Shia. We have a civil war here; it is only a matter of time, and some peppers to provoke it."

AFTERWORD

IN APRIL 2003 I MOVED into Baghdad's upscale Mansur district, where I lived with other journalists in a house that had a small swimming pool. I sat at the pool every night and watched bats swoop down from palm trees to sip the water or catch insects. In the distance I could hear the chatter of automatic weapons, as the anarchy that began with the American occupation turned violent. I would walk home from the main street, which by May of that year was already bustling again, as new businesses and restaurants opened. The house had one somnolent guard, armed with a Kalashnikov to protect against robbery, at night. That first month, there were still impromptu gun markets on street corners, and not far from my house I could have purchased a rocket-propelled grenade launcher for fifty dollars as well as a machine gun for a similar price. As the occupation persisted I stayed in less luxurious accommodations but often visited Mansur, and in April 2006, as I was driving through the district's main shopping drag, I passed two bullet-riddled corpses in the middle of the road.

In October 2007 I once again moved to Mansur. This time I lived in an ostentatious mansion obscenely decorated with every style imaginable, from Baroque to Arabic, with kitsch being the only unifying factor. The house had belonged to a Baathist before Westerners rented it. In the first three years of the occupation, Mansur was teeming with middle- and upper-class shoppers sampling from the expensive clothing and shoe boutiques, appliance stores, fresh juice bars, and the famous Al Rawad ice cream shop. Thursday evenings were the busiest. Now the shops that lined the long streets were shuttered closed all day and night. The wide boulevards were patrolled by equally unpredictable bony stray dogs and Iraqi security forces. The Mahdi Army and al Qaeda were said to control various parts of Mansur. As in other cities that had gone through civil wars, such as Beirut and Mogadishu, the posh central areas were devastated and new centers were built in the periphery, in this case in the Sunni and Shiite areas. One month later when I returned, the lower half of Mansur, which was under Shiite influence, was bustling once again. The upper part, still said to be in the hands of al Qaeda, was deserted. Sunni Iraqi soldiers stood watch, but they too were afraid.

While I was in Baghdad several controversies were distracting the media. Blackwater, the private security company, had once again massacred Iraqi civilians while guarding American diplomats. Private security companies, accused of brutality, lawlessness, and subversion of the American mission, became the latest scapegoat for the American failure in Iraq. It was forgotten that since April 2003 hundreds of thousands of American and British soldiers had participated in the country's occupation, that American soldiers regularly opened fire on innocent Iraqis, killing them. The Iraqi government attempted to ban Blackwater from Iraq, but it was overridden or ignored by the American occupiers.

Turkey meanwhile was enraged that its Kurdish separatist group, the PKK, had a fortified base in the mountains of Iraqi Kurdistan and that PKK fighters were crossing the border into Iraqi Kurdistan to rest and to go to the Makhmur refugee camp, where they recruited or visited relatives. Many Iraqi Kurdish militiamen from Masud Barzani's Democratic Party of Kurdistan had also fought with the PKK. Some of them now worked for private security companies. As Turkey threatened to invade Iraq, the Americans who had invaded in 2003, on the false pretext that a threat emanated from Iraq, warned that a Turkish invasion would provoke instability. Instead the Iraqi prime minister Nuri al Maliki and his government promised the Turks that they would put an end to the PKK. But the Iraqi government has no authority in Kurdistan. In Erbil, Suleimaniya, and other Kurdish cities there is no sign of the Iraqi state, no Iraqi flag, and no Arabic language. The border between Kurdistan and the rest of Iraq is treated by the Kurds with the same vigilance as an international border. But it is unlikely that even Iraq's Kurds could easily dislodge the PKK, which had firmly ensconced itself in remote mountains expecting the Americans to evict it since 2003.

While the American military touted the success of the "surge" and the American media dutifully parroted this, if indeed violence had gone down in Baghdad, it was not a sign of success. The violence in Iraq was never senseless. It was logical and teleological, and like war, it was about politics through other means. In Baghdad and other cities, Sunnis were removing Shiites and Shiites were removing Sunnis. Christians and Kurds were also victimized in some places. Violence between Iraqis had decreased only because there were fewer people to kill. The division of Iraq into ethnic or sectarian homogenous zones had nearly been completed. Militias had begun to consolidate control over neighborhoods and had been successful in killing or expelling all unwanted groups. As a result there were up to two million Iraqi refugees in Syria and one million Iraqi refugees in Jordan alone.

In October 2007 some Sunnis still lived in Rusafa, or east Baghdad, in the neighborhoods of Fadil, Zayuna, Baghdad Jadida, Sinaa, Karada, Waziriya, Adhamiya, Shaab, Kahera, Hai Tijar, Jisr Diyala, Nahrawan, and Sleikh while west Baghdad, or Karkh, had Shiites remaining in Alawi Hilla, Rahmania, Shawakeh, Karaimat, il Fahameh, il Aitaifiya, Kadhimiya, Shalchiyeh, Tochi, Iskan, Washash, Harthiya, and Mansur. Though Sunnis had traditionally dominated Karkh, Shiite militias now controlled most of it, and the only true Sunni strongholds remaining were Amriya, Hai Jamia, Khadhra, Mansur, Nafaq al Shurta, and Ghazaliya. Shiites were still being expelled from Abu Ghraib in western Baghdad as well as Ghazaliya, Mansur, Dora, Sahat al Talaya, Sheikh Ali, and Mushahada. Sunnis were still being expelled from Shuula, Dora, al Iskan, Washash, Tobchi, and Palestine Street.

Moqtada al-Sadr had officially imposed a cease-fire on his militia, the Mahdi Army, but only to disassociate himself publicly from what he, along with the other main Shiite Islamist sectarian political parties that dominated the Iraqi government, privately supported: the removal of Sunnis from Baghdad. The Mahdi Army dominated Baghdad. Sunnis were hunted not only by Shiites in and out of the government, but their battles with al Qaeda had weakened them and made them vulnerable on two fronts. The Mahdi Army, never very disciplined or hierarchical, had descended into localized gangs, and even if ordered to cease fighting by Moqtada, it would be unlikely to heed his orders. Instead, Moqtada was merely a symbol for the warlords who fought in his name. Sheikh Raad Hamid Eissa and his assistant Abu Tufuf led the Mahdi Army's office in Kadhamiya, which controlled the militiamen fighting in Shuula and Ghazaliya as well and planned attacks against the Americans in parts of western Baghdad. Sheikh Raad and Abu Tufuf held meetings in a house behind the Baghdad Department of Health in Kadhamiya, and Raad, who is sought after by the American military, drives a white Toyota. In Washash, a neighborhood close to Mansur, Sheikh Hakam Abu Ali led the Mahdi Army. While I was in Baghdad, Hakam executed two Shiites because they belonged to the Iraqi National Guard. Hakam, who had just been appointed to his position in mid-October, viewed the Americans as his primary target. In Iskan, also close to Mansur, Ahmad Khazal led the Mahdi Army. He lived behind a school in that area and had been appointed when his predecessor, Hamudi Naji, had been killed by a suicide motorcycle attack.

Moqtada appointed Sheikh Abbas al Kufi to investigate the

misdeeds of Mahdi Army members. Kufi was head of "special groups" for the Mahdi Army, which acted as bodyguards for Moqtada, protected holy sites, and conducted investigations. Kufi appointed Sheikh Ahmad Kamel Yaaqubi as head of the "Golden Group," another special unit of the Mahdi Army. Yaaqubi had been trained in Iran by the Revolutionary Guard, and had visited Mecca with Moqtada for the Hajj pilgrimage. Abbas al Kufi had recently killed thirty-three Mahdi Army leaders. He had tried to persuade Moqtada to disband the Mahdi Army and establish a new militia called Jeish al Tahrir, or the Army of Liberation, which would focus on fighting the Americans. Moqtada had refused, explaining that the Mahdi Army had done a lot for Shiites.

Shiite militiamen knew that the only obstruction on the road to full control over Iraq was the American occupation. It took the Americans longer to realize that they had tried to play sectarian politics and lost, betting that the "good" Shiites would cooperate against the "bad" Sunnis. They had not counted on Shiite recalcitrance to cooperate fully. As a result, and because of fear of Iran and pressure from "moderate" Sunni allies in the region, the Americans were backing the creation of Sunni militias. It was a temporarily expedient measure. It had indeed reduced the level of attacks against the Americans and their allies in the coalition and the private security companies that guarded their convoys. But the creation of more warlords only guaranteed that Iraq would never exist as a state and promoted the same fissiparous tendencies that caused the civil war. At the most cynical level, instead of allowing for a winner in the civil war, it would prolong the fighting and resembled the American dual-containment strategy of the 1980s. The United States now backed the Shiite government in Baghdad and its Shiite militia-dominated security forces, while also backing Sunni militias whose ultimate ambition was to receive funding, weapons, and other assistance from the Americans so they could fight the Shiites. Such was the case of Abu Risha, a member of the Sunni resistance who used to attack

American convoys for his own profit, thus alienating the resistance. After al Qaeda killed his relatives he went to war against them. The Americans and other tribes invented a title for him and the fiction that he was a leader, and he led the main Sunni militia in the Anbar province until he was assassinated.

Elsewhere the Sunni militias had imposed a reign of terror on their neighborhoods. In Amriya, a western Baghdad neighborhood long since emptied of Shiites and controlled by militias, during the last high school examinations, Sunni students came, many with their parents, to take their tests. Three gunmen entered the high school and kidnapped two students. They beheaded one and sent the other one back within an hour with a warning that this was the fate of those who crossed al Qaeda. Then another militia showed up, this one belonging to the Islamic Party. Its members rounded up all the students and led them to the yard, shooting into the air, separating the females from the males, and threatening to kill the males. Many parents, including mothers, were waiting outside for their children. The brother of the beheaded student led the militiamen and told the terrified students that they would be killed because they had done nothing when the al Qaeda kidnappers took his brother. Then the powerful Sheikh Abdallah Janabi showed up with his militia. Janabi, also known as Abu Muhamad, had led the mujahideen in Falluja. He ordered the men not to kill other Sunnis. Janabi had previously collaborated with al Qaeda.

At the same time some of the mothers called the Iraqi National Guard, who showed up before Janabi's militia blocked the walls that surrounded Amriya. Janabi told the National Guard to wait outside. The guard agreed and offered to help should it be needed. Janabi told the Islamic Party to give him some time, and its members also agreed. His men soon returned with eight al Qaeda members, the men who had beheaded the student. The al Qaeda men explained that the boys had been writing anti–al Qaeda slogans on walls and that one of them had a brother in the Islamic Party, so they had to make an example. Janabi told them that he would make an example of them. They were executed and then hung in front of the school and all the people gathered there.

The Islamic Party fought with al Qaeda in Amriya and pushed al Qaeda out. The two groups also battled in the volatile Dora district, but neither al Qaeda nor the Islamic Party, led by Sheikh Ali Juneid, could succeed in defeating the other. Meanwhile Sunnis were still persecuted by Shiite militias as well, and the Mahdi Army stopped a bus in Seidiya, pulling out three Sunni girls and executing them for not wearing the hijab.

Another alternative the Americans were hoping to provide to the Shiite militiamen who dominated Iraq was Ayad Allawi, the former Baathist and CIA collaborator who was appointed interim prime minister until the elections of 2005. Allawi was said to have been engaged in numerous meetings with former Baathists in Jordan, London, and Lebanon. He was now trying to rebuild the Baath Party with the backing of Iraqi politicians such as Adnan al Dulaimi and Tariq al Hashimi, and allegedly even had the support of the KDP's Masud Barzani. Adnan Janabi and the former minister of interior Falah al Naqib assisted Allawi. He wanted to lead the party just as Saddam had.

TALK OF A COUP TO replace Prime Minister Maliki failed to understand that Maliki was irrelevant anyway. Gone were the days when Baghdad was the only major city in Iraq and whoever controlled Baghdad controlled the country. Now Iraq was a collection of city-states: Basra, Amarra, Ramadi, Kirkuk, Mosul, Erbil, Suleimaniya, and others, each independent of the other. Maliki may well be the last prime minister of Iraq. They cannot run elections in Iraq anymore. When he is run out there will be no new elections, and the pretense of an Iraqi state will be over.

It has become popular with former supporters of the war, including Thomas Friedman of the *New York Times* and Democratic presidential candidates Barak Obama and Hillary Clinton, to blame the Iraqis for the American failure. The Iraqis did not choose democracy or Iraqis did not choose freedom, Americans like to say now. The Iraqis have to decide to stop killing each other, they like to say. Or Iraqis have to step up. These statements are dishonest and misplace the blame. Sunni and Shiite Iraqis were protesting the American occupation as soon as it began, demanding elections and sovereignty. I saw the demonstrations along with other journalists. We the Americans ignored their demands and imposed a dictator, Paul Bremmer, on them, hoping he would pave the way for the right Iraqi strongman to rule in our stead. Iraq is not Rwanda, where Hutus and Tutsis slaughtered each other and America could pretend it had no role. Iraq had no history of civil war or sectarian violence until the Americans arrived. America caused the civil war.

The flow of fighters into Iraq and of millions of refugees out of Iraq, the smuggling of weapons and even sheep, and the export of dangerous ideas such as sectarianism and jihadism demonstrate that the Iraqi civil war has become a regional conflict formation, which, according to Barnett Rubin and Andrea Armstrong of New York University's Center on International Cooperation, is a set "of transnational conflicts that form mutually reinforcing linkages with each other throughout a region, making for more protracted and obdurate conflicts. . . . Networks of armed groups, traders, leaders, and states within a region use violence to achieve political, ideological, and economic goals. They often capitalize on social relationships that extend influence across borders and operate within the territory of a failed state without reference to legal authorities. Certain cross-border groups, such as traders engaged in smuggling, who facilitate conflict in some circumstances may seek and promote the stability needed for state reconstruction in others." Elements of regional conflict formations also include "the involvement of neighboring states, to the alliances of armed groups, to the operation of the transnational informal economy." Rubin and Armstrong warned, "The collapse of some states within a region accelerates the regional spread of conflict."

I met Barnett Rubin, an expert on Afghanistan, in his NYU office. "Iraq under Saddam created a kind of balance," he told me. "It existed as a strong Sunni state that controlled its borders and acted as a separator between different regions. It kept Iran away from Shiite populations in the Gulf, it created more security in Turkey because Kurdish guerrillas did not have a secure foreign sanctuary, and you had a system of Arab states, all Sunni dictatorships, based on inheritance. Then we destroyed this state, dismantled the army, destroyed the bureaucracy. Then you wonder why people join ethnic militias." The situation in Iraq reminded Rubin of Afghanistan, where the arming of militias prevented the establishment of a government and led to foreign sponsorship of the militias.

The surge was merely a way to kick the problem of Iraq down to the next administration, but the truth is American soldiers will never leave Iraq. The large bases in the Anbar province such as al Asad and Taqadum are built to last. They will be "an enduring presence," as one marine officer told me. Located in the remote desert, impregnable, and only occasionally targeted by mortars, these bases will remain for decades, but the Americans may eventually withdraw from Iraq's urban areas. Any real withdrawal from Iraq, through the treacherous roads of the Anbar to Jordan, through the south past Shiite militias on the way to Kuwait, or even through the so-called Sunni triangle, Samarra, Tikrit or Mosul to Kurdistan or Turkey, would be a withdrawal under fire. There is only ignominy left for the Americans and slaughter for the Iraqis. Iraq has been killed, never to rise again. The American occupation has been as disastrous as the Mongols' raid on Baghdad in the thirteenth century. Iraq's human capital—all its intellectuals, professionals, the educated, the moneyed classes, the political elite—has fled. These people will not return. Instead of creating a neoconservative utopia with a flat tax, a peace agreement with Israel, and Ahmed Challabi as the benign dictator, we have betrayed the hopes of all Iraqis who wanted a new start after Saddam, without Baathists or Americans. Only fools spoke of "solutions." There was no solution, and the only hope was that perhaps at least Iraq could be contained. In late 2007, thanks to the Mahdi Army's temporary freeze and the rise of Sunni militias, Iraqis began to cautiously reemerge in Baghdad, but it remained to be seen if this was a mere lull in the fighting or a glimmer of hope for the first time since 2003.

GLOSSARY

amir One who gives orders, a commander or a prince.

awar al dajal The blind giant, akin to a Muslim Antichrist.

dinar The Iraqi currency. In the 1980s one dinar was worth three dollars. In April 2003 one dollar was worth three thousand dinars. It has since stabilized and one dollar is now worth about fourteen hundred dinars.

dishdasha The long gown traditionally worn by Arab men.

diwan A traditional meeting hall or guest room.

ebaya The long black cloak worn by Muslim Iraqi women, especially Shias, that covers the head and body, leaving an opening for the face. Also known as *chador.*

fadil Generous.

faqih A religious jurisprudent.

faudha Chaos, the perpetual state in postwar Iraq.

Fedayeen "Those Who Sacrifice Themselves"—a militia established by Saddam.

fitna Internal strife, a condition Islam eschews.

Fudala "The Generous Ones"—a political movement founded by Ayatollah Muhammad al-Yaqubi.

hawza "Circles of learning"—the Shia seminary based in Najaf.

hawza natiqa The outspoken or politically active *hawza.*

hawza samita The silent and politically docile *hawza;* a disparaging term.

ihtilal Occupation.

intiqam Revenge, a main motivator for the resistance.

kaffiyeh The head scarf, often checkered, worn by traditional Arab men.

Kalashnikov The most common weapon in Iraq.

khutba The sermon given at the Friday noon prayer.

maku "There is no . . ." —the most common refrain in postwar Iraq.

manbar The seat of the cleric in the mosque.

marja A Shia cleric who can issue religious verdicts on matters of jurisprudence and who is to be emulated by his followers.

mu'dhin The man who calls others to prayer from a mosque.

mujahid A holy warrior.

mujahideen Holy warriors.

muqawama Resistance.

peshmerga "Those who face death"—Kurdish guerrillas.

sahel An Iraqi dialect word referring to the act of dragging a corpse in public.

shaqi An Iraqi tough guy. *Shaqis* would go on to lead resistance units.

Sharia Islamic law.

tahrir Liberation.

ACKNOWLEDGMENTS

I COULD NOT HAVE GOTTEN TO IRAQ, nor remained there, nor succeeded as a writer, without the help of so many people I cannot remember most of them. I owe a debt to Scott Armstrong, who ignored my mother's plea not to help me to go to Iraq and was a second father to me. My mother was a tireless supporter and it is thanks to her efforts that I am where I am now. My brothers were always loyal friends and challenged me to prove every assertion. Howard Chua Eon believed in me and gave me the chance to fulfill my ambitions. Chris Varhola, Glenn Schweitzer, and Jacek Orzol were generous friends. My family around the world gave me sanctuary when I needed it; I thank them all: Ahmad, Nick, Marko and the Theroses, Amer, Matt, Cinar, my close friends who helped me so much. Sy Hersh, David Remnick, Sharon Delano, Gerry Marzorati, Scott Malcomson, Peter Bergen, Tony Karon, Andrew Meier (whose idea this was), Lourdes Lopez (my tireless agent). Thanks to Mark Levine, Juan Cole, Amazia Baram (who was essential with background on Falluja), Joost Hiltermann, David Patel, As'ad Abu Khalil, Robert Pelton. Thanks also to Steve Clemons and Sherle Schwenninger of the New America Foundation for supporting my work. Thanks to the Lombardi family for their generosity. I must have driven my editor Bruce Nichols insane, and I apologize and am forever grateful for his patience and the opportunity he and Free Press gave me. To the many people who helped me, housed me, and cared for me along the way. To my parents and brothers, I'm sorry I abandoned you and caused you such great worry. To the memory of my friends who died in Iraq's violence. To my friend Meitham, I owe my success and my life to your efforts. To my wife, Tiffany, my best friend and soul mate, it was all worth it.

INDEX

ABOUT THE AUTHOR

NIR ROSEN is a journalist whose work has appeared in *The New Yorker, The New York Times Magazine, Time, Harper's Magazine, The New Republic,* and *Salon.* In addition to English, he speaks Arabic, Farsi, and Hebrew. In April 2003, he moved to Baghdad to cover the American-led intervention in Iraq and spent a year and a half under occupation with the Iraqi people. He has also reported from Afghanistan, Pakistan, Somalia, and the Congo. He is a fellow at the New York University Center on Law and Security. He lives with his wife, Tiffany, in Istanbul.